Scholarly Leadership in Higher Education

Perspectives on Leadership in Higher Education

Series Editors: Camilla Erskine, Tanya Fitzgerald and Jon Nixon

Perspectives on Leadership in Higher Education provides a forum for distinctive, and sometimes divergent, ideas on what intellectual leadership means within the context of higher education as it develops within the 21st century. Authors from across a number of nation states critically explore these issues with reference to academic and research-informed practice and development, institutional management and governance, the remapping of knowledge as well as sector-wide policy development.

Also available in the Perspectives on Leadership in Higher Education series

Cosmopolitan Perspectives on Academic Leadership in Higher Education, edited by Feng Su and Margaret Wood
Leadership for Sustainability in Higher Education, Janet Haddock-Fraser, Peter Rands and Stephen Scoffham
Leadership in Higher Education from a Transrelational Perspective, Christopher M. Branson, Maureen Marra, Margaret Franken and Dawn Penney
Mass Intellectuality and Democratic Leadership in Higher Education, edited by Richard Hall and Joss Winn
Exploring Consensual Leadership in Higher Education: Co-operation, Collaboration and Partnership, edited by Lynne Gornall, Brychan Thomas and Lucy Sweetman

Scholarly Leadership in Higher Education

An Intellectual History of James Bryan Conant

Wayne J. Urban

BLOOMSBURY ACADEMIC

LONDON • NEW YORK • OXFORD • NEW DELHI • SYDNEY

Bloomsbury Academic
An imprint of Bloomsbury Publishing Plc
1385 Broadway, New York, NY 10018, USA
50 Bedford Square, London, WC1B 3DP, UK

www.bloomsbury.com
BLOOMSBURY and the Diana logo are trademarks of Bloomsbury Publishing Plc

First published 2020

© Wayne J. Urban, 2020

Wayne J. Urban has asserted his right under the Copyright, Designs and
Patents Act, 1988, to be identified as Author of this work.

Cover image © Jobalou / iStock

All rights reserved. No part of this publication may be reproduced or transmitted
in any form or by any means, electronic or mechanical, including photocopying,
recording, or any information storage or retrieval system, without prior
permission in writing from the publishers.

No responsibility for loss caused to any individual or organization acting on
or refraining from action as a result of the material in this publication can be
accepted by Bloomsbury or the author.

A catalogue record for this book is available from the British Library.

A catalog record for this book is available from the Library of Congress.

ISBN: HB: 978-1-3501-2928-3
ePDF: 978-1-3501-2929-0
ePub: 978-1-3501-2930-6

Typeset by Deanta Global Publishing Services, Chennai, India
Printed and bound in Great Britain

To the students in the history of higher education class at the University of Alabama, 2006–2016.

Contents

Series Editor Preface	ix
Author Preface and Acknowledgments	xi
Introduction	1
1 James Bryant Conant, 1893–1933	9
2 The Harvard Presidency in the 1930s	25
3 The Second World War, the Cold War, and the Nationalization of Harvard	67
4 General Education: An Increasing Priority	103
5 Extra-Harvard, 1933–52	135
6 Educational Statesmanship and Its Discontents, 1955–71	163
7 James Bryant Conant and Educational Statesmanship	189
Bibliography	205
Index	211

Series Editor Preface

The prime purpose of the series is to provide a forum for different and sometimes divergent perspectives on what intellectual leadership means within the context of higher education as it develops within the twenty-first century. The series draws on interconnections between intellectual histories and intellectual leadership in the field.

What are universities for in the twenty-first century? This is a question that is now debated not only within universities themselves but also within wider society and across the political spectrum: we can no longer assume a consensus regarding the ends and purposes of higher education or the role of universities in fulfilling those ends and purposes. Consequently, leadership within higher education cannot simply be a matter of effectively managing the status quo. Leadership necessarily involves an analysis of trends and changes in the global twenty-first-century world and of how the university might contribute to its central mission as the critic and conscience of society. In short, it requires *intellectual leadership* that is both strategic and programmatic: strategic in its understanding of the present and future impact of globalization and programmatic in its grasp of how universities might respond to that impact. Importantly, this necessitates an understanding of the intellectual history of the field and the mapping of the changes, continuities, and challenges that have marked universities as sites of knowledge.

What might constitute intellectual leadership? This series aims to address that question directly with reference to (1) historical shifts and changes in the field, (2) leaders and leadership of institutions of higher education, (3) the remapping of knowledge of the field, and (4) interrogating critical issues that impact on the role of universities in wider society. It aims, in other words, to explore the following questions:

- What characterizes intellectual leadership and how can the dispositions necessary for intellectual leadership be understood?
- What is the role of leadership as intellectuals and public individuals?
- How can universities help us reshape our understanding of the changing landscape of knowledge and of its mandate to act as the critic and conscience of society?
- How might an intellectual history of the field be mapped and understood?

Central to all these questions is the importance of interconnectivity in a context of increasing institutional and global complexity: interconnectivity within and across institutions, regions, and cognate fields. The gathering of agreement is one of the prerequisites of intellectual leadership at every level—and that requires an understanding of different viewpoints and opinions, some of which may be in direct conflict with others. The capacity to balance, respect, and contain these differences is what constitutes intellectual leadership.

Scholarly Leadership in Higher Education: An Intellectual History of James Bryan Conant offers a unique contribution to this series and its renewed direction. The author, Wayne Urban, examines the university presidency of James Conant (1933–53) and offers a critical and compelling narrative of the role and place of an elite institution within American higher education. Notably, Urban highlights the central link between academic leadership, research, scholarship, and public engagement. The analysis presented in this book further emphasizes the importance of university leaders connecting with faculty and the wider community and the importance of a reorientation from an almost exclusive preoccupation with management systems and organizational structures. Thus, the book resonates with a number of contemporary leadership and policy issues that have dominated the international higher education landscape for the past three decades.

The key focus that Urban brings to this work is his own scholarly attention to the unusual nature of Conant's presidency. Conant was a Harvard graduate but not a member of one of the elite families that dominated the institution: the hallmark of his presidency was not to preserve elite traditions but to modernize the university, its student body, and faculty and to invoke a level of education reform. Equally important to Conant's scholarly agenda was his own pursuit of knowledge as a scientist and humanist. As Urban concludes, it was this combination of intellect and agenda that was unusual not only for a president at this time but one that is rarely seen in present day university leadership.

The historical insights offered into the leadership of a university as well as the challenges and dilemmas of a leader have resonance for the higher education sector. As Urban cogently highlights, leaders, leadership, and educational institutions have increasingly been diversified and stratified, ostensibly to better serve their communities. This is not a text that echoes the importance of elite institutions and elite higher education but rather opens up debates further about the nature and importance of higher education and leadership that is scholarly in its focus and direction.

Tanya Fitzgerald, Helen M. Gunter, and Jon Nixon

Author Preface and Acknowledgments

I have been working on James Bryant Conant for much more than a decade. The length of time that I have spent on this project deserves some explanation. My interest in Conant originated in some work I was doing at the turn of the twenty-first century on the Educational Policies Commission (EPC), a high-status group of educational administrators and a few university presidents sponsored by the National Education Association (NEA). Its purview was to comment on policies and practices, mainly in the public schools, and to recommend changes in those policies and practices. In my reading of the verbatim minutes of the EPC,[1] I came across the significant contributions of Conant who was a member for most of four four-year terms in the 1940s and 1950s. Conant was by far the most active university president on the EPC and it is through reading his contributions to that body that I developed an interest in his larger educational views. My early work on Conant, stemming in part from the EPC minutes, focused on his ideas on K-12 education, beginning with his participation in the landmark 1944 EPC report, *Education for All American Youth*.[2] This work continued through studies of his later writings on the K-12 sector, most especially on various aspects of the American high school through the 1950s and into the 1960s.[3] Though I was working diligently on Conant, the way that that work might bear fruit in a larger manuscript was never very clear to me.

That murky situation became a bit clearer over the period from 2006 to 2016 when I started teaching multiple sections of the History of American Higher Education to graduate students, mainly in the higher education administration program, at the University of Alabama. At about the time I went to Alabama, I took a research trip to Harvard University to work in the primary sources related to Conant. One of the most valuable of these sources turned out to be his presidential reports, published each year from 1933 to 1952. These reports were also available electronically, so I could use them in my courses at Alabama. What was remarkable to me then, and became increasingly evident as I went over the reports with students, was the wide range of Conant's educational interests. He commented on all sorts of educational issues, including those in play at Harvard and those of note outside of Cambridge. Further, his comments were engaging to me, and to the students, engaging enough that I used the reports in my classes for most of my decade of teaching at Alabama. Beginning with those reports, and using other primary sources, some of which came from the Conant Presidential Papers at the Harvard Archives, I slowly developed several chapters on Conant's Harvard presidency. Those chapters represent the core materials of this book.

The consideration of the Harvard presidency was exceptionally beneficial for me, in that it gave me a path to what I think is a contribution on Conant that has some scholarly significance. Two things stood out about Conant that hampered my early effort to achieve what I hoped would be a solid analysis of the man and his ideas. The first is that there were already two enormous volumes on Conant and his work, one by Conant himself and another originating from a Harvard undergraduate thesis.[4] That situation was compounded by the publication in 2017 of a comprehensive biography of Conant by his granddaughter, a noted historian who had published several other volumes, including two on different aspects of the development of the atomic bomb.[5] The large books on Conant, with the exception of his autobiography, concentrated mainly on his work as a scientific administrator in Washington, DC, for the federal government during the Second World War, especially the development of the atomic bomb. Since these two works on Conant, by his granddaughter and by James Hershberg, both dealt much more with Conant's activities for the federal government, developing the atomic bomb in the Second World War and serving as a diplomat in West Germany in the mid-1950s, I concluded that a work that concentrated on Conant as an educator, both as Harvard president and in his educational analysis and advocacy mainly in regard to the comprehensive high school in the 1950s and 1960s, would overlap little with the two already published volumes. While my volume does overlap substantially with a good portion of Conant's autobiography,[6] the lapse of nearly fifty years since its publication and the background and viewpoint I bring to the analysis I hoped, and do still hope, justifies my effort.

The second problem for me in dealing with Conant was more personal. In my early work, though I had developed substantial respect for Conant and his view of education, I had reason to question the adequacy of those views, particularly his attitudes toward the high school and teacher education. That is, Conant claimed to take a democratic approach to American education, and he made this claim honestly; that is, he really believed it. The problem for me was what seemed to me to be his "elitism," as illustrated in his advocacy of education of the gifted and talented and his interest in standardized testing and the institutionalization of that interest in the creation of the Educational Testing Service (ETS). While I can do no more than state the nature of my reservations about Conant here, I

Author Preface and Acknowledgments xiii

will return to the issues of elitism and standardized testing periodically in the rest of this manuscript. The point I want to stress in this preface is that Conant's infatuation with standardized testing and advocacy of education for the gifted seemed, at the least, in tension with, if not contradictory to, his stated advocacy of democratic education.

An overly simplistic summary of the issue would be that I didn't like Conant's views on the American high school. It is not that one needs to like one's subject in order to spend the time on him requisite to a thorough analysis, but it is difficult to work on someone for whom one has substantial questions about one of his core commitments. The chapters in this volume will show that my respect for Conant increased as I discovered various aspects of his Harvard presidency, including his attempt to "diversify" the student body, largely through the use of standardized tests. Another of Conant's core values, respect for faculty and faculty scholarship, also appealed greatly to me as a university faculty member. My respect for these and other of his presidential commitments and accomplishments grew and I came to increasingly appreciate Conant's work as a leader in higher education.

Added to my problems with Conant was the issue of his rather severe personality. It might be a slight exaggeration, but a very slight one, to say that Conant had a likeability problem. In her biography, his granddaughter referred to him as "cold-blooded" in describing his dealings with some Harvard faculty. His other biographer discussed his "Yankee starchiness, discomfort with emotions and sensitive personal issues, . . . and the sacrifices he willingly made . . . to satisfy his thrusting ambition" all as handicaps in his personal relations, beginning with those between himself and his sons.[7] His New England ancestry, dating almost back to the Puritan original settlers, undergirded the rather stiff formality he exhibited in many of his personal relations, especially with those whom he had less than intimate contact. My problem with Conant's personality, however, was modified significantly by my studies of his actions and interactions as Harvard University president.

It wasn't that Conant was any more likable as a president than he was in any other of his several roles. What stood out to me, however, was that Conant represented, consistently, in his university presidency a series of values and priorities that appealed to me as a longtime (almost fifty years) university faculty member. Conant was a scientist, a scholar, and an intellectual. He was a chemist who rose to the chairmanship of his department at Harvard largely through his research and publications. After becoming president of Harvard, he gave up research and publication in chemistry, but he turned his attention to teaching the history of science and to systematic analysis and published commentary on various aspects of American education, initially about American higher education but eventually about elementary and, particularly, secondary education. So, he became a scholar of a very different sort from the one that he was prior to the presidency. But he never gave up his stated devotion to scholarship and actions, particularly publications, in pursuit of that devotion.

Perhaps the best way to summarize my regard for the Conant presidency is to state that the Conant I uncovered as Harvard president was a man for whom I would have liked to work. He was a scholar who valued scholarship first and foremost and sought to institutionalize scholarly excellence in the Harvard faculty. He respected his faculty, especially its leading scholars, and tried to facilitate their work. This did not mean that Conant was particularly interested in faculty power on campus. On the contrary, he, as will be shown, managed to alienate a large portion of his faculty on more than one occasion. Yet, Conant respected the scholars at Harvard and did his best to free them to expand their scholarly influence and interests. While Conant was himself an award-winning scientist, he had a wide-ranging intellect even as an undergraduate and allowed his broader concerns to dominate during his presidency. Thus, though he clearly valued educational accomplishment in the sciences, he also sought excellence in the humanities and social sciences and in the professional schools at Harvard. In fact, as a university president, he continued to think and to publish in the larger arena of American educational policy and in American science pedagogy and policy. His breadth of interests outside of his own area of chemistry was evident from the beginning of his life. That breadth sustained him during his presidency and allowed him to see that presidency in a larger light than is common among university presidents, in his own time and, certainly, in later times.

Historical scholarship is a lonely effort but one that also cannot be undertaken alone. Acknowledging those who have helped is always a pleasure. I made three visits to the Harvard University Archives for this project and was helped immensely by the staff at the Archives. While I was never able to obtain permission to quote from the Conant Personal Papers, I was fortunate to be able to use, and to benefit greatly from, the Conant Presidential Papers. Conant's autobiography and the annual president's reports he wrote during his presidency are other primary sources that helped me immensely. The main, non-Harvard primary source collection that I used was the Carnegie Corporation collections at Columbia University. Carnegie archivist Jennifer Comins was especially helpful to me, before, during, and after my visit. I am extremely grateful to her for all her efforts on my behalf.

Author Preface and Acknowledgments xv

In addition to archivists, historians, like many scholars, depend to a large extent on librarians. Benita Strnad of the Education Library at the University of Alabama provided information when I needed it, suggestions for sources of various kinds, and insightful responses to sometimes incoherent questions. I was on sabbatical from the University of Alabama for one year working on this project and was fortunate to spend a good part of that year working in the Emory University Library. Then Emory provost, and now president, Claire Sterk, helped me to get situated in the library and the staff members at the Woodruff library were all helpful in aiding my research. In the latter stages of my work, reference librarian Denise Dimsdale of Georgia State University tracked down several sources for me and uncovered a few new ones.

I owe a large debt for the completion of this project to colleagues and students at the University of Alabama. Particularly helpful was Sarah Wever who served as a research assistant and organized an enormous amount of material quite effectively. As discussed earlier, this project would not have been completed without the participation of students in my history of higher education classes in Tuscaloosa. They read Conant's presidential reports with insight and enthusiasm and provided me with intelligent and convincing reactions to what they had read. Without their input, and insight, I would not have completed this work. I dedicate this volume to those students, many of whom have wondered, and worried, about its completion.

Colleagues at Alabama—Karri Holley, Philo Hutcheson, Stephen Tomlinson, and others—were likely taxed by my frequent and sometimes oblique references to Conant and his work. I thank them for listening. Kate Rousmaniere of Miami University (Ohio) read most of this manuscript and made comments that improved it greatly. The late Harold Wechsler of New York University also read the entire manuscript and commented critically in ways that helped me move forward. And, at a critical time for me, Terry Parsinnen, historian at the University of Tampa, read the manuscript and boosted me with his enthusiasm for the work. Of course, errors or misinterpretations are mine, not of any of the already mentioned readers or others who read at least a part of it, including Craig Kridel of the University of South Carolina, Robert Hampel of the University of Delaware, and my abovementioned colleagues at the University of Alabama.

Notes

1 The verbatim minutes of the EPC meetings are available in the NEA Archives, now housed at George Washington University.

2 Educational Policies Commission, *Education for All American Youth* (Washington, DC: National Education Association, 1944). Also see, Wayne J. Urban, "Social Reconstructionism and Educational Policy: The Educational Policies Commission, 1936-1941," in K. Riley, ed., *Social Reconstructionism: People, Politics, Perspectives* (Charlotte, NC: Information Age Publishing, 2006).

3 Wayne J. Urban, "James Bryant Conant and Equality of Opportunity," *Paedagogica Historica* 46 (February–April, 2010): 193–205.

4 James B. Conant, *My Several Lives: Memoirs of a Social Inventor* (New York: Harper and Row, 1970); and James Hershberg, *James B. Conant: Harvard to Hiroshima and the Making of the Atomic Age* (New York: Alfred A Knopf, 1993). Conant's autobiography was 700 pages long and the Hershberg volume was nearly 1000 pages long.

5 Jennett Conant, *Man of the Hour: James B. Conant: Warrior Scientist* (New York: Simon and Schuster, 2017). Jennett Conant had earlier published *109 East Palace: Robert Oppenheimer and the Secret City of Los Alamos* (New York: Simon and Schuster, 2005) and *Tuxedo Park: A Wall Street Tycoon and the Secret Palace of Science That Changed the Course of World War II* (New York: Simon and Schuster, 2002). She also published two books on espionage in the World War II era. *Man of the Hour* came in at a relatively modest near 600 pages, compared to its two predecessors.

6 Conant discussed four lives in his autobiography, that of a chemist, a university president, a diplomat, and an educational analyst, in addition to his life as a government scientist in the Second World War. I deal mainly with the second and the fourth lives in this volume.

7 See Jennet Conant, *Man of the Hour*, p. 157; and Hershberg, *James B. Conant,* p. 104.

Introduction

This book appears in a series on leadership in higher education. It directly addresses issues of leadership rarely, however. In an era when, at least in the United States, we sometimes turn to sport coaches for lessons in leadership, or look to compile or discuss lists of "exemplary" leadership qualities, James Bryant Conant's career presents a welcome antidote to such inanities. Conant was first and foremost a scholar and an intellectual, and this quality was exemplified throughout his career at Harvard and in its educational aftermath. Conant's major priorities as a university president were academic and, again, provide a contrast to much of what is currently going on in higher education, at least in the United States.

I intend to provide an intellectual history of James Bryant Conant as the president of Harvard University, concentrating both on the institution itself and the mind of its leader. The point of this is to show that this university president was marked as much or more by his desire to succeed academically outside of his presidency, as well as within it. Conant's ambitions were realized through a lengthy publication record while he was leading Harvard, much of which will be analyzed herein. His presidency involved a consistent adherence to academic excellence at Harvard, as evidenced most significantly in its student body and its faculty. I will also discuss a number of Conant's other presidential priorities on issues such as athletics, the professional schools, public policy, the public schools, the Divinity School, and the Graduate School of Education. These discussions will show that Conant wanted a Harvard that was engaged in the public life of American society in ways that would lead that society toward democratic ends. And Conant himself was engaged, publicly, politically, and intellectually, in actions that sought a better society.

Conant's presidency was, to me, largely a success, for reasons that will be developed in this analysis. That success was institutional; that is, Harvard became a much more noted university nationally during his presidency than it had been beforehand. Conant was also an intellectual success as president of Harvard, using his position to advance a variety of views on American education, society, and politics. It wasn't always that people agreed with him; of course, they did not. Rather, it was that Conant offered thoughtful analyses and insights into a variety of intellectual problems and issues, as well as positions on the timely issues in American politics and policy. His views earned serious attention, if not always agreement. And one of the major attributes of Conant as an intellectual and political analyst and advocate was that he understood that not everyone would agree with him. Thus, there was an intellectual aspect of respect for other points of view in Conant's presidency that appealed a great deal to me; and I spend substantial time in the succeeding pages documenting that part of his life.

Conant was a successful president, even though he spent considerable, if not enormous, amounts of time away from Harvard. These absences were frequent throughout his presidency but especially prevalent during his half-decade in the early 1940s as a scientific administrator in Washington, DC. He worked for the federal government in many wartime capacities including the Manhattan Project that developed the atomic bomb used to end the Second World War. Conant devoted at least half of his time beginning in 1940 and continuing into 1945, to work in Washington or elsewhere away from Cambridge, Massachusetts. In reality, it was often more than half of his time but the stated situation was that he was a half-time president. Thus, though he remained quite interested in Harvard and its well-being, and did his best to stay involved in institutional affairs, Conant was never a hands-on manager. He was confident enough to leave the presidency for national service, trusting that his policies would guide the institution in spite of his absence. And, if things went off-track, in his mind, he was confident enough either to let them continue until he could return to deal with them or, perhaps, even, to consider that they might result in positive outcomes for the institution. To say that this is an unusual attribute in a university president, particularly in a time like our own when we seem to see presidents as, unavoidably, the face, maybe even the body, of their institutions, is to understate the significance of Conant's presidency. To suggest that current presidents, perhaps inordinately enamored with their own significance, might learn from the actions of a man who often, perhaps even usually, spent only part of his time on the job is to have one's tongue partially in his cheek. Nevertheless, Conant's approach and his accomplishments are clearly significant and I want to make them available for study, even, and perhaps especially, to those who spend countless hours on their job.

Perhaps the best way to summarize my regard for the Conant presidency is to state that the Conant I uncovered as Harvard president was a man for whom I would have liked to work. He was a scholar who valued scholarship first and foremost and sought to institutionalize scholarly excellence in the Harvard faculty. He respected his faculty, especially its leading scholars, and tried to

Introduction

facilitate their work. This did not mean that Conant was particularly interested in faculty power on campus. On the contrary, he, as will be shown, managed to alienate a large portion of his faculty on more than one occasion. Yet, Conant respected the scholars at Harvard and did his best to free them to expand their scholarly influence and interests. While Conant was himself a scientist, he had a wide-ranging intellect even as an undergraduate and allowed his broader concerns to dominate during and after his presidency. Thus, though he clearly valued educational accomplishment in the sciences, he also sought excellence in the humanities and social sciences and in the professional schools at Harvard. In fact, as a university president, he continued to think and to publish in the larger arenas of American educational policy and science history and policy. His breadth of interests outside of his own area of chemistry was evident from the beginning of his life. That breadth sustained him during his presidency and allowed him to see that presidency in a larger light than is common among university presidents, in his own time and, certainly, in later times.

An exceptionally attractive side of Conant as Harvard president, and in his work outside the presidency, was his wide-ranging intellect. In addition to his own disciplinary excellence in chemistry, Conant was interested in issues and concerns that brought him into contact with scholars from other disciplines at Harvard. For example, in his early years on the chemistry faculty, he participated in the founding of an interdisciplinary discussion group called the "Shop Club," which involved him with scholars from many disciplines, "scientists, economists, historians, classicists, literary scholars." The group met monthly for dinner, a presentation from one of the members on a topic of interest to all, and discussion of that presentation.[1] And Conant as president, in one of his first acts, moved to bring to the Harvard campus university professors, who would pursue their own interests, as researchers and teachers, without the institutional confines of a departmental appointment.[2] These "roving professors" were to receive a substantial salary and research funds to teach and do research wherever on the campus they felt comfortable, in multiple departments or in no department.[3] This was at the same time that Conant understood that the disciplinary excellence that undergirded much scholarly accomplishment was to be found largely in academic departments, particularly in the faculty research done in those departments and the doctoral study that flourished alongside of that research. While the university professors were to be free not to be bound by departmental restrictions or restraints, the department members were also free; in fact, they were encouraged to carry on the research and teaching that they believed would enhance their disciplines.

In another example of intellectual breadth, from the beginning of his presidency, Conant sought to undergird the education at his institution, and outside of it, with a historical foundation. Conant advocated work in the history of science, at both the undergraduate and graduate levels, early on in his presidency. He learned the importance of this history of science from his father-in-law and department chairman, Theodore Richards, who developed a course in the history of chemistry. Also, at Harvard he learned from the noted historian of science George Sarton, who developed a doctoral program in the history of science, as well as an undergraduate concentration for a few exceptional students beginning in t936, with Conant's support. While that program failed to spring into a robust health, with large numbers of students, its very existence at Harvard, when counterparts were all but nonexistent, testifies to the affinity of Conant for a larger view of his own field and its relationship to other fields.[4]

Conant also sought to foster study in American history, both at Harvard and outside of it, in the interests of the creation of a healthy, stable, and prosperous American society. In the late 1930s, Conant tried to create a series of volumes in American cultural history, based on the success of the Harvard (literary) classics created by Charles W. Eliot in the late nineteenth century. Though this effort failed to prosper, Conant's support for the enterprise indicated the importance to him of historical studies and other humanistic pursuits. His acceptance of failure in this effort indicated not that he changed his ideas about history's importance but that as president he knew when to end an effort that would not bear fruit.

Conant's wide-ranging intellectual interests and priorities were sublimated during his half-decade of work for the federal government during the Second World War. During that period, he managed, however, to appoint a faculty Committee on General Education at Harvard that produced a landmark account of needed changes in general education, *General Education in a Free Society*.[5] He provided a preface to the published version of the committee's report and, while serving as president, developed a course in the history of science that was one of the courses recommended by the committee to reinvigorate general education at Harvard. As we will describe at length, Conant taught the course for three years and made it a foundation for several of his publications in the history and philosophy of science in the late 1940s and early 1950s. Thus, Conant was able to succeed in fostering the humanities and a humanistic approach to his own field at Harvard, less than a decade after his failed experiment in cultural history.

The point of all of this discussion, and the substantive elaborations of it in the chapters of this book, is that James Bryant Conant was much more than a university administrator and much more than a scientist and scientific

Introduction 5

administrator engaged in service to the federal government. He was a scholar and an intellectual devoted to the notion that the life of the mind should be accessible and attractive to a large swath of the American public. Further, the Harvard presidency gave him a pulpit from which to preach the sort of intellectual excellence and substance that he valued. And, most importantly, this approach to the life of the mind undergirded the success of his presidency during, and after, his twenty years in that office.

My analysis of Conant contains seven chapters that follow this introduction. The second chapter deals with his childhood, education, and experience prior to becoming Harvard president in 1933. It shows how his early experiences paved the way both for his success in the sciences as a faculty member and his wide-ranging perspective on Harvard and its role as an educational leader in the nations that animated his presidency.

The third chapter considers the first decade of Conant's presidency, highlighting the theme of Conant's pursuit of excellence in faculty and student body. It shows his devotion to academic merit in both students and in faculty, and it outlines a variety of initiatives he undertook in pursuit of this priority. It also shows him to be a leader of his university who was first of all an intellectual colleague of his faculty. And, in addition, it recounts a major clash with his faculty in which Conant was forced to "apologize" for some of his actions as president. This apology was a Rubicon moment in his leadership of Harvard and its faculty, allowing him to continue in his larger efforts for another fifteen years. The chapter then discusses a variety of his interests and commitments at Harvard, all of which indicated how his long intellectual reach undergirded his approach to the job of president.

The fourth chapter covers the succeeding years of Conant's presidency, from the early 1940s to 1952, showing both a continuity of themes over all his years in that office and the newer issues he confronted during wartime and the postwar years of his term in office. The inauguration of coeducation at Harvard was one of the unintended but progressive results of wartime conditions on campus. Conant's concern for academic freedom and the integrity of Harvard as an educational leader caused him to frequently question the possibility of federal overreach in to academic matters at the same time that Harvard, like many American universities, was close to being taken over by the federal government. This concern over federal control of academic institutions carried over into the postwar years when Conant presided over Harvard in its rise to preeminence in American higher education. Conant's ambivalence over federal involvement in higher education was real and was prescient. It showed another aspect of his leadership, a willingness to not only engage his institution with his government but also to be gravely concerned about the consequences of that engagement.

The fifth chapter deals with general education, one of Conant's persistent major priorities, in the Harvard College curriculum and outside of it. It describes the genesis of the Harvard faculty report on general education in the early 1940s and shows Conant's involvement, indirect but real, in the ideas contained in the report. This chapter also details Conant's work teaching a course in the history of science that was among the new Harvard general education offerings that resulted from the Harvard Report. Coming after his long period of absences from Cambridge, this effort reiterated Conant's respect for and commitment to the faculty role at the same time that it represented his own reimmersion in campus educational affairs. It also showed the depth of his own intellectual commitment to history of science as an integral part of the larger scientific effort, one that had emerged in the early years of his presidency. Conant's participation in the intellectual life of his institution reiterated his commitment to the life of the mind, for students and faculty, a commitment that was clearly fundamental to his view of his role as leader of Harvard.

The sixth chapter discusses Conant's ideas and actions extra-Harvard, that is away from or independent of the Harvard campus, during his presidency. They built on interests and commitments he developed during his presidency and they enabled him to contribute to educational affairs long after it ended. These activities included service on various boards of government and nongovernment agencies, as well as increasing activity in pursuit of both academic excellence and democratic access in the public schools, particularly the public high school. This chapter also discusses Conant's activities as a quintessential cold warrior, a participant in pursuit of the ideological conflict of the United States with the Soviet Union that began in the late 1940s and continued for the rest of his life. Though Conant was a longtime opponent of communism, he also had to deal with the intrusion into campus affairs, at Harvard and across the nation, of Wisconsin senator Joseph McCarthy and his anti-communist crusade. Conant's protection of faculty from the intrusion of McCarthyism was a major priority, but he also was inconsistent at times in his defense of academic freedom. That inconsistency was something he later acknowledged, with a tinge of regret. Equally controversial was Conant's conflict with the Roman Catholic Church, particularly the archbishop of Boston, over the issue of federal aid to Catholic schools, a policy that he thought threatened the well-being of the public schools. This latter clash characterized the distance that Conant had come, away from Harvard affairs and into the larger arena of public policy, showing both the

Introduction 7

breadth of his intellectual interests and the potential negative consequences of those interests for the leader of a large elite private university.

The seventh chapter describes and evaluates Conant's postpresidential activities, primarily those in the area of public secondary education. He left Harvard at the end of 1952 for a diplomatic post in Germany but began almost immediately to plan for his efforts on behalf of the comprehensive public high school not long after his arrival on the continent. Those efforts continued his pursuit of both intellectual excellence and democratization through the public high school. They resulted in Conant becoming, through studies of American schools, a sort of de facto leader of American public-school supporters. At the same time, however, he was moving to a position more critical of the leaders of American public schools, as exemplified in the National Education Association and its leading constituency of American public school administrators. Conant's pursuit of academic excellence through the public schools was a flawed effort, but it showed him to be a fervent supporter of public education as the best way to achieve his twin goals of academic excellence and democratic equality. The chapter ends with a discussion of Conant's final two published volumes, one on educational policy and policy making and the second, a lengthy autobiography that was much less successful than his earlier works.

The final chapter assesses Conant's efforts and accomplishments as an educational leader, during and after his presidency of Harvard. It reiterates his commitments to academic excellence and democratic equity, at Harvard and in his post-Harvard years. It shows how those commitments, along with his broad intellectual interests and respect for faculty, characterized a largely successful leadership of Harvard. It also reiterates some weaknesses in the Conant academic legacy, including the tension between the commitments to academic merit and democratic education that he both fervently espoused, the institutionalization of that tension in the creation of the Educational Testing Service (ETS) and the easy access to the largesse of the Carnegie Corporation that allowed him to ignore it. Away from Harvard, Conant pursued, though not successfully, the development of the comprehensive public high school. More successfully, he was involved in the creation of the Education Commission of the States, an intergovernmental body that sought to realize a meaningful educational policy at the national level in a governmental system that hampered such development. In large part, he earned the label of educational statesman that allowed him to continue the leadership he had begun at Harvard and carried into affairs away from Harvard during his presidency.

Notes

1 Hershberg, *James B. Conant*, p. 59.
2 Letter from President Conant about the new University Professorships at Harvard, (May 28, 1935), Conant Presidential Papers (hereafter called Presidential Papers), Box 121, Folder 4, Harvard University Archives.
3 This initiative is discussed at length in Chapter 2.
4 Conant, *My Several Lives,* p. 86. The development of the program in history of science is discussed by Hershberg, in *James B. Conant*, pp. 407–409. Hershberg not only attributes the birth of the program to Conant's support but also notes Conant's lack of support for program expansion, largely because he thought it to be an area in which students would not likely find future employment or other support.
5 Committee on the Objectives of General Education in a Free Society, *General Education in a Free Society* (Cambridge: Harvard University Press, 1945).

1

James Bryant Conant, 1893–1933

My goal in these pages is to provide a comprehensive account of the educational career of James Bryant Conant. The major focus of this account will be four substantive chapters on Conant's leadership of Harvard University during his presidency of that institution from 1933 to the end of 1952. An account of his advocacy and research on American public education, especially the American high school, is a second topic of concern here, addressed in one chapter. Much of what Conant did in leading Harvard, and in analyzing the high school, and many of the reasons for his doing this educational work, can be understood through a discussion of his prepresidential years, which began with his birth in 1893. They are the focus of this chapter.

James Bryant Conant was born in Boston and raised in the Massachusetts town of Dorchester, much more of a distant outpost of the city of Boston than the integral part of the city that it is today. Though born in Boston, Conant begins his autobiography noting that "I make no claim to being a proper Bostonian."[1] Conant did this to distance himself from the Brahmin elite that ruled Harvard before his presidency. However, the chapter in that autobiography describing his early childhood is entitled "A Yankee Childhood." Thus, Conant claimed to be a Yankee but not a proper Bostonian. These claims are not opposed to each other, but they also point to an ambiguity in Conant's background that is relevant in explaining his social position before becoming the Harvard president. That ambiguity was in Conant's class background and social prestige and particularly in the way he saw his background. Conant stressed his non-Boston Brahmin roots to claim affinity with less-than-elite groups that had been excluded from Harvard through much of its history or discriminated against even if they were admitted. Yet Conant's colonial Massachusetts roots indicated something very close to an elite background, particularly when connected with his parents' relative affluence. The same ambiguity that Conant experienced in his personal life characterized what Conant saw as the "democratization" of Harvard that he advocated during his presidency. That is, at the same time that Conant was advocating the democratization of Harvard, he was seeking that democratization through the admission of students like himself, qualified academically but not in terms of their social background. What Conant never addressed was the fate of those less qualified academically, either at Harvard or in the rest of American higher education, or the reliability of "qualifications" as a valid predictor of future success for all students.

Though Conant's ancestors never came to social prominence within the city of Boston, and thus never were part of the Boston Brahmin elite that ruled affairs in the capital city of the state of Massachusetts as well as at Harvard University, both his parents had a long, and distinguished, Massachusetts lineage. On his father's side, that lineage could be traced back to Roger Conant, who founded the city of Salem, Massachusetts, early in the seventeenth century. The Salem City Guide notes that Roger Conant "built the first Salem house" and adds that Conant's signature was on "the building contract for enlarging the meeting house" that became the first church in Salem.[2] There is a statue of Roger Conant facing the Salem town common that was erected in 1913.

Conant traced his mother's ancestry, not quite to the Mayflower but to the ship that sailed to the New World immediately after the Mayflower had landed. Thus, both sides of the Conant family can be linked to the famous early settlers of the Massachusetts Bay Colony.[3] This ancestry marked Conant as a traditional New Englander with strong roots in the Puritan ethos, which characterized the early settlers and marked their descendants. What Conant's background did not represent, however, was the old wealth and social prominence that characterized the prestigious Boston families that dominated both the city and Harvard University through most of their first 300 years of existence. Conant's ancestors lived in villages near Plymouth and Bridgewater, Massachusetts, both historic settings south of Boston that were overshadowed socially and economically by the capital city. Conant himself was raised in the town of Dorchester, still south of Boston but closer to the capital than the families had been before. To Conant, the Dorchester in which he was raised was "a farm town in which a few wealthy Bostonians built estates." One of his biographers, however, referred to Dorchester as "a working-class" Boston suburb.[4] While it would seem difficult for Dorchester to have been both a farm town and a working-class suburb, its evolution in the twentieth century probably testifies to the accuracy of both labels, though not at the same time. That is, as it grew in size and increasingly came to be a part of the greater Boston area, the town gave way to the working-class suburb. Whether working-class suburb or farm town, Dorchester was

James Bryant Conant, 1893–1933   11

not Boston and was seen by proper Bostonians as peripheral at best, clearly overshadowed by the capital city.

Conant described his own Dorchester house as large but not a lavish estate like those of the wealthy Bostonians who also lived there. It was, however, large enough to house both the Conant family of mother, father, son, and two daughters and his maternal grandparents. Conant's grandparents, on both sides, were Swedenborgians in their religion. Emanuel Swedenborg had been raised in the Lutheran Church but left it for his own vision of a Christianity that emphasized both the human and the spiritual aspects of life and saw no conflict between science and religion. Conant's parents stopped attending the Swedenborgian church in Roxbury, Massachusetts, at about the time that he entered school. His mother, who with his maternal grandmother and sisters were dominant presences in his early childhood, never tried to make him a Swedenborgian. Rather, she informed him about that faith and its relation to other Christian faiths. What was important, at least to Conant in telling his own story, was that his mother abhorred "all trinitarian doctrines" and tried to be nonjudgmental in evaluating other aspects of religion. In her old age, she "attended a Unitarian Church" and Conant usually characterized himself as a Unitarian. Conant stressed that his mother was "a dissenter." He added that though she was gentle, she was a person with firm ideas that were freely spoken to her family.[5] Conant, thus, was basically raised in the belief that "dissent was not only respectable but usually morally correct."[6]

Politically, the Conant family was staunchly Republican, with an abolitionist bent, though his mother was implacably opposed to the imperial designs of Republican presidents William McKinley and Theodore Roosevelt. Even more contention in the family arose politically when Conant's maternal grandfather Bryant espoused strong democratic beliefs and supported the Great Commoner Williams Jennings Bryan in the 1896 presidential election. Conant's father was mostly silent in the wake of the strong opinions of his wife and father-in-law, preferring to pursue his economic interests outside of the household to involving himself in the strident political discourse of its other adult inhabitants.

James Scott Conant sought to be an artist but wound up as an engraver, a skilled craftsman whose talents were widely acknowledged. Taking advantage of the economic development in turn of the century Dorchester that arose from the placement of its Ashmont station on the railway to Boston, he became a builder-developer of the new housing going up in the community. He built new houses in Dorchester to sell to the families that sought to live there in proximity to the work that could be found in and around Boston. As a builder, he had considerable economic standing in the town, and as an engraver, he had a skilled craft that linked him to the working people who bought his homes. He encouraged his son's scientific interests in childhood by setting up a small shop for the young lad in the basement of their home. Here the boy could experiment to his heart's content and entertain other neighborhood children with his wizardry. The young Conant was also impressed by his father's membership in the Union Army during the Civil War, choosing to ignore the lack of actual combat time in the elder Conant's service record.[7]

One of Conant's biographers summarized his early life as an illustration of the traits that would characterize his adult existence. Specifically, "avid curiosity, and breadth of interest, skepticism toward religious or political dogma, obedience to authority, fascination for military affairs, admiration for intellectual excellence, rigorous self-discipline and devotion to duty, awareness and a desire to participate in an epoch of accelerating technological change" were in the makeup of the young man from a very early age.[8]

Conant attended the public elementary school in Dorchester for all but one of the first six years of his education. At the end of his sixth year, however, he faced a choice that needed to be made. As Conant recounts things, "At that time in Greater Boston, the shift to a college preparatory school for the last six years of secondary education was almost compulsory for anyone who intended to go to college."[9] Remaining in public grammar school and attending the local public high school meant little chance for a student to go on to higher education. Neither of Conant's parents had any higher education, but they were affluent and cultured enough to have already sent one of Conant's older sisters to Smith College.[10] They thought enough about the academic promise of their son that they planned to have him attend the prestigious Milton Academy, a private, preparatory school relatively close to Dorchester where his older sister was then teaching. The son, however, had a different destination in mind. Following the lead of one of his classmates and friends in Dorchester, Conant chose the Roxbury Latin School for his secondary education.[11] Roxbury, despite its title as a Latin School, had a strong science program that Conant wanted to use to build on his childhood interests. In addition to science laboratories and instruction in chemistry and physics, Roxbury Latin had the usual emphasis on the classics and traditional subjects related to college preparation such as Greek and Latin, German or French, and mathematics.

While Conant's granddaughter noted that Roxbury Academy was a "part of the Boston public school system," it was a far cry from the public high school that Conant would have attended if he had stayed in Dorchester and

James Bryant Conant, 1893–1933   13

academically superior to most, if not all, other high schools in the area, private or public.[12] Modeled on the Boston Latin School, which was in turn modeled on English public schools that were public only in the sense that they trained students for public leadership, Roxbury's curriculum was set to facilitate entry to higher education, especially to Harvard College. Roxbury Latin was free to inhabitants of the surrounding area who could gain admission but any student who sought to enroll had to pass a set of rigorous entrance tests. Roxbury Latin was, and is, controlled by a self-sustaining board of trustees who were steeped in its academic ethos rather than by a board or school committee, geographically or otherwise chosen to represent the interests of its community. If one considers public schools to be free, compulsory, universal, tax-supported locally usually through a property tax, and managed by a politically chosen body, Roxbury fails on all but the first count. The school history of Roxbury Latin, published on the occasion of its 300th anniversary in 1945, describes it as an "independent" school. While noting that it was free to boys of any means qualified to enter, it also adhered to a highly restrictive admissions policy. The school's uniqueness was attributed in its published history to its purpose. "This purpose is to provide for gifted boys, regardless of their means, in a thoroughly democratic atmosphere the very best type of modern education to prepare them for college education and eventual leadership in their communities."[13]

Roxbury Latin was akin to the prestigious, expensive private academies in Massachusetts and other New England states that prepared students for admission to the Ivy League and other prestigious private colleges that were prominent in the region. While it did not charge the considerable tuition that private institutions charged, it was, and sought to remain, "independent" of public management that might compromise its goal of providing for, and only for, the academically gifted male student. This rather lengthy discussion is important for its relation to one of Conant's major innovations at Harvard during his presidency, the National Scholarship Program, which he advocated as a way to "democratize" Harvard. This will be discussed in the next chapter.

Conant did well in most of the exams for admission to Roxbury but failed the spelling test. His mother's entreaties on behalf of her son to school authorities persuaded them that the failure in spelling could be remedied and that the excellent performance on most of the other tests, particularly the science tests, merited admission. Conant's record at Roxbury Latin showed that his mother was an accurate analyst of her son's potential. Conant did relatively well at Roxbury Latin School, especially after he encountered Newton Henry Black, a teacher of chemistry and physics. It was Black who turned Conant's experimental urges from electricity toward chemistry. The young man prospered under Black's tutelage, learning much more from the man himself, through experiments and understanding of those experiments, than through any courses in the subject. Conant described how he passed a chemistry test for Black before engaging in any study of the subject. After this, his chemistry studies were largely advanced, tutorial, and heavily involved with laboratory experimentation.[14] Conant called Henry Black "the teacher who had the greatest influence on my life."[15] Black, who had recently received an MA in chemistry from Harvard, was instrumental in getting Conant an entrance examination from the Harvard chemistry department. Conant's performance on the examination was good enough to enable him to enter Harvard and to skip introductory science courses and enroll in advanced courses in chemistry from the time he was admitted.

The young man had many interests other than studies in science, however. At Roxbury Latin, his was a frequent presence in the school library. He also participated in the school's rowing crew and the football team. He was active in school plays and was a writer for, and editor of, the school's newspaper.[16] Thus, from very early in his educational career, Conant valued studies other than the sciences and sought out participation in extracurricular activities. This combination of excellence in science and a wide-ranging profile outside of it also characterized his experience at Harvard College.

James Bryant Conant enrolled in Harvard College in 1910, one year after Abbott Lawrence Lowell became its president. Lowell was intent on reforming education at Harvard College, which had taken a back seat to graduate education under his predecessor Charles W. Eliot. Studying in chemistry, Eliot's own discipline and one that was of minimal interest to Lowell, Conant reaped the benefits that academic specialization as offered in Eliot's university provided. As he had done at Roxbury Latin, however, Conant tried at Harvard to achieve in areas outside of the sciences. He studied economics with Frank Taussig, one of the leaders in the field nationally and one of the prominent members of the Harvard faculty. Similarly, he enrolled in a history course taught by Frederick Jackson Turner, recently come to Harvard from the University of Wisconsin, whose scholarship had proclaimed the dominance of the frontier in American economic, cultural, and political development. He studied with one of Harvard's eminent philosophers, George Herbert Palmer, and also took courses in French and Italian. He avoided the English department, perhaps because he was confident of his writing skills. Following his experience at Roxbury Latin, Conant sought to participate in important activities outside of the classroom at Harvard. He had two stints on the Harvard newspaper, the *Crimson*, and eventually made it to the editorial staff as assistant managing editor. Though he was enthusiastic about the theater, he did not make Hasty Pudding, the prominent theatrical club on campus. Probably because of his service on the *Crimson*, he was invited to join the Signet, a literary society with considerable prestige on campus.[17]

Conant was enthusiastic about the value of the Signet in his own education. "Here I found my general education. In this club, around the luncheon table, conversation was kept at what we believed to be a highly sophisticated level." He referred to the Signet discussions as "far more significant in broadening my interests than all the courses I took to fulfill distribution requirements."[18] He concluded this discussion with a reference to an important course he took in Italian Renaissance art and culture, on the advice of an upper classman in the Signet group. Conant was attempting to supplement his excellent education in chemistry with wide-ranging studies outside the sciences and participation in activities that spoke to general intellectual excellence as well as to achievement in a special field. The emphasis on scholarly specialization characterized his faculty career at Harvard while the concerns about general education were extremely important during his presidency. He happily referred to his ability to have two sets of friends at Harvard, one group made up of the older advanced chemistry students who he joined from the beginning of his freshman year and a second group consisting of those outside of chemistry, whom he met in the dormitories and at the *Crimson*, and who were more his own age but who also had interests quite different from students in the sciences.[19]

Conant was made aware of the social deficiencies in his background from the first days of his enrolling at Harvard. He did not qualify, socially, for one of the prestigious "clubs" that more established Bostonian students joined easily. Instead, he began life in the college dormitories and later lived in one of the rooming houses close to the campus. He was acutely conscious of this situation and, in later years, recalled how he lived with the social misfits near Harvard Square.[20] One way to deal with the social snobbery he encountered was to throw himself into academic work.

Despite his interests outside of chemistry, Conant from the beginning, with a strong push from Newton Henry Black, knew that his future lay in advanced study in this subject. Initially, his mentor in chemistry was Theodore Richards, a specialist in physical chemistry, an eminent scholar who Conant described as a "passionate investigator" of subjects such as the atomic weights of chemical elements. Richards received a Nobel Prize for his research work in 1915.[21] He was the most prominent member of the faculty in the Department of Chemistry, chairman of the department, and a model of what Conant aspired to be from the first days of his enrollment at Harvard. In his junior year, however, Conant discovered the work of Elmer Kohler, an organic chemist recently arrived at Harvard who was a prolific researcher but an even more accomplished teacher. Conant began to work with Kohler and to study organic chemistry as well as physical chemistry. Conant continued to study with both Richards and Kohler after he received his BA in chemistry and immediately went on to doctoral study.

In his doctoral work, Conant engaged with the research of both of his mentors but also drifted off in a direction unknown to them. Perhaps because of the craftsmanship and entrepreneurial bent of his father, Conant was always interested in the practical aspects of what he studied, in addition to the theoretical concerns of the subject. Neither Richards nor Kohler embraced the applied ramifications of their subjects, though they did not actively denigrate chemists who wandered from the road to academic excellence. Conant himself was attracted to industrial chemistry and found a position in a steel plant in the summer of 1915, one year before he received his PhD. He remarked that he quickly forgot what he learned about steelmaking but added that what "I learned about the inner politics of a manufacturing plant remained with me ever since."[22] After his doctoral studies finished, Conant went into the private sector with two of his fellow Harvard students, setting up a company to produce chemicals that were in scarce supply in the United States because of the involvement of Europeans in the First World War. He had two forays into the production of chemicals, both punctuated by explosions in the factories established and one of which resulted in the death of one of his colleagues, a close friend.[23] Conant had left the factory prior to the fatal explosion to return to Harvard to a faculty position in the chemistry department, but he never lost respect for chemists who sought to apply their work in industrial contexts. He commented on the move toward more practical applications as becoming more prominent in the years after 1917 than before.[24]

Of course, the primary event of the later years of the second decade of the twentieth century was the First World War. Conant left Harvard for service in the Bureau of Chemistry of the federal government but, to his chagrin, was not engaged directly in war work. After that he shifted to work in Washington, DC, addressing how to provide defense against the poison gases that Germany had introduced into the First World War battlefields. Finally, he became a commissioned officer engaged in work on mustard gas. He was commissioned to a plant in Willoughby, Ohio, that was charged with developing a new poison gas called Lewisite.[25] According to one of his biographers, Conant's work in Washington and Willoughby opened his eyes to new prospects and fueled new

James Bryant Conant, 1893–1933 17

ambitions in the young chemist. The work "put him in touch with movers and shakers in science, business, the armed forces, and politics. . . , exposed him to the possibilities of applied research and to the methods and tactics of secret wartime scientific administration and research."[26] While this taste for wartime work paved the intellectual road for the biographer's concentration on Conant's work for the federal government in the Second World War, it also suggested a value to the applied and the practical that would show itself directly in Conant's educational concerns and pursuits as president of Harvard and later as an analyst of the American high school.

The war ended before Conant's wartime research could show results in combat. He then flirted, though briefly, with staying in industrial chemistry but, instead, returned to Harvard to a faculty position in the Department of Chemistry. He quickly rose through the ranks to a position of prominence in the field. Conant's ascent was certainly not inhibited by his personal life. He courted and eventually married Grace Thayer Richards, the daughter of one of his mentors and the chair of his department, Theodore Richards. After his marriage in 1921, Conant and his new wife embarked on a trip to Europe, which Conant appreciated as the birthplace of the profound theoretical accomplishments in his own field, as in many other scientific fields. They spent time in England, France, Italy, and Switzerland, alternating periods of academic discussions and encounters in the sciences with visits to museums and other cultural centers.[27]

Conant returned to Massachusetts and settled into the academic life of a scientist at Harvard. From his earliest days as a faculty member he saw research as his greatest undertaking, one that was far more important to his own advancement in his discipline than undergraduate teaching. This weighting, as we will see, also undergirded many of his presidential actions, though he never derided the importance of a Harvard College education. As a faculty member, he pursued several objectives that would characterize his presidency. For example, he supported expanding scholarships to Harvard undergraduates that would open the institution to students outside the Boston social elite. This plan did not meet with President Lowell's approval and, thus, was to be put on a shelf to be taken off later when Conant was the chief executive. As he had done as a student, Conant sought intellectual enrichment outside of chemistry, reading widely in history and the humanities. He was one of the founders of the Shop Club, a discussion group of a few dozen "scientists, economists, historians, classicists, and literary scholars," which met monthly for a dinner and a presentation. Notable among the luminaries of this group were Lawrence Henderson, a

18   *Scholarly Leadership in Higher Education*

biochemist and Conant's uncle by marriage, and Arthur Schlesinger, Sr., noted historian and chair of the History Department.[28]

Conant was consistent, both in pursuing excellence through research and theoretical accomplishment in chemistry and in seeking contact in the intellectual world outside of his field. He remarked in his autobiography that his experiences outside of academic chemistry nourished "a cherished ambition to try my wings some day in other fields than the scientific." He apprised his wife prior to their marriage of the specific nature of these ambitions when he told her that for the distant future he had three goals: "The first was to become the leading organic chemist in the United States; after that I would like to be president of Harvard; and after that, a Cabinet member, perhaps Secretary of the Interior."[29] These priorities would be fulfilled to a large extent in the coming decades.

In pursuit of the first priority, excellence in chemistry, Conant undertook research in several areas, including the making of rubber and the properties of chlorophyll. Additionally, he cooperated in research in the field of biochemistry with two friends in the Medical School and also worked on a research project with Percy Bridgman in physics. In the mid-1920s, he undertook a trip to Germany, by now more open to American visitors than it had been in the immediate post–First World War years. Conant revered German scientific accomplishment and had wanted to study there at the doctoral or postdoctoral level, a desire thwarted by the war. Though his father-in-law had political reservations about the trip, he provided an entrée for the young chemist to a number of the most famous German chemists. Conant acknowledged Germany as responsible for top accomplishments in organic chemistry. He attributed that achievement to the German university system that required two doctorates for full professorial status, granted that status to only one professor in a given field at any university, and was extremely rigorous in evaluating scientific accomplishment. Senior professors dominated academic studies in Germany, and they were devoted evaluators of those who worked for them, as well as of all academics in their field. Conant was impressed with the laboratories of German chemistry professors because of the outstanding qualifications of those who worked there. Rather than being staffed by graduate students, as was the case in the United States, German professors could, and did, hire chemists with doctorates who provided outstanding assistance in conducting research. In fact, Conant tried, unsuccessfully at first, to hire chemists with doctorates for his own laboratory at Harvard, succeeding only when he had an offer for a full professorship at Cal Tech. Harvard's counter offer to Conant included a full professorship, a

James Bryant Conant, 1893–1933   19

substantial raise, and money for several research assistants, including those with doctorates.[30]

Conant presided over a productive research laboratory and that productivity was acknowledged by a prodigious publication record. He reaped a sizable number of research grants and used those grants to increase the amount of work in his laboratory. Conant's eminence in his field was recognized in 1929 when he became the Shelden Emery Professor of Chemistry at Harvard. He also became chairman of the Department of Chemistry in 1931, confirming his leadership in his field.[31] In 1932, he received the Chandler Medal for chemical accomplishment, causing the *Boston Globe* to describe him as "one of the most brilliant of the younger organic chemists this country has produced."[32] He continued to lead his department for another year, when a vacancy in the Harvard presidency occurred.

When, in 1932, Abbott Lawrence Lowell announced his intention to retire, Conant chose not to indicate any interest in the position. He thus seemed to demur on this chance to achieve the second goal he had disclosed to his wife a decade earlier. Instead, Conant announced his support for the candidacy for the position of Kenneth Murdock, a professor in the English Department and a personal friend who had been the best man at his wedding. As a chair of one of the large science departments at Harvard, and a distinguished faculty member, however, Conant was contacted by those involved in the search process for Lowell's successor for information on the various qualities that were needed in the presidency and the qualifications of those who were being considered for the position. The members of the Harvard Corporation, the smaller and more prestigious of the two boards that constituted the management of the university, were charged with selecting the new executive. That selection would then be ratified by the larger governing board, the Overseers.

Conant had rather strong views about Harvard, views that had been shaped by what he considered the problems of the university under President Lowell. Lowell, as already noted, had instituted reforms that sought to restore the prominence of Harvard College, which had been overshadowed by the innovations in graduate education under his predecessor, Charles Eliot. Eliot's institutionalization of a radical elective system for undergraduates meant that they were free to follow their interests, whether serious or frivolous, and had few specific requirements to meet to get their degrees. Lowell instituted two major changes to support undergraduate education, the residential house system, wherein undergraduates lived together on or close to campus and the tutorial system, whereby undergraduate education was handled by tutors chosen as much for their commitment to teaching as for any excellence in research. In the

20 *Scholarly Leadership in Higher Education*

curriculum, Lowell also instituted a system of concentration and distribution requirements, which brought some coherence to undergraduate studies. Conant supported the house system as a way to encourage intellectual communities in the undergraduate student body. His chemistry department, however, was one of the few departments that refused funding to hire tutors for undergraduates, because they compromised, according to Conant, the high standards for promotion that prevailed in the research-oriented department.[33]

Conant had the chance to voice his views on Harvard as it sought a new president to one of the corporation members, Robert Homans, with whom he had several discussions about the situation. Conant found that Homans agreed with him that the university was first and foremost "a collection of eminent scholars." Further, "if the professors were the most distinguished in the world, then the university would be the best university. The quality of those appointed to life position was therefore fundamental." Conant criticized appointments that had been made for personal reasons at Harvard under Lowell. Even if appointments were made for things as laudable as being helpful to one's department, or "for devotion to Harvard, then Harvard to that extent was betraying its trust." Conant called on his "own experience as a scientific investigator" to indicate to Homans that there were "few positions . . . in 1932 in the United States where a professor could carry on research." He added that "to fill one of these positions with a second-rate person was to betray a trust—to be guilty of almost criminal negligence." Conant also voiced concern over the importance of the academic caliber of the student body as an indicator of institutional excellence, but he reiterated to Homans that "I was speaking first about appointing professors who should be outstanding scholars."[34] Homans, impressed with Conant's ideas, asked if he himself had interest in the job. Still committed to Murdock's candidacy, Conant replied that he "certainly did not want the job, but if it were offered, I would take it."[35]

Murdock had strong qualifications for the leadership of Harvard. He had been dean of the faculty (of Harvard College) in the latter years of the Lowell regime. He was described as "a gravely ironic professor of colonial and literary history with the stiff-backed stride of an ex-ensign, an adroit, precise intelligence, and a taste for Mozart and Keats." He and Conant had been friends since undergraduate days at Harvard. Those seeking a new direction for Harvard, however, looked askance at Murdock, because of his service in Lowell's administration. His candidacy was damaged irreparably when he was observed in the company of a woman other than his wife on a transatlantic trip to the continent. Murdock was not made aware of this discovery, at least during the time before presidential selection. When he failed to become president and, instead, Conant succeeded to the office,

James Bryant Conant, 1893–1933   21

Murdock "never forgave his onetime friend . . . for his failure to persuade the men around Lowell of his fitness to succeed to the presidential office."[36]

Conant's persuasiveness in advocating academic excellence in faculty as a major presidential priority caused Homans to have other members of the corporation discuss the presidency with the relatively young chemist. Those discussions seemed also to be well received and Conant's own candidacy became strengthened. The issue of one's disciplinary background is often contentious in presidential selection politics, particularly among faculty members. Conant, as a scientist, represented a group of scholars who felt they had been neglected by the Lowell regime. Thus, his candidacy found favor among scientists who saw it as a way to redress their grievance. On the other side of the ledger, however, the humanists instinctively feared any scientist as a narrow specialist opposed to intellectual accomplishment other than in the laboratory. When noted philosopher Alfred North Whitehead heard of the possibility of Conant becoming president, he was appalled. Narrow empiricist scientists were the least qualified of all the scholars to lead a university, according to Whitehead. When reminded that Charles W. Eliot, a chemist like Conant, had led Harvard for forty successful years prior to Lowell's ascendancy, Whitehead responded that this was because Eliot was a "bad chemist."[37] The poet, Robert Frost, was equally offended by Conant's scientific parochialism. He considered Conant to be narrow-minded, "a Puritan and a prude, if not a prig."[38] Thus, the fight in the faculty over Conant's candidacy pitted the scientists against the humanists, longtime faculty enemies in fights over curriculum, expenses, personnel policies, and numerous other issues.

The decision over who to hire as Harvard's next chief executive was not made by the Harvard faculty, however, but by the two governing boards of the institution, the corporation and the somewhat larger Board of Overseers. And Conant's stock rose as he talked with more and more of the members of these two groups. Eventually, President Lowell, who had tried to stay out of the deliberations over his successor, at least publicly, entered into the discussions. While he was no great advocate of Conant, as the chemist grew closer to the presidency, the existing president chose not to intervene. The Overseers eventually closed ranks in support of James Bryant Conant as the next Harvard president and sent President Lowell to deliver the news. He vowed to Conant that he would stay out of the way of the new president, unlike the situation he had encountered with his own predecessor. And, to a considerable extent, Lowell honored that commitment, though he was at least partly aware of Conant's ideas of what needed changing at Harvard and that some of his own achievements might be modified considerably, if not simply discarded.[39]

Conant was overtly ambivalent about the presidency. He knew it would be a tough job and, while he relished the challenge, he also was aware of the considerable downside that came with the position. He described the presidency as "an awful job—if you take it you have to be willing to knife your best friend."[40] He alerted the governing boards of his intent to make improvements at Harvard. To do this he thought he had to stem an academic decline, to hold the budget in check in the midst of the Great Depression and, most importantly, to increase faculty quality. Studentwise, Conant identified with the "'meatballs'— the ambitious, middle class students, the first- and second-generation ethnic immigrants who worked overtime to overcome prejudice . . . so as to enter the establishment at Harvard and then, with their degrees, . . . the outside world." Theodore White, journalist and popular historian of a series of the *Making of a President* books in the late twentieth century, was an undergraduate during the early years of Conant's presidency. White recognized Conant's affinity for the student without the social pedigree that many brought to Harvard. White recalled that "Conant was the first president to recognize that meatballs were Harvard men too," adding that he himself [White] was "a hungry, ambitious, Jewish meatball from Boston."[41] While as a student Conant himself was a long way from being a "meatball," he was also a long way from being a typical Harvard student, with a social pedigree and an income to match it. Conant's affinity for the meatballs would be realized in several of his actions as president.

It is to those actions, especially in relation to the makeup of the student body and the faculty, that we turn in the next chapter. The Conant presidency was punctuated by his search for faculty and student excellence, the latter as a way to democratize Harvard. That presidency was also characterized by Conant's own commitment to general education as a significant priority for the students of Harvard College, one that would undergird their own possibilities for leadership in American society.

Notes

1 Conant, *My Several Lives*, p. 3.
2 "Welcome to Salem Massachusetts," https://www.salem.com/guide/roger.php.
3 Hershberg, *James B, Conant*, pp. 12–13.
4 Jennett Conant, *Man of the Hour*, p. 12 and Conant, *My Several Lives*, p. 7. One paragraph before describing Dorchester as a farm town, Conant referred to the time of his childhood as the age of the growing low-income suburb.

5 Ibid., p. 10.

6 Conant, *Man of the Hour,* p. 20.

7 Conant, *My Several Lives*, pp. 11–12.

8 Hershberg, *James B. Conant*, pp. 12–13.

9 Conant, *My Several Lives*, p. 14.

10 Conant, *Man of the Hour*, p. 23.

11 James Bryant Conant, "An Autobiographical Fragment," in Robert J. Havighurst, ed., *Leaders in Education*, The Seventieth Yearbook of the National Society for Studies in Education, Part II (Chicago: University of Chicago Press, 1971), p. 116.

12 Conant, *Man of the Hour*, p. 22.

13 Richard Walden Hale, Jr., *Tercentenary History of the Roxbury Latin School* (Cambridge: Riverside Press, 1945), pp. 1, 161.

14 Hershberg, *James B. Conant*, p. 16.

15 Conant, *My Several Lives*, p. 15.

16 Conant, *Man of the Hour*, p. 29.

17 Ibid., p. 39 and Hershberg, *James B. Conant*, pp. 26, 29.

18 Conant, *My Several Lives*, p. 24. Distribution requirements across the curriculum were one of the major reforms President Lowell introduced into the Harvard College curriculum, in an effort to tame the specialization and whimsy of the free elective system of his predecessor, Charles Eliot.

19 Ibid., p. 25.

20 Conant, *Man of the Hour*, pp. 12–14.

21 Conant, *My Several Lives*, p. 29.

22 Ibid., p. 39.

23 Ibid., pp. 42–45.

24 Ibid., p. 25.

25 Ibid., pp. 48–51.

26 Hershberg, *James B. Conant*, p. 48.

27 Conant, *My Several Lives*, pp. 53–55.

28 Hershberg, *James B. Conant*, p. 59.

29 Conant, *My Several Lives*, p. 52.

30 Ibid., pp. 67–75.

31 Conant, *Man of the Hour*, p. 107.

32 As quoted in Hershberg, *James B. Conant*, p. 93.

33 Conant, *My Several Lives*, p. 82.

34 Ibid., p. 83.

35 Ibid., p. 87.

36 Richard Norton Smith, *The Harvard Century: The Making of a University to a Nation* (New York: Simon and Schuster, 1986), p. 103. Smith cited "confidential sources" for his account of the Murdock–Conant tension.

24   *Scholarly Leadership in Higher Education*

37   Samuel Eliot Morison, "The Harvard Presidency," *The New England Quarterly* 31 (December, 1958): 444.

38   Hershberg, *James B. Conant*, p. 93.

39   Conant, *My Several Lives*, pp. 89–91.

40   As quoted in Hershberg, *James B. Conant*, p. 103.

41   Ibid., p. 80. White discussed Harvard under Conant in his autobiography *In Search of History: A Personal Adventure* (New York: Harper & Row, 1978), pp. 40–44.

2

The Harvard Presidency in the 1930s

When James Bryant Conant was poised to become the president of Harvard University, he had a clear vision of not only what he intended to accomplish but also a sense that he needed to proceed carefully along the path he had chosen. His overall goals were excellence for Harvard, excellence in the faculty, excellence in the student body, and national leadership for the university. In pursuit of these goals, he brought to the presidency a good bit less formality than characterized the tenure of his predecessor Abbott Lawrence Lowell. Yet, he understood that there was little to be gained in antagonizing Lowell.[1]

Lowell had provided a strong fiscal and material foundation for Harvard, in relatively good economic times, during his term in office. He was a careful steward of Harvard's finances; at the same time he presided over a significant building program on campus. One of his major educational goal was to rescue the Harvard College curriculum from the radical elective system instituted by his predecessor, Charles Eliot. His pushing through a system of concentration and distribution requirements for students in the college ensured, he believed, that they would emerge with both a major field of study and a sound background in other fields when they graduated. Just as, or more importantly, he instituted a "house" system whereby students of the college lived with each other in physical settings that encouraged social and intellectual interaction. To establish the house system, he found a donor to fund the construction of seven new houses at Harvard in 1928, with a $13 million contribution.[2] In housing and in all areas, Lowell was a careful steward of Harvard's wealth, and he entrusted to his successor an institution in a state of strong financial balance when he retired. This allowed Conant to move beyond the bricks and mortar and dollars and cents orientation of his predecessor and to turn attention to the direction he would emphasize in his presidency, the people who would work and learn at Harvard.

Conant quickly initiated more direct contact with Harvard faculty than had been the case with Lowell, seeking to engage them in his campaign to improve the university. For example, from his earliest days in office, as president of the university, he presided over the meetings of the various schools and colleges, something his predecessor had not done for many years.[3] Conant wanted the faculty to come to know their president and he, in turn, sought contacts with the faculty. Dealing with university faculty is a delicate task for any president, particularly the president of Harvard University. And Conant wanted to make sure the faculty were aware of his interest in them and their work, especially given the plans he had for faculty enhancement.

Improving the Harvard faculty was a long-term, multifaceted task, and Conant had indicated to the Harvard Corporation members and Board of Overseers that the faculty needed improvement and, further, that the improvement would come mainly through the area of research and scholarship. He began almost immediately to reform the retirement system at Harvard. When Conant came into office, Harvard could have been described as having "no retirement age." He moved carefully to establish a system whereby the normal retirement age was sixty-six, another two years were to be granted if warranted, and exceptional faculty members might extend their service until age seventy-six. As retirement changes were being considered, the makeup of the existing faculty had to be kept in mind to avoid opposition. Sixty-six and sixty-eight were relatively uncontroversial ages to retire for those then on the faculty. The maximum of seventy-six, however, could have proved to be more of a pitfall. Two of the leading scholars on the faculty, Frank Taussig in economics and George Kittredge in English, were both approaching the new, final retirement age. Conant cautiously contacted both of these men about retiring and persuaded them to announce their own forthcoming retirement voluntarily, rather than have it come due to a new "rule."[4]

Retirement changes were but one part of a larger plan to improve the Harvard faculty. More generally, achieving national leadership at Harvard meant, for Conant, that the institution needed to overcome its parochialism. That parochialism was centered on Boston, on Massachusetts, and, to a lesser extent, on New England and the rest of the Northeast. Early twentieth-century Harvard, despite the significant changes in the direction of graduate study and the adoption of the elective system for undergraduates during the lengthy presidency of Charles W. Eliot, was still an essentially local institution. The locality centered on Cambridge, and its larger neighbor Boston, and the Brahmin families who were prominent in the history of those places as well as in the state of Massachusetts. Conant's immediate predecessor, Abbott Lawrence Lowell, was a scion of those families who cemented their hold on Harvard through maintaining their dominance in the makeup of the Harvard student body and the orientation of Harvard College. Lowell's changes in Harvard College did nothing to disturb the social hierarchy within the college that stratified the student body along the same social lines that stratified Boston and Massachusetts society. This stratification supported Harvard's dependency on the old families that had been associated with the institution for generations. Another strong pillar of Lowell's Harvard was the Divinity School, which he valued as a bulwark against the intellectual diversity sought by Eliot. Lowell's Divinity School faculty consisted of mainly old-line Massachusetts Protestants such as Unitarians and Congregationalists, with a smattering of other Protestants and a token Roman Catholic and Jew as members.[5] Thus, the Divinity School reinforced the same religious distinctions and hierarchy that existed in the surrounding town, city, and state.

Conant's view of the situation was a good bit different from Lowell's. He acknowledged the historic affinity between Harvard College and Massachusetts Puritanism and its religious descendants. He remarked that while the historic purpose of Harvard to advance learning was conceived in an environment where education and theology were inseparable, "today learning has become secular." For Conant, to a large extent, universities had replaced religion and the churches as seats of social solidarity and leadership. In support of this conclusion, he noted that "the universities are now the residuary legatees of many of the spiritual values which were guarded by the church three centuries ago." Given this reality, he added that what was needed now was "a true reverence for learning."[6]

In many ways, Conant was the anti-Lowell. Like Eliot, he was a chemist; the two were different in background from Lowell who had a law degree and a faculty appointment in the government department. As shown earlier, Conant was not a Boston Brahmin, again in contrast to his predecessor, Lowell, as well as to Eliot. As seen in the previous chapter, Conant came from a more modest socioeconomic background than that which characterized the old Boston families and grew up in the then distant Boston outpost of Dorchester. The major religious flavor in Conant's upbringing, Swedenborgianism, was seen as, at best, odd by the orthodox Boston Christians who dominated the Harvard campus. Personally, Conant displayed an informality in style that was in direct contrast to what might have been called the stuffiness, perhaps even the pomposity, of his predecessor.[7] This difference led to the campus traditionalists calling their new president Greasy Jim.[8] Longtime Harvard faculty member John Finley described the difference between Lowell and Conant as follows. Conant's "scientific rigor replaced the Puritan vision of an austere God."[9]

The major external issues with which Conant coped during his presidency included the Great Depression of the 1930s, the Second World War, and its aftermath, and the early years of the Cold War. While these three phases meant quite different challenges for the university, challenges that were met, though not completely successfully, Conant's own major commitments were unwavering throughout the period. They were enunciated at the beginning of his presidency and continued in the foreground through most of the rest of it. Conant was devoted to a vision of making Harvard an institution of excellence, academic excellence, especially in its student body and its faculty. Achieving that excellence would ensure that Harvard would assume a leadership role in American higher education and American society. Conant's pursuit of what has come to be called "meritocracy" encompassed both a student dimension, as evidenced most specifically in a national scholarship program, and a faculty dimension, as evidenced in a variety of cross-departmental initiatives and a tightening up of promotion and permanent employment policies. These twin priorities for pursuing excellence at Harvard constituted the largest single thematic element in Conant's presidency, one that he pursued from its very inception.[10]

In his first report as the president of Harvard University, covering the years 1932–33, Conant outlined the essential direction that Harvard would follow: "To accomplish its mission, Harvard must be a truly national university."[11] For Conant this nationalization encompassed three major particulars, two of which have already been mentioned: the improvement of the student body and the scholarly upgrading of the faculty; the third priority meant the involvement of Harvard faculty in external affairs and assuring that Harvard students had an education that prepared them for national leadership. Achieving the first two of these goals, national scholarships and faculty improvement, occupied the major part of Conant's attention in the 1930s and into the early 1940s. The third, national impact, took center stage during the Second World War and proceeded to intensify during the rest of his presidency. The final years of his presidency involved extensions of, and/or variations on, these three major emphases.

Walter Lippmann described the change sought by Conant during his presidency, especially as it related to the orientation of the Harvard College student body.

> To discharge the responsibilities which have been thrust upon us by the modern
> world, we shall have to change the outlook of young men. We can no longer allow
> them to believe that the normal career of a college man is to go out and make a

private fortune. . . . It is in the administration of President Conant that the first generation of Harvard men will be trained for these newer responsibilities.[12]

In discussing the prescience of this quote, one author noted that "Conant's presidency would be the first to train college men for careers useful to the public."[13] As part of changing the major objective of Harvard College graduates away from personal gain and toward more civic and national responsibilities, one thing that Conant needed to do was to improve drastically the academic quality of those students.

National Scholarships and Standardized Tests

It was clear, at least to Conant, that achieving an intellectually superior student at Harvard necessitated the geographical diversification of the Harvard College student body. According to one history of Harvard, when Conant took the presidency, 40 percent of Harvard's students came from its home state, Massachusetts, the largest percentage of any major college in the United States. Further, according to the same account, the student body was not particularly accomplished academically, since at least "30 to 40 percent of freshmen had unsatisfactory records."[14] The first step to improving the situation, Conant argued, was that Harvard needed to attract the most intellectually capable students from areas outside of New England. The specific goal, in Conant's own words, was that "any man with remarkable talents may obtain his education at Harvard, whether he be rich or penniless, whether he come from Boston or San Francisco."[15] Conant sought to institutionalize a process to achieve this objective through the development and implementation of a national scholarship program.

Through this program, Conant meant to take advantage of what he considered a significantly enhanced pool of high school graduates, made possible by the enormous increase in high school enrollment achieved during the early twentieth century.[16] Through national scholarships, Harvard sought to attract able youth, particularly those from outside New England and the Northeast, who lacked the financial resources to enroll. Of course, identification of the winners of national scholarships required Harvard to ponder and decide the criteria on which they were to be selected. Conant was aware that there was some slippage in academic rigor that had accompanied increased high school enrollment, most particularly a diminution in enrollment in foreign languages and in advanced mathematics and science courses, especially in the larger public high schools. When seeking students from outside of New England for Harvard, Conant also had to contend with the lack of alignment between high school curricula in the rest of the country and Harvard admissions criteria. Harvard and other like-minded universities, such as Yale and Princeton, had developed a series of subject matter examinations through the auspices of the College Entrance Examination Board (CEEB) that aligned quite nicely with both the colleges' priorities and the curricula of New England private preparatory schools. Their lack of fit with large public high schools that were characteristic in much of the Midwest and far West, Conant's initial primary target for new students, was clear.[17]

To cope with this situation, Conant early on became an advocate of standardized ability or "aptitude" tests that purported to identify academic ability, regardless of subjects studied in high school. He went on record with his optimistic view of the validity of tests like the Scholastic Aptitude Test (SAT) in the Harvard admissions process a few years after the inauguration of his national scholarship program. He reported to the Harvard community on the progress of the national scholarship program during the academic year 1936–37:

> It is becoming increasingly clear as we proceed with our scholarship plans, that we are providing opportunities for certain youths who would otherwise not have been able to attend any institutions of higher learning. Those of our staff engaged actively in the selection of scholarship holders . . . have been impressed with the large number of able youths throughout many sections of this country whose financial resources are too scanty to allow them to proceed with a first-class education.[18]

In expanding on the reasons for his support for this approach, Conant added that conditions in the Depression decade were such that opportunities for the poor student to work his way through college had been severely diminished and that, therefore, "Harvard College is rendering worthwhile service to the nation by widening opportunities for higher education." For Conant, this policy was in keeping with what should be undertaken by a large endowed university like Harvard, which had "a very special social obligation to widen the opportunities of education, regardless of residency, birth, and financial circumstances."[19] Harvard achieved this extension of opportunity through national scholarships that encompassed what now would be called a needs-based approach, one that increased the amount of a scholarship according to the student's financial need for support. The poorer the student, the greater the amount provided by his scholarship. Those students who qualified for a scholarship academically but

The Harvard Presidency in the 1930s   31

had substantial financial resources would be noted as Harvard scholars but would receive little or no financial aid.

Conant continued to expand and emphasize Harvard's national scholarship program throughout the 1930s. In his 1938–39 presidential report, for example, he noted that availability of the national scholarships had been expanded to students in seventeen states and that further expansion would be undertaken when more funds became available.[20] What had hampered the program was the economic stasis of the 1930s, a situation in marked contrast to that of the previous decade. Conant was optimistic, however, that the situation would improve and that Harvard would increasingly enroll exceptional students whose economic status would have precluded them from considering the school. He was able to institutionalize standardized testing as a major part of the admissions process in Harvard College through his appointment of admissions officers, like Henry Chauncey, who recognized the power of that testing and worked hard to increase its use on campus.[21]

In spite of Conant's enthusiastic advocacy of standardized testing, Harvard lagged behind other prestigious universities, like Yale and Columbia, in its familiarity with and consequent reliance on them. A 1934 Carnegie Corporation study of the newer standardized aptitude tests noted Harvard's hesitancy and attributed it, in part, to a lack of testing-related infrastructure at Harvard, in marked contrast to bodies like the Bureau of Statistics at Yale.[22] That agency had made possible a detailed study of the relationship of tests to student success at Yale, one that saw significant results for the standardized measures in predicting that success. To bring Harvard's record up to par with that of Yale and Columbia, the Carnegie Corporation sought to employ Conant's favorite staff member in admissions, Henry Chauncey, to do a comprehensive analysis of Harvard's experience with measures like the SAT.[23]

Harvard College was not the only setting in which Conant sought to institutionalize the criterion of academic excellence through standardized testing in admissions. Another favorite place for excellence and institutional expansion, in the early years of his presidency, was graduate education. As a chemistry faculty member, Conant had been exposed to the necessity of research and graduate education to the pursuit of the intellectual accomplishment that he treasured. As president, he sought to expand admissions to graduate departments through procedures and policies akin to the national scholarships, procedures that recognized academic merit as the major qualification.[24] In this arena, the Graduate Record Examination (GRE) was Conant's standardized test of choice. He endorsed the GRE, like he favored the SAT for undergraduate study, because it eliminated, or at least mitigated, the variability between various backgrounds in a discipline that candidates for graduate study often presented. A study of the validity of the GRE at Harvard early in 1940 found that the GRE alone was "practically as effective as the undergraduate record in enabling one to predict the graduate school averages of . . . students." While this was the case, the GRE was less predictive of success than the student record of Harvard College undergraduates but "far more effective than the undergraduate record . . . in predicting the graduate averages of students coming from colleges that usually send only a very few students to Harvard."[25] Increasing the reach of Harvard for graduate students nationwide, like the pursuit of the most capable undergraduates then, meant increased reliance on standardized tests like the GRE.

Unlike in the undergraduate arena, however, in graduate study, Conant had to contend with the positions of graduate faculty members in the many disciplines, who often questioned the recommendations for more standardized testing coming from administrative admissions officers appointed by and responsible to the president. Faculty members, in general, were much more skeptical of standardized tests than was Conant. In 1937, for example, he commiserated with Ben Wood of the Carnegie Foundation for the Advancement of Teaching on the reluctance of historians and other social scientists to participate in developing standardized tests in their field.[26] Conant was savvy enough as a president, however, to know that he could not defeat faculty in any direct confrontation over standardized testing in relation to admissions to graduate study. He preferred, instead, to work with graduate faculty and try to sell them on the benefits of standardized procedures, as, at the least, a supplement for the more faculty-favored policies such as academic record, interviews, and letters of recommendation.

In his final presidential report, Conant critically assessed the results accomplished by the national scholarship program. He remarked that the money to support the program at the level it needed had not been forthcoming. Further, those who were supported by the program did not attract enough other students from regions such as the West and the South to make a regional presence visible on the campus. Finally, the program reinforced a notion that Harvard was for straight A students, a criterion that Conant, due to a variety of factors such as differing academic standards and extra academic qualities and orientations often exhibited by future leaders, found severely wanting as a sole guide for selection. He suggested that alumni might be able to help in recruitment of students from other regions but cautioned that alumni recruitment efforts were more likely to result in solicitation of athletes than of scholars.[27]

The Harvard Presidency in the 1930s   33

In spite of this legitimate concern about undue influence in admissions from alumni with distinctly nonacademic preferences, Conant was also a realist who understood that completely discarding the traditional Harvard priorities was economic suicide for Harvard. His actions on the admission of Jewish students to Harvard, a group that quite often seemed to embody his meritocratic values, deserve close attention in this regard. Ostensibly, Conant's devotion to meritocracy precluded moves to restrict Jewish admissions, since Jews were often high scorers on standardized tests. And, in comparison to his predecessor, Lowell, Conant differed in his policies. During a period when Jewish enrollment in Harvard College reached 25 percent, Lowell had proposed an outright quota system for Jewish admission that would basically halve the number of Jewish students.[28] Though his faculty voted strongly against quotas, and Lowell backed down from a formal quota policy, the actions of the admissions apparatus during his presidency followed Lowell's priorities and meant that there would be a rather rigid limit, though not an official quota, on the number of Jews allowed to enroll.[29]

Conant's administration had a very different public face on the Jewish question from that of Lowell. He assiduously advocated the admission of the best qualified students and seldom, if ever, made remarks about Jews or any other ethnic or minority group. Yet, the difference in the two leaders was not as stark as defenders of Conant might wish to make it. When Lowell proposed the quota on Jews to the Harvard faculty, Conant, then a chemistry faculty member, voted for it. He never addressed the reasons for his vote, so speculation about them is just that, speculation. As president, Conant acted, ostensibly at least, quite differently from Lowell, seeking the best students wherever they could be found, particularly in non-New England areas. Yet the reality of admissions under Conant was not too different from that under Lowell. Conant, in spite of his stated preferences for merit, had also to contend with the political and economic realities surrounding Harvard. This meant that the Boston Brahmins and other privileged New Englanders and wealthy and powerful men in the rest of the Northeast, who wished to send their offspring to a Harvard not significantly unlike the institution that they attended, and who constituted a significant portion of the private givers to the institution, needed to be acknowledged in some form. Thus, alongside of the stated preference for the best students stood the very real need for students who would represent the past and likely support the future financial welfare of the university. Many prominent Harvard alumni, then, feared the significant alteration of the political and social climate of Harvard undergraduates, seen as a likely prospect with the admission of large numbers of the newer, eastern European immigrant descended Jews. During

34 *Scholarly Leadership in Higher Education*

Conant's days as a student and young faculty member, Jewish students, mainly from the Boston area and descended from the older western European Jewish migration, attended Harvard as commuter students. Their presence thus did little to alter the social life and mores of the residential students. Newer Jewish students were distinctly different, however, often coming from places like New York City, from eastern European backgrounds, and consequently much less assimilated than their forebears at Harvard and therefore much more of a threat to the established undergraduate mores.[30]

Conant himself had little to say about any of this, publicly or privately; however, looking at the reality of who was and who was not admitted to Harvard, at least in the first decade or so of Conant's presidency, leads to a conclusion that mitigates his stated devotion to the best students, regardless of background. In a relatively recent study of admissions discrimination at Harvard, Yale, and Princeton, the author concluded that Conant and his admissions officers, at least in the first decade of his presidency, "continued to set a ceiling on Jewish enrollment." He went on to add that, in spite of Conant's devotion to seeking students with the best qualifications, "not all qualified students who could pay their own way were highly sought after." Rather, "some such students—especially of Jewish origin and relatively unassimilated eastern European backgrounds — were welcome only in limited numbers." Thus, Conant's devotion to academic excellence had its limits, its distinctly ethnic limits, though he diligently searched for talent outside of those limits during most of his presidency.[31]

One must conclude this discussion with reference to Conant's own background as a guide to his presidential actions. He himself was a bright student who had to talk his way into Harvard, or at least his mentor Henry Black had to talk Conant's way into Harvard. And Conant used a test of chemistry knowledge to buttress his own admission. While this test was not a standardized test, it was a more objective measure of knowledge than what he might have experienced if he had not had the sponsorship of Black. Conant's affinity for the "meatballs," noted earlier, undergirded his support for admission to Harvard for those academically excellent students of whatever economic background from wherever in the nation. He saw the test that had secured his own admission as a way to secure the admission of others who might not be admitted. While the standardized tests he advocated were not subject matter tests, they shared with those tests the reliance on student achievement over social and academic pedigree that characterized the admission of many, if not most, Harvard students prior to his presidency. The ability of this approach to democratize Harvard, as Conant frequently averred, is a subject for consideration throughout much of the rest of this book.

Roads to Faculty Excellence

The second major objective of Conant's drive for excellence at Harvard, and the one that attracted much of the favorable attention to his presidential candidacy, was to significantly improve the intellectual caliber of the faculty. Again, in contrast to Lowell's concentration on undergraduates and buildings, Conant believed that an essential attribute of a new Harvard was a reconstruction of a faculty that was in decline. In tandem with his discussion of national scholarships, Conant enunciated his desire for faculty improvement at Harvard in his first presidential report for 1932–33. He remarked that Harvard must have the most distinguished faculty that it could get, a faculty made up of "great scholars and investigators." Such a faculty was the sine qua non for improving Harvard. He noted, "If we fail in this regard, there are no educational panaceas which will restore Harvard to its position of leadership." The environment for faculty excellence at Harvard had suffered under Conant's predecessor. Lowell's devotion to the college and his signature contributions, the House system and the tutorial method, as well as the curricular changes represented by concentration and distribution requirements, all dealt with undergraduates. Lowell did little to advance faculty scholarship at Harvard. Conant was clear in enunciating his own counter-priorities. The "academic life at Cambridge must be made more satisfactory in a number of ways. Sufficient time should be allowed for writing and investigation; a satisfactory balance must be struck between teaching and research."[32] And that balance for Conant was, if anything, weighted more heavily on the research side. In considering the problems of instruction in Harvard College, he concluded, "I have only one firm conviction: namely that the final solution must not in any way interfere with our aim of having in the Faculty of Arts and Sciences the most distinguished body of creative scholars which it is possible to obtain."[33] To those who argued that research did not necessarily mean good teaching, Conant's answer was "excellent teaching would not, in itself, assure a young man's career promotion."[34]

Under Lowell, that balance had been tilted away from research and investigation, especially in the Faculty of Arts and Sciences. Lowell had a strong preference for teaching and a disdain for research. That disdain was registered in many ways, including his stated loathing of the PhD degree. In opposition to doctoral study, Lowell founded the Harvard Society of Fellows, a body that used a variety of informal criteria for admission and which sought to reward scholarship, a term that implied, at least for Lowell, much more than research. The Society of Fellows was established as a clear rival in emphasis to the research

36   *Scholarly Leadership in Higher Education*

orientation of the PhD. Further, Lowell was peremptory in his decisions about keeping faculty, relying mainly on his own judgment, as superior to any other more objective criterion such as contribution to knowledge. Lowell's resort to personal authority in faculty matters was "astonishing," according to one history of Harvard. When he found out that a young instructor whom he liked very much was leaving campus, Lowell "granted him tenure on the spot."[35] The Harvard faculty during Lowell's presidency, had exhibited little intellectual distinction. Harvard had earned only one Nobel Prize during Lowell's administration; that belonged to Theodore Richards, Conant's early faculty adviser, his predecessor as Chemistry Department chair, and his father-in-law. When Conant began his presidency, the Faculty of Arts and Sciences was notable mainly for its mediocrity. Its most famous members, Frederick Jackson Turner in history and Alfred North Whitehead in philosophy, had earned their reputations on work done before they came to Harvard, rather than during their years in Cambridge.[36]

Conant moved forcefully, but not too precipitously, to reverse the trend toward what he feared was mediocrity in the faculty. He began, as noted earlier in this chapter, with a reform of the retirement system at Harvard. He described the situation he was facing with further changes in faculty personnel policies and indicated the obstacles to improvement in his 1934–35 presidential report. "In any university today, there are two great obstacles to stimulating teaching and imaginative research." The first obstacle for Conant was "the present division of the faculty into a multitude of special departments which have all too little contact with each other."[37] This situation was related to increases in university size and in organized knowledge that were then taking place. While departmental specialization was essential for effective graduate education, it was far less important at the undergraduate level. Conant supported the "explorations toward breaking down departmental lines for undergraduate concentrations" that were being undertaken by several committees.[38] The second obstacle to excellence on the faculty was "a lack of flexibility which manifests itself particularly when new appointments or promotions are to be made."[39] Conant moved to combat both of these problems with new initiatives.

Shortly after beginning his presidency, he announced his desire for the beginning of a program of "University Professorships." The idea behind this proposal was that "great minds today should not be contained by specialized boundaries." He described the key consideration for university professors when he remarked that they needed to be "free from departmental restrictions."[40] These professorships were for "roving" professors, not attached to any academic department. The professorships would free those who held them to investigate any problem or issue that interested them, regardless of its relation to any department's priorities. Further, university professors would be allowed to teach whatever topic they wished to teach to any students who chose, or were chosen, to study with the professor. Conant sought to repudiate, or at least to mitigate, the undue influence of academic departments and the specialization that much of the work of their faculty represented. What this specialization meant, for Conant, was that the departments had "all too little contact with each other." University professors would help bring various fields of knowledge into relationships with each other, which might encourage productive interaction by faculty specialists. University professorships could be used to recruit a "number of mature scholars and scientific investigators . . . who would probably be loath to accept academic positions because of a feeling that their intellectual activities might be too rigidly confined within departmental limits." Such a "professorship without portfolio, free from departmental restrictions, and with ample salary and research funds would appeal to men with broad imagination who now regard the teaching profession with only slight interest."[41]

Conant went on to describe a specific example of one who might be a university professor and what he might accomplish. A lawyer, also trained as a historian, with a career in public service and an interest in public problems, could come to Harvard and teach in the law, business, and arts and science faculties. He could also work with advanced students in government, sociology, or elsewhere. "All through his academic career as a University Professor he is free to teach what he feels is at that time of his life is the vital subject in which he is interested." Additionally, he "has time and money to prosecute his scholarly activities. He is here and there in one library or another; . . . he has no departmental connections but he is welcomed as a member of the departments and faculties in which he offers courses and with which he becomes associated in connection with his research." His graduate students, for there was no doubt in Conant's mind that his new university professors would have a large role in graduate education, would "come up for their advanced degrees through the regular channels of perhaps two faculties." In short, the university professors would be able to provide a discrete and definite intellectual boost to Harvard, to its undergraduate and graduate students, and a prod to other Harvard faculty members to venture outside of their parochial, disciplinary interests and get involved in the important research work that often crossed departmental or disciplinary boundaries.[42]

Conant understood the milieu and priorities of an academic department, having lived in, worked in, and led one during his first fifteen years at Harvard.

The personnel problem with departments was that, too often, they thought in parochial ways that centered mainly on the advancement of their own discipline, rather than the advancement of knowledge. Further, academic departments, though no strangers to conflict, often became centers of work and workers who preferred the status quo to any significant alteration in their lives that might come from significant changes. Issues of promotion and other remuneration, monetary and nonmonetary, were quite often the occasion for conflict between an administration and a department. Conant saw himself as a leader in the move to bring new life to Harvard through hiring the best faculty members available and often saw departments as bodies that were quite willing to promote good faculty members with whom they could, and did, coexist rather than to take a chance on excellence coming from an unknown quarter.

University professorships were not the only, or even the most important, way that Conant sought to control the influence of departments. Early on in his presidency, he established advisory committees to the president in the sciences, the social sciences, and in the humanities. These groups were used for advice on "appointments, honorary degree recipients, and research support." He consulted frequently with those committees on diverse topics and urged them to voice their concerns, when asked and when not asked, about the present and future of Harvard. The distinguished scholars chosen for these committees by Conant, and their willingness to accept appointment, indicated the significance of those bodies and the empathy of those selected with the concerns of the president. Conant also reinvigorated visiting committees to departments from Harvard's Board of Overseers. If these visiting committees were treated seriously, as Conant intended them to be, they could persuade the academics in departments to confront concerns and priorities that they ignored, primarily because of narrow, disciplinary affiliations.[43] None of these movements indicated severe or profound antipathy to departments on the part of the president. What they did indicate, however, was his understanding of normal academic conventions and habits and how they might provide obstacles to his pursuit of excellence. And Conant saw the most important role that he could play as president was to make sure that promotion and tenure were geared to establishing excellence. He noted that the "relationship of the President to the faculties is a peculiarly important part of the Harvard tradition" and added that "it is essential that he should devote as much time as possible to a consideration of promotions and appointments, consulting with the Deans and the individual members of faculties."[44]

Thus, Conant sought to regularize employment and retention procedures in ways that sought to appoint the most qualified person to any available position and to also make sure that the standards for retention of those seeking promotion reflected that same criterion. In his own words, Conant noted, "I had expressed the view that every permanent position should be filled only by an outstanding scholar and teacher."[45] It was in the retention area that Conant would face the first major controversy of his presidency. Given the grave economic conditions of the depression, disqualifying a faculty member for further appointment, either through a temporary or more permanent process, was a daunting task. The realities of this situation meant that when Conant took office, and during the first few years of his presidency, several faculty members, particularly instructors in the Faculty of Arts and Sciences, were on appointments that lasted well beyond the four-year limit that had been suggested for these positions. The good economic times of the 1920s, the tendency of President Lowell to leave appointments to deans and faculty committees, the tutorial system, the natural tendency of groups of men to maintain their work life, especially given few pressing reasons to change a situation, and the Oxford-Cambridge tradition that junior academics could stay in their positions without being promoted, all contributed to what the new president saw as an untenable situation in Cambridge. Without addressing the situation, Harvard, for Conant, was moving to a place where men of comparable age would be making disparate salaries and facing quite different work situations, as some were promoted to the senior ranks, with accompanying salary raises, while others simply stayed on in the junior ranks.[46]

Conant discovered that a disproportionate number of these junior appointments beyond four years were in a few departments. In 1936–37, he decided to do something about the situation and let a number of the long-term but temporary instructors know that they would receive one more temporary appointment. After that, however, they would no longer be employed. The economics department was one of the departments with a significant number of temporary instructorships and several of those instructors were offered final, two-year appointments. Among them were Raymond Walsh and Alan R. Sweezey, who soon became a cause célèbre in the Harvard community. Walsh and Sweezey were known for their left-wing politics as well as for holding office in a recently established Harvard teachers' union. The termination of their appointments was portrayed as the administration retaliating against the leaders of the fledgling faculty group. The two economists approached senior colleagues, in their own department and elsewhere in the Faculty of Arts and Sciences, for support in contesting the non-reappointments. A committee of nine senior faculty members from several departments called on the president with a petition that had been given to them on behalf of the two economists and over a hundred other members of the teaching staff that asked for an inquiry into the presidential actions on appointments. In what seemed an astute move politically, President Conant appointed the nine members (soon to be eight because of the death of one of them) as a committee to investigate the appointments of the two economists and of all other junior faculty (instructors and assistant professors).[47]

The Special Committee Appointed by the President of Harvard University issued a report on the specific appointments of Walsh and Sweezey on May 24, 1938. That report, which was eighty-six pages long, including appendices, found that the president did not act in any prejudicial way toward the two young economists such as in retaliation for their union activities. The report also found, however, that the actions of the president, in direct contradiction of the departmental recommendations for continuation of the two scholars for another term, could be construed as being inimical to them, their scholarly record and qualifications, and to thereby harm their future employment prospects. The report recommended that the departmental recommendation for reappointment be followed, rather than the president's recommendation for a terminal appointment.[48] Conant's responses, as noted in a letter to the Harvard Board of Overseers, were to accept the report, answer its contentions regarding his actions toward the faculty members by writing a letter to the two economists stating that he had no negative opinions as to their scholarly worth, remind the Overseers that the committee had exonerated him from political bias and retaliatory action and restate his original recommendation that the two-year reappointments be final. In essence, then, Conant accepted the committee's report at the same time that he rejected the committee's recommendation and refuted its contention, and the department's recommendation, that the circumstances surrounding the situation required reappointment of the two professors.[49]

The acceptance of the president's recommendations by the Board of Overseers provoked significant negative reaction, among the committee members as well as in the larger Harvard faculty. Still, the committee appointed by the president continued its work and produced a second report that recommended, among other changes, a five-year term for faculty instructors with no reappointment. This confirmation of what Conant called "an up or out" policy was accepted enthusiastically by the president, who also reported that he had discussed the issue with several faculty and concluded that there was a consensus among the faculty in support of the new policy. Given that it would be administered by a new dean of the Faculty of Arts and Sciences, a member of the committee who

The Harvard Presidency in the 1930s   41

had made the suggested changes, the president reported that the situation had been resolved, finally and favorably.[50]

That proved to be a drastically overly optimistic reading of the situation. At a called meeting of the Faculty of Arts and Sciences on October 8, 1939, the faculty restated their negative reaction to the new appointments policy of the president and the new dean. At a second meeting the following week, three department chairs demanded a reversal of decisions that had adversely affected their young faculty and a report from the new dean outlining how those decisions had been made. Less than a month later, another meeting of the faculty was held and an acrimonious split between some faculty members and the president was laid bare. The first thing that the faculty did at this meeting was to abolish the Faculty Council, a representative group recommended by the president early in his term of office that had acted on behalf of the full faculty. A second motion was offered to appoint a committee to investigate the recent change in appointment procedures that had taken the power of appointment away from the faculty and vested it in the president and the Board of Overseers. This threatened directly the very power of the presidency, as well as the principles of excellence in appointment that Conant had fought for, and implemented, since his coming to the job. The dean of the Business School advised the president that what he needed to do was apologize to the faculty for the heavy handedness of his recent actions. Conant accepted that advice and, before the recommendation regarding investigating faculty prerogatives in appointments could be voted on, he apologized directly to the faculty. He admitted that he had made errors that were directly responsible for the current tension in the faculty but "asked the faculty, however, not on account of my mistakes, to take a hasty step which might affect Harvard adversely for years to come." After his statement, a motion to table the issue was made and adopted by voice vote.[51] President Conant had dodged the proverbial bullet and kept intact an appointment and promotion procedure that would be adopted, in conjunction with its alignment with policy adopted by the American Association of University Professors two years later, by most colleges and universities throughout the nation. To a large extent, it is still the policy for promotion and tenure that is in place at those institutions.

Subsequently, after a little more than a decade of his presidency, Conant institutionalized the presence of extradepartmental influence in the permanent appointment of Harvard faculty when he put in place a system of *ad hoc* committees to be involved in the hiring. He described his experience with permanent appointments to the Harvard faculty with two conclusive statements. The first was that "there cannot be a uniform procedure for making life appointments applicable to all parts of a complex university." He then stated that, in his experience, "nine times out of ten the normal forces working within any special segment of the University makes for a good appointment, *but against an excellent appointment*." To make sure that excellence, not just goodness or competence, was the criterion that would be followed at Harvard, Conant remarked that starting in the past few years "all recommendations for permanent positions are reviewed by an *ad hoc* committee chosen for the special purpose of considering the merits of the department's choice as well as the qualification of possible candidates outside the university." The *ad hoc* committee was appointed by the president with consultation from the dean involved. It usually contained one senior member from the department involved and two scholars from outside of the department.[52] As this system evolved, and largely because of the support of the committees by the president, the *ad hoc* committee came to become the final arbiter of the appointment process and to outstrip the department faculty in the choice of permanent colleagues.

Given this rather lengthy account of Conant's sometimes adversarial relationship with departments and their faculties, particularly on the terrain of appointments and promotion, it may seem odd to conclude that, generally, Conant had great respect for and good relations with Harvard faculty. Conant understood, and respected, the university as an institution and was familiar with its history back to medieval times and with the tradition of faculty control that characterized most of the earliest universities in those times. During his presidency, one source notes that "when push came to shove in his dealings with deans or departments, Conant was likely to lose." In contrast, "in disputes with his supposed overlords, the Corporation and the Board of Overseers, he always won." This discussion ends with the following conclusion: "Power at Harvard— such as it was—flowed up from below."[53] Conant's major priority was to make sure that Harvard would have the best scholars available on its faculty. In addition to the use of *ad hoc* committees to assure this process, he was reported to have a tendency to appoint weak deans who would not be able to contest his final decisions in hiring.[54] Once hired, however, Conant was content to let faculty go in whatever directions they thought appropriate for their work. Other than various attempts, mostly unsuccessful, to institutionalize cross-departmental work, he left faculty to their own devices, providing whatever support he could to those who worked on projects he valued, and not interfering with the work of any faculty member, even if it did not follow his own preferences.

In the immediate post–Second World War years, when the Cold War was heating up and universities, most of which were just getting back on to their feet

The Harvard Presidency in the 1930s   43

and all of which were contending with enormous enrollment pressures from veterans, Conant restated his basic position on the nature of a university and its relationship to a faculty free to investigate what they wanted. "The bedrock on which the scholarly activities of a university are founded is a charter of free inquiry; without this you may have an institution of advanced education, a technical school or a military college, for example, but you do not have a university."[55] A year later, he described Harvard as follows:

> This university is composed of ten faculties, each one of which is to a large degree a self-regulating community of scholars; the permanent members carry forward the ancient tradition of independence, the hallmark of the university of the Middle Ages. These ten faculties with their respective student bodies are the essential core of Harvard; everything else is secondary.[56]

He went on to enumerate the ten faculties and spell out several of the things that were secondary, including "endowments, administrative officials, Governing Boards," and specified that these are "either accessory apparatus or channels of communication with the body politic which these faculties seek to serve."[57]

Non-Priorities of President Conant

Thus far, the primacy of Conant's meritocratic vision for Harvard has been stressed, as well as his specific actions taken on behalf of that vision in the recruitment of students and the appointment of faculty. It might be well to take a moment, while still concentrating on the early years of Conant's presidency, to indicate the things that Conant did not pay great attention to in his administration. First, in that regard, is the area of fundraising. Contrary to many of his contemporaries, and certainly contrary to most university presidents in the twenty-first century, Conant paid minimal attention to raising money. Of course, the depression, which confronted Conant and Harvard with possible dire consequences from the time he took over the presidency, hampered any large fundraising campaigns. The numbers reflected that reality. Harvard's gift and bequest income that stood at $15.6 million in 1931, the year before Conant's appointment, had dropped to $2.6 million in 1935.[58] This, of course, was not a reflection on Conant or his presidency, but it did indicate that something needed to be done.

Conant was persuaded to use the coming 300th anniversary of Harvard's founding, which was to be celebrated formally in 1936, as a platform from which to try and increase giving substantially. As to the specifics of how funds sought through the tercentenary were to be used, Conant asked his departments to prepare proposals for needed funds to be raised through the tercentenary. When departments responded with a batch of proposals totaling $81 million in needed new funds, he ignored them and produced his own proposal for $30 million for national scholarships and university professorships. Even this reduced amount turned out to be "a farcically unrealistic goal." By the end of 1936, only $5.5 million had been raised. As was often the case, fundraising under Conant was clumsy and halting, suffering from poor planning as well as poor execution of plans.[59] Of course, given the realities of the Great Depression of the 1930s, it was difficult to envision a substantially more rosy result. This situation, as will be shown in Chapter 3, changed a good bit for the better in the years after the Second World War.

In spite of his lack of success in fundraising, Conant did not harm Harvard financially in the initial years of his administration, marred economically by the high tide of the Great Depression. He benefited from Lowell's stewardship and inherited an institution that was basically in good financial health. Conant's own frugality with the budget was acknowledged across the campus. In deference to the depression, and to signal a change away from the formality and formalities that had characterized the Lowell administration, Conant eschewed an inaugural ceremony and celebration. The Sunday teas that Lowell had held for undergraduates were considerably less elaborate under Conant, and other rituals favored by his predecessor were either diminished in significance or stopped completely. In describing the situation on campus in general, one history of Harvard noted that under Conant, "charm had taken a sabbatical." It added, however, that the "echo of Eliot's assertive baritone" was present.[60] Under Conant, Harvard was able to sustain itself through the worst of the Great Depression. Faculty wages were not reduced, though staff wages were cut. There was no resort to layoffs, of faculty or of staff, though as we have seen Conant encountered resistance to his attempt to strengthen faculty retention standards. The financial resilience of Harvard during the depression lay primarily in the steadiness of tuition income. There was no reduction in tuition for Harvard students at any time in the decade.[61] Conant, thus, presided over a relatively healthy Harvard, money wise, and contributed to the maintenance of that health with his own penchant for counting pennies, as well as dollars.

In addition to relative unconcern with fundraising, Conant was basically uninterested, again in contrast to Lowell, in erecting buildings that would provide a physical legacy of his administration. Few buildings were constructed during Conant's first decade as president, and the few that were built supported other of Conant's priorities more than reflecting any general "edifice complex." Noted Bauhaus architect, Walter Gropius, appointed by Conant to head Harvard's School of Design, planned and constructed a new home for the Law School that embodied his own innovative, and functional, design.[62] Similarly, a new home was constructed for the Littauer School of Public Administration (to be discussed in the next section of this chapter) but again to support the efforts of the fledgling school and its interdisciplinary thrust rather than to adorn either the campus or the president's legacy.

Nazi Germany cast a shadow over Conant's Harvard, most controversially through its political intrusion into the tercentenary celebration when a Harvard alumnus who was a Nazi functionary sought a prominent role.[63] Conant was a great respecter of the scientific accomplishments of German universities, particularly their scientists. His respect made him much slower to condemn Nazi intrusions into German university life, and much more willing to send Harvard representation to German university celebrations, even when evidence of a Nazi takeover was strong. Nazi persecution of Jews began during the Lowell administration and it and the later Nazi takeover of German universities meant a large number of German Jewish scholars seeking appointments to American university faculties. Harvard was anything but a leader in the employment of these refugee scholars in the 1930s. Lowell simply refused to employ Jewish refugee scholars. Conant was not as flat-footed in his stance. When asked to employ one or more refugee scholars, he demurred unless the particular individual was the "best qualified" for a particular position on the Harvard faculty. When most controversy over the anti-Semitism of the Nazi regime had diminished, especially in academic circles, and the Nazi persecution of Jews became widely acknowledged, it "still was Harvard policy in 1940 that no refugee would be appointed unless his department or school was ready to support him to the end of his working life."[64] In spite of this the German refugee presence on the Harvard faculty grew in the late 1930s, though two of the most prominent refugees appointed to the faculty, Walter Gropius in the School of Design and Robert Ulich in the School of Education, were not Jewish. Harvard's record on hiring German Jewish refugees under Conant was not exemplary. It contrasted with what went on at the University of Chicago, for example, and at other prestigious American universities. Still, Conant was not a consistent or even a vigorous anti-Semite. In fact, he helped get two Jewish students admitted to Harvard in this period, one indication of his willingness to act on behalf of the persecuted as an individual, even if the willingness was not otherwise evident.[65]

His mixed record on Jewish students and faculty was echoed in his dealings with other minority groups. African American students were not denied admission to Harvard, but neither did they constitute a priority for the institution. And the Conant administration also took a relatively indifferent stance toward African Americans on the faculty. A proposal was made to Conant in 1935 that Harvard invite Alain Locke, noted African American philosopher and Harvard graduate and doctoral recipient, for a visiting lectureship. Conant consulted a Harvard philosopher who was lukewarm about Locke's suitability for the post and eventually said no to the request, though he did not preclude an invitation in the future. This reluctance to act positively in the racial arena characterized other of Conant's activities. In the early 1940s, he ignored the nascent civil rights movement, fending off more than one request to act to ameliorate the condition of African Americans. In 1943, however, as the Second World War made clearer the mistreatment of African Americans and enhanced the voices of those who sought to end it, Conant took a positive position and signed a petition sponsored by the president of Smith College deploring a race riot in Detroit.[66]

Conant's position regarding the significant Roman Catholic presence near Harvard was one of diffidence but not of overt hostility. Catholic enrollment at Harvard was small under Lowell and remained limited under Conant. Yet neither administrator wanted to antagonize the significant Catholic population in Cambridge and Boston. Lowell had maintained amicable relations with the archbishop of Boston, based as much on their mutual adherence to conservatism in most aspects of life as on any other factors. Conant, in turn, kept up a steady relationship through an Irish-Catholic Harvard alumnus, who advised him on the nuances of the political relationship between Harvard and the Irish Catholic–dominated government of the city of Cambridge.[67]

Conant had one significant non-priority that indicated another clear difference with his predecessor. Conant had little use for athletics, particularly for intercollegiate athletics. He seldom attended Harvard athletic contests of any kind, even the annual football game with archrival Yale. Early on in his presidency, in the midst of the Great Depression, he announced that athletic funding would be cut. The depression had turned football from a money maker into a part of a larger financial problem for athletics. Conant used the situation to bring the football program under much tighter financial control.[68] He added that, in his mind, cutting the athletic budget would not significantly harm opportunities for the undergraduate students. Conant also remarked that not cutting funding for athletics would support "the hand-to-mouth policy of old days which must eventually lead any institution to have far too great

The Harvard Presidency in the 1930s   47

concern with football gate receipts."[69] A few years later, he declared that the state of athletics on campus was good and added that stressing the importance of intramural athletics over intercollegiate athletics had helped the situation. He reinforced his belief in intramural, as opposed to intercollegiate, athletics, when he concluded that "athletics for all is more than a slogan in modern Harvard; it is very close to being a description of reality."[70] Conant never wavered from his devotion to intramurals, and his suspicion of intercollegiate athletics, throughout his presidency. He discussed athletics in his penultimate presidential report in words that echoed his ideas of the 1930s. He remarked that the essence of a policy on scholarships for athletes agreed to by Harvard, Yale, and Princeton was that athletes have the same opportunities for financial assistance as "other students whose interests and abilities have been shown in other activities." He concluded that athletes "shall be neither penalized nor favored because of their athletic ability."[71]

Another major non-priority for Conant was the Divinity School. Conant was not a religious person, and he had little desire to help the Divinity School, which struggled for funds throughout his presidency. Early on in his presidency, he acted on his suspicion of religion at Harvard when he decided to end an early morning bell ringing at the Memorial Church that, since 1760, had announced the Morning Prayer service. He also told the dean of the Memorial Church at Harvard that if Christian symbols like a cross or candles were ever displayed on the communion table at the church, "he would not again show his face in the church." Conant did attend church services, on occasion, however, being the happiest when the sermon given was of intellectual substance such as that given by visitors such as the noted philosopher and theologian, Reinhold Niebuhr. It was reported, however, that Conant allowed his son to read detective stories during sermons and that he had no interest in issues related to things such as Baptism rites.[72]

Conant maintained his suspicion of, if not direct antipathy to, the Divinity School throughout his presidency. He flirted more than once in his twenty years in office with trying to close the Divinity School. In the early 1940s, for example, he set up a committee to solve the problems of the Divinity School, hoping that it would find them unsolvable and recommend closure. Much to his disappointment, the committee recommended instead an increase in internal institutional funding and a campaign to raise outside funds for the school. Conant gave a definite negative answer to the first recommendation and acquiesced, however not with great enthusiasm, in the second. Needless to say he was not surprised when the increased endowment effort bore little fruit, though he also

48   *Scholarly Leadership in Higher Education*

understood that wartime conditions hampered the effort severely.[73] In the final year of his presidency, he argued with the men of the Harvard Corporation who aided him in governing the university over the fate of the Divinity School. This time Conant's diffidence to the school was counteracted by the offer of two of the corporation members to lead a $2 million endowment campaign.[74] In the last year of that presidency, he noted with some chagrin that during his term in office, all but three professional schools, Divinity and two others (which he did not name), had increased their budget. He added that in his two decades as president, "all the professional faculties (except Divinity) have lived on their own."[75]

The Tercentenary Celebration

While the fundraising aspect of the 300th anniversary celebration has been discussed, for Conant it was much more than an effort to raise money. It allowed him to provide a stage on which to celebrate his own historical commitment to the university as an essential institution of Western culture. Conant threw himself into preparations for the coming celebration but concentrated much more on the actual celebration activities than on any fund raising that they would facilitate. Various commemorative activities took place throughout the tercentenary year, 1936. The highlight, however, was a several days long Conference on the Arts and Sciences held in early September. Seventy-one scholars presented papers, with equitable representation from the arts and letters, the physical sciences, the biological sciences, and the social sciences. Included among the presenters were Arthur Eddington and Arthur Holly Compton, two physicists, the first from England and the second an American Nobel Prize winner; Jean Piaget and Carl Jung, eminent European psychologists; and the anthropologist Bronislaw Malinowski, the historian Frederick Meinecke, and the philosopher Etienne Gilson, all Europeans. These scholars, and many others, gave a series of lectures and other presentations that reflected the historical eminence of Harvard as well as the significance of scholarship itself, in Cambridge and elsewhere. Additionally, President Franklin Delano Roosevelt, a Harvard alumnus, spoke at a session open to alumni as well as to scholars. Roosevelt was an obvious choice to speak; however, his participation aroused the ire of many conservative Harvard alumni, including former president Lowell.[76]

    Conant's own presentation at the tercentenary conference restated his belief in the historical and contemporary importance of Harvard and other universities

The Harvard Presidency in the 1930s   49

and of the scholarship done by their faculties. He argued first that the university from its medieval inception to contemporary times had four major emphases: knowledge for its own sake, the liberal arts, education for the professions, and a vigorous student life. These four emphases needed to be in balance for the most effective university life. At times, such as when liberal education for undergraduates dominated, the balance was lost, and "the stream of learning and research inevitably dries up." Such was the case in the ideas of John Henry Newman, author of *The Idea of the University*. Newman believed that to discover and to teach meant a university as "a place of teaching universal knowledge for the diffusion and extension of knowledge rather than the advancement."[77] Institutions that concentrated on research and discovery alone were also out of balance, best described not as universities but as research institutes or academies. The contemporary scene, especially in the United States, was another instance of an unbalanced educational effort at universities. The problem here was the dominance of the professional motive, especially that of the newer, more directly applied professions such as engineering. Conant called this view, looking at the university "through the dull glasses of immediate utility."[78]

Even more threatening to the health of the university for Conant was that "a wave of anti-intellectualism is passing round the world."[79] While he did not name the source of this anti-intellectualism, there is little doubt that he was referring first to Nazi Germany and its acolytes or allies in Spain and Italy and to a lesser extent to communist nations such as the Soviet Union. The result of this kind of anti-intellectualism was intellectual and educational chaos. "To bring order out of educational chaos," he added, was "the mission of the liberal arts curriculum of our universities." The traditional liberal arts agencies by which to bring such order were the classics and mathematics that provided a common background to all who were educated. This solution had been made obsolete, however, by the explosion of knowledge in other areas such as the sciences and the social sciences.[80]

The goal for Conant was to find the modern equivalent of the unifying force of the classics and mathematics. While he was not clear on the specifics of the solution, he was clear that mere sampling of university history, general science, and arts and literature was insufficient. More satisfactory and a beginning point for contemporary reform in the liberal arts was the emphasis on "the thorough study of at least one discipline." Here Conant was unveiling his own interest in general education, an interest that would eventually result, as we will see in a later chapter, in the publication of the Harvard Redbook on general education and his own teaching of a general education course in science.[81] Conant also spoke of another theme that would capture much of his intellectual attention when he alluded to the important goal of "development of a national culture based on a study of the past."[82] The last few pages of Conant's address were devoted to intellectual freedom, in the case of the universities to academic freedom, as the sine qua non for any genuine university accomplishments. And the goal of these accomplishments, for Conant, was to be found in the one-word motto of Harvard University "Veritas," or truth. The search for truth was the fundamental activity of universities since their inception, and that search for truth was, if anything, even more important in the conflict-ridden years of the 1930s.[83]

Interests in things like truth, academic freedom, liberal education, and national and cultural history were certainly not what the critics of Conant as a narrow natural scientist would have expected to hear. We will show later in this chapter and in subsequent chapters, however, that they constituted a considerable part of his intellectual interests, concerns, and commitments as the president of Harvard University. James Bryant Conant as the president of Harvard had a wide-ranging view of the university and of higher education elsewhere in the United States and throughout the world. The particulars and contours of that view are the particulars of the rest of this analysis. Some were in unexpected areas such as education and public policy.

Other Priorities: Education, Public Administration, History

In a direct contrast to his negative attitude to athletics and the Divinity School, Conant repeatedly voiced his support for different parts of the university and frequently advocated experimenting with change in Harvard's curriculum during the 1930s and after. During the first decade of his presidency, Conant had a chance to indicate the parts of the university that he had great interest in and which he earnestly wanted to succeed. It should not be surprising, given what has been said about his somewhat jaundiced views of departments, that none of the disciplinary departments was favored consistently by the chief executive. Conant was careful not to go overboard in his discussion of various academic programs or priorities, knowing that as president he was responsible for all of the campus. He did, however have a few favorites, and they were located most often in the professional school arena. In keeping with his desire for cross-departmental, interdisciplinary efforts, for example, Conant took a distinct interest in the birth and development of the field of public administration.

The Harvard Presidency in the 1930s   51

In 1934, Carl Friedrich of Harvard's Government Department proposed an institute of public administration wherein Harvard training would meet the need for better educated public officials to lead various areas of civil service, especially in the national government. Conant demurred on the new institute, because of financial difficulties, but endorsed the idea of such training. A year later, Lucius Littauer, a distinguished alumnus and former Republican congressman, offered a gift of $2 million for a Graduate School of Public Administration. Conant ignored the politically partisan undertones (anti-New Deal) of the giver of the gift and quickly accepted the money and proceeded with plans to develop the new school.[84] The school hired no new faculty and admitted no degree students. Rather, in company with Conant's interdisciplinary ideas, it took an all-university approach to the training of students for government service. It utilized faculty from numerous parts of the university, most particularly from the Economics Department and the Government Department, as well as the Business School. Initially, the enrolled students in the Littauer School were on leave from government positions, with an intention not to seek degrees but to improve their own approach to their work. The Littauer gift was used to put up a new building large enough to handle both the students from government service enrolled and other students from arts and sciences departments and professional schools such as the Business and Law School who were interested in public administration.[85]

The Littauer School embodied several of Conant's treasured academic priorities. It crossed departmental and disciplinary lines in its faculty and it enrolled working professionals interested in improving the public good, as well as or in place of seeking their own personal advancement. Additionally, the Littauer School declined to follow, at least initially, the traditional academic model of degree studies, hewing more closely to an education that would improve the understanding and the skills of students who came from positions in public service. All of these qualities indicated why the Littauer School ranked high on the list of Conant's priorities and also that it would suffer from debates and disputes from its various participating academic sponsors over the years. Additionally, the vagaries of a core student body that came from the world of work, and was dependent on release from that world for enrollment, meant that the school would eventually have to depend more on normal graduate students and degree studies for its survival. Only when the Littauer School evolved into the Kennedy School, after Conant had left Harvard, did it achieve the success that Conant and its initiators had envisioned.

The second professional school in which Conant showed great interest was one that was already in existence when he ascended to the Harvard presidency.

52   *Scholarly Leadership in Higher Education*

This school was not in the best of repute across the campus, the Graduate School of Education. Conant's view of the field of education when he was a chemistry faculty member was the conventional view among arts and sciences faculty. He described this point of view as follows: "There was no excuse for the existence of people who sought to teach others how to teach." He added that his own knowledge of chemistry and his coauthorship of a high school chemistry textbook, with his high school chemistry teacher, meant that he knew what there was to know about teaching that subject. For Conant, when "any issues involving benefits to the graduate school of education came before the faculty of arts and sciences, I automatically voted with those who looked with contempt on the school of education."[86]

When he became the president of Harvard, however, and the head of all the faculties in the university, his position changed. He remarked that it "soon became evident that the antithesis between the views of the professors who taught the usual college subjects and those who were instructing future teachers in those subjects was not as simple as I thought." He went on to state that the result of his thinking along these lines was to attempt to create mutual understanding between these two groups through the establishment of a joint Master of Arts in Teaching (MAT) program. This program was to replace the MA programs in the various subject matter fields used as a credential by many to obtain high school teaching jobs and the Master of Education degree in the School of Education offered for similar purposes. Conant formally proposed the MAT in his 1934–35 presidential report.[87] This joint program made the arts and sciences faculty responsible for the subject matter content of the teachers in training and the education faculty responsible for the educator preparation aspects of the program. To consider the particulars of the new joint program, he appointed a committee of seven faculty members, four from arts and sciences and three from the School of Education.[88] While the committee's makeup may have reflected Conant still leaning toward arts and sciences, it produced a program that was approved by both faculties, one that was quickly implemented. Conant was proud enough of the MAT program to proclaim it as one of the major social inventions of his career in his autobiography.[89] MAT programs have proliferated, though not necessarily flourished, since Conant's invention at Harvard, most often in institutions of higher education that have emphasized the arts and sciences in undergraduate and in graduate studies.

In 1933, Conant had briefly outlined a program for a School of Education that would concentrate on the development of psychological tests to help with admissions decisions that facilitated innovations in admissions such as the national scholarship program at Harvard. Other considerations he thought worthy of the School of Education included concentration on the challenges presented by the backgrounds of many of the students who were to be taught in the schools and more practical work on the techniques of teaching. Adding to these concerns an emphasis on a thorough mastery of subject matter (to be gained largely in arts and sciences), Conant concluded with a recommendation for less emphasis on philosophy and psychology, as well as on training for school administrative work in the School of Education.[90]

Later in the 1930s, Conant's mind about the mission of a School of Education had changed or at least was in the process of changing. A long discussion of secondary education led off the presidential report for 1937–38. He began by arguing that the high school was becoming increasingly important nationally and then reviewed statistics on high school enrollment indicating a tenfold increase in total enrollment from 630,000 in 1900 to over 6 million in 1936. This increase included a new kind of student who was less or disinterested in academic success and more interested in practical survival, including occupational and economic betterment. To serve these new students, whom Conant believed to be a clear majority, especially in the public schools, new curriculum was needed as well as a significant expansion of vocational guidance services. He noted that while the academic subjects were still important, "the educational problems of the second type [non-academic students], however, are infinitely more significant if we lift our eyes from our immediate task to consider the total load carried by the secondary schools of the country." He added that not just Harvard but American universities in general had avoided paying attention to the public schools. In regard to schools of education, he noted, "There can be no question today that the study of education as a social process—quite apart from the training of teachers—is as important as the study of law or of business administration."[91]

Conant remarked that most teachers were then trained in normal schools, where larger concerns such as he had discussed were overshadowed by the battle to provide the number of teachers needed for the burgeoning public high, and elementary, schools. In fact, education faculties in general were too concerned with maintaining legislative mandates that teachers for the public schools be trained in normal schools and/or in teacher education programs managed within education departments of schools at other institutions of higher education. Compounding the situation was that the new problems of organization and administration that attended the mass increase in school enrollment were neglected by arts and science faculties. The Harvard Graduate School of Education was a body that Conant wished to see rise to meet the challenge of new conditions. The problem was that the school was "one of the youngest of our graduate schools" and its faculty was "small and its resources totally inadequate for the position which it should occupy both within the Harvard family and in the nation." He added that while the joint MAT degree was in keeping with his priorities, the Graduate School of Education needed to do much more in the areas of research and service. He concluded this discussion with the statement: "We can hardly hope that Harvard may play a significant part as a national institution unless prepared to cope adequately with one of the most important of national problems, and one at the center of our primary concern, education."[92]

How had Conant progressed, or at least changed, in his thinking from the standard arts and sciences faculty suspicion of the School of Education, to an advocate of a joint MAT teacher training program, and to an analyst of changes in public school enrollments that provided stark challenges to those in the fields of study encompassed by any school of education? The complete answer to this question is not known, but the significance of the change in Conan's views of public education is beyond doubt. He began during the 1930s an interest in American public schools, and the institutions like the Harvard Graduate School of Education that trained teachers and administrators for those schools, which would last for the rest of his life.

Conant's own explanation for the change in his thinking, at least as it was taking place within Harvard University and its Graduate School of Education, involved his interactions with the two leaders of the school in the 1930s and very early 1940s. He remarked that during the 1930s, he began to mitigate his criticism of the Graduate School of Education through discussions with its then dean, Henry Holmes. Conant remarked that Holmes taught him "more about the tasks facing a teacher in a high school which was not selective, and, therefore, quite unlike the school I had attended." Conant added, however, that in spite of its selectivity, the high school had a "democratic tradition" and, further, that he himself was interested in a school having a greater variety of backgrounds in its student body. Finally, he applauded the fact that his high school, "the Roxbury Latin School, was free for children of families living in Old Roxbury," those students who could pass the admission examination at least. Conant surmised that "Dean Holmes must have recognized my antiaristocratic bias and played on it for all its worth."[93] Conant had inherited Holmes as dean of the Graduate School of Education, but the two evidently got along personally well enough that they could interact intelligently with each other, to the benefit of Conant's understanding of the new challenges facing American public schools as well as

The Harvard Presidency in the 1930s   55

to the Graduate School of Education's standing with the president, if not with the rest of the university.

Late in 1939, Holmes decided to resign as dean, perhaps in order to get someone newer to continue the president's education on educational affairs. Conant had someone in mind from the beginning of the search for Holmes's replacement. That individual, Francis Spaulding, was already on the education faculty. Conant broke a few eggs in selecting Spaulding, however, declining to fully involve the faculty in the search.[94] In spite of this, the search resulted in the choice of a well-qualified candidate who was acceptable to the faculty. Francis T. Spaulding was an alumnus of Harvard College who had earned both a master's and a doctoral degree in education at Harvard and been on the School of Education faculty since 1924. His major areas of expertise were school administration and leadership. In 1938, Holmes had chosen Spaulding as associate dean for the school and began to involve him in discussions about educational policy with the president. In fact, Spaulding had helped Conant with his discussion of the high school in the latter's 1937–38 presidential report, discussed above. And it was Spaulding who had specifically suggested the inclusion in the report of the term "study of education as a social process," which indicated that the school was to go far beyond a focus on teacher training and far beyond what Conant had contemplated earlier in the decade.[95] Finally, Spaulding had been the author of a two-volume survey of education in New York State, mentioned specifically in Conant's 1937–38 report as a prime indicator of the direction to take in a School of Education focused on research and service.[96] Spaulding was officially installed as dean of the School of Education in 1940.

Conant and Spaulding agreed on more of a social science orientation and research focus for the Graduate School of Education, along with a renewed emphasis on the training of administrators for the public schools and other educational leadership roles. It should be noted that in his dealings with the Graduate School of Education Conant was able to foreground his own oft-stated interest in interdisciplinary efforts, as institutionalized in the MAT degree. The interest in the social sciences, especially as evidenced in cross-disciplinary initiatives, was, as noted earlier, also characteristic of the early development of the Littauer School. The social sciences were particularly attractive to Conant in the first decade of his presidency, as he sketched out other initiatives and developed his own sense of his educational priorities.

In fact, the social sciences, or at least a social science approach, even invaded Conant's involvement in his own area, the natural sciences. Conant waxed eloquently on the importance of an historical understanding of the university and of the academic scholarship that was its fundamental activity. He thought that such an understanding might mitigate the feuds between academic departments on turf issues through "an appeal to a common family tradition." He added that the "line of descent is the same for all," and that for a genuine development of the history of scholarship, "it is first necessary to train the future professors of this much neglected subject." Given that academic research and scholarship was most advanced as an enterprise in the natural sciences, to accomplish the objective of charting and understanding that development, he announced that Harvard had established a PhD program in the "History of Science and Learning." Those responsible for the new doctoral degree were also developing a new field of concentration for a few "undergraduates of high rank" in the history of science. Careful experimentation by teachers of this subject should also lead, said Conant, to a demonstration of the "value of the History of Science as a part of the college curriculum for any large body of students."[97]

Prefiguring his own involvement in history of science courses for nonscientists in the next decade, Conant added, "I can conceive of a course in the History of Science elected by large numbers of students without scientific bent which would test the powers of even the habitual crammer." He added that such "a course in which various phases in the development of science were thoroughly explored might serve as an introduction for non-scientists to the methods of science."[98] Thus, Conant, the chemist who could no longer maintain a program of research in chemistry, found an outlet for his scientific endeavors in advocating and developing programs in the history of science at the graduate and undergraduate levels. He conflated in his own mind the history of science and the history of scholarship, and facilitated this conflation through encouraging work in the history of science, for scientists and for nonscientists.

Conant's choice to lead the new program in history of science was already at the university, though not in a regular faculty position. George Sarton was a Belgian who had emigrated to the United States in the 1910s in flight from the war being waged on his nation by Germany and its allies. Sarton was a giant in the field of history of science, founder and editor of its leading journal, *Isis*, and a prolific scholar. He had a doctorate in chemistry from the University of Ghent in Belgium and agreed with Conant that a scholar in the history of science needed a background in one of the sciences. Further, the two agreed that this background might best be filled in chemistry, a field bound by relationships to both biology and physics. Sarton had come to Harvard in 1916, under sponsorship and with financial support from the Carnegie Institution, one of the many philanthropic institutions founded by Andrew Carnegie. Sarton received a place in which to

The Harvard Presidency in the 1930s 57

conduct his research in the history of science in the Widener Library at Harvard, the title of lecturer, and a small stipend to give a few lectures in his subject during the academic year. Conant attended a few of those lectures near the end of his doctoral studies in 1916.[99]

Conant noted that in the second year of his presidency, attempts began to be made to make Sarton a more regular member of the faculty. Those attempts came to fruition when in 1940 Sarton became a permanent member of the Harvard faculty. In between those two developments, a program in the history of science was established at Harvard, mainly at the doctoral level, and a standing committee on the history of science was established in the Faculty of Arts and Sciences. The program never grew to the extent that Sarton, or Conant, envisioned, graduating only two PhDs in the next decade.[100] Conant's explanation for the lack of program development resided in a lack of outside funding for the program itself. In addition, Sarton's disinterest in pursuing that funding, establishing productive relationships with historians and with scientists on campus, and pursuing an undergraduate program in the field that Conant felt was imperative for program success did not help the situation.[101] The result was that Sarton continued to give his lectures and advise only a few students until his retirement in 1951. Conant remarked that Sarton's lectures to undergraduates in the history of science were extremely well attended in the immediate post-Second World War years, the enrollment growing to 300 students, triple what it had been in the 1930s.[102]

History of science was not the only application of the social sciences that Conant supported in the early years of his presidency. He had much bigger goals for the historical approach to understanding society, goals geared to the improvement of Harvard College and for improving life outside of Harvard College as well. He thought that history properly taught should result in an "educational virus which alone maintains its potency throughout life—the virus of a self-perpetuating liberal education." He remarked that it was "possible that in the study of our national cultural history we may find the principle that is needed to unify our liberal arts tradition and to mold it to suit this modern age." He added that a "true appreciation of this country's past might be the common denominator among educated men which would enable them to face the future unified and unafraid." He made sure that it was not academic historians or history majors who were the object of this effort. "It is not to those who are concentrating in history that such a proposal should appeal. It is rather a suggestion to the non-historian. Here is a vitally important aspect of his liberal education which he might at least start developing during his college years."[103]

58   *Scholarly Leadership in Higher Education*

Thus, like the history of science, cultural or social history had for Conant a larger appeal to nonspecialists, and the development of that field, at least on the undergraduate level, should be undertaken by both specialists and allies in related fields. Such an undertaking for Conant was at the core of what would be a meaningful liberal education, the essence of the education offered at Harvard College.

One year later, Conant took his advocacy of the development of American cultural history a step beyond Harvard College. He restated his belief that a thorough knowledge of economic, political, and cultural history was desirable for every college graduate and added that separate academic coursework in the area was not the answer to achieving this objective. Rather, true understanding would be obtained better through the stimulation of reading in this area of study. In pursuit of that objective, he announced creation of a faculty committee to develop the Harvard Reading List in American History and an examination and prizes based on that examination for those who scored the highest on it. Taking the list, and the reward system, off campus was also a goal for Conant. He advocated distribution of the reading list as a means of adult education and added that noncommercial broadcast of a number of faculty lectures on topics related to the list had been undertaken.[104]

Conant had to admit the ultimate failure of his desire for innovation in cultural history, on and off campus, later in the 1930s. He prefaced his admission with a restatement of his view that special consideration should be given to American cultural history. This time he stated more explicitly what tied his advocacy to both liberal education at Harvard and other colleges and to adult education outside of colleges and universities: "It is my belief that only by a deep immersion in our cultural history—the political, social, scientific and literary history of the country—can an *education for citizenship* be achieved." Having finally specified a concrete goal of citizenship education as the objective of his efforts in this endeavor, he had to add that his efforts to increase the voluntary study of American history by Harvard undergraduates had failed. This outcome was clear in spite of the placement of a counselor in history as a resident in the Harvard Houses for the last two years.[105] In spite of the failure of his plan for cultural history on campus, Conant in this case exhibited an intellectual curiosity and commitment to an idea that seemed unusual for a university president, one that revealed a commitment to advancing liberal education in unusual ways. That commitment would be successfully institutionalized in the regeneration of general education at Harvard, to be described in a later chapter.

Both the history of science and cultural history were for Conant intellectual vehicles by which to improve the liberal education offered at Harvard College. While the former effort had succeeded, at least initially through the hiring of a faculty member and the institution of a doctoral degree program, that program never flourished at Harvard. The latter program had failed completely. Of course, trying to stimulate intellectual work outside of the curriculum, at Harvard or at any other institution of higher education, was a herculean task, and Conant's failure in this regard should not be seen as a repudiation of its importance. His own analysis of the situation at Harvard led him to conclude that resistance to initiatives such as the extracurricular study of American history was due in greatest part to the "penetration into the liberal college of university functions." By this he meant that specialization, a sine qua non of most graduate programs, was the source of the resistance to, and repudiation of, broad areas of study such as cultural history. He was so opposed to this rigid, disciplinary specialization that he contemplated battling it where it originated at Harvard, in the graduate school. Cognizant of the opposition that any initiative to liberalize graduate education would face, he advocated not the radical reform of graduate curricula themselves but minor alterations. Conant remarked that it was "at least worth discussing whether the candidate for the PhD should not be required to keep alive at least some minor interest in broad general fields of culture, entirely apart from their specialty."[106] Again, Conant's lack of success in this endeavor did not belie the intellectual significance of the effort.

Conant had another suggestion to combat overspecialization in graduate programs. He wished to see the intimacy and constancy of interaction that was encouraged for Harvard College students through the residential House Plan incorporated into graduate studies. This meant the erection of two or more houses for graduate students in Cambridge where the students could eat, and meet, with each other in settings that encouraged discussion across their disciplinary boundaries. Such an initiative could try to combat what Conant described as the "academic nationalism" that excessively narrowed the views of graduate and professional students.[107]

Conant understood that graduate studies, clearly under the control of graduate faculty, might be beyond the reach of his cultural history and other interdisciplinary initiatives. He acknowledged as much when he remarked that departmental autonomy was essential at the graduate level but not as essential for undergraduates. He added that "explorations toward breaking down departmental lines for undergraduate concentrations are being explored by committees." Such explorations were being undertaken, not just because of the

60   *Scholarly Leadership in Higher Education*

wishes of the president but because the students themselves were unhappy with aspects of the curriculum. A student committee in 1939 decried the failure of Harvard College to provide "an intelligible and broad view of the main areas of learning" as well as the "present system of concentration as leading too often to narrow specialization." The problem with the concentrations, one vehicle that President Lowell had introduced as an antidote to the principle of completely free electives for students, was that they were almost completely in the fields in which a "student in the Graduate School of Arts and Sciences may study in order to obtain a PhD." Doctoral majors were most often too narrow in focus for undergraduate concentrations. What Conant advocated was to add fields that were broader in scope, allowing students to relate their courses to later study in professional schools and not be bound by the narrower concerns of doctoral major fields.[108]

All of this is to say that Conant, in his first decade as president of Harvard University, exhibited a range of intellectual interests far beyond what might be expected of a university president in this or any other era and an especially wide range of interests for a president with a scientific background. Additionally, the interests and orientations identified here continued to animate Conant's presidency in its next, and final, decade. Conant's interest in excellence in the student body and in the Harvard faculty, his suspicion of intercollegiate athletics and of theological concerns as evidenced in the Divinity School, his interest in history of science for graduates and undergraduates, and his devotion to cultural history as a liberating study, not as a specialist endeavor, all testified to the breadth of concerns that motivated this university administrator. The successful establishment of the Littauer School and his advocacy and interest in the School of Education indicated an educational executive who was able and willing to expand his own intellectual horizons. Finally, his understanding that his ideas more often than not could, and would, be debated and found impractical or inappropriate, and his willingness to accede to the judgment of his opponents that his ideas were not as convincing as he thought them to be, testified to an intellectual and/or political willingness to accept defeat that is not often found in college and university executives, in Conant's day or in subsequent eras.

Conclusion

In most ways, Conant's first decade as a university president was successful. He sought, and obtained, an increase in quality of the student body and a marked

The Harvard Presidency in the 1930s 61

improvement in the scholarly credentials of the Harvard faculty. He reined in the athletic program without completely alienating the alumni. He oversaw the establishment of the Littauer School and the widening of the scope of the Graduate School of Education, both examples of his intent to extend the influence of Harvard beyond Cambridge proper. And he put into action his own intellectual questioning of the specialist impulses that pervaded graduate education and threatened undergraduate education in ways that did not attempt to cow the specialists but to engage them. The meritocratic vision and modernization agenda of Conant, then, survived his first decade as president largely intact. As we will see in the next chapter, they would go on to be important in the second decade of his presidency. Two negative aspects of his presidency, his, at the least, mild and veiled anti-Semitism and his tendency toward single-mindedness in his approach to faculty personnel policies, also remained in evidence in the second decade, though in different ways and with different results. The second decade, as described in the next chapter, differed from the first decade in many ways, especially in the impact of the preparation for and conduct of the Second World War on the university. And the Cold War climate of the last five years of Conant's presidency also had profound consequences for Conant and for Harvard. Elaborating on these differences, and identifying the thematic similarities in Conant's leadership of Harvard in the two decades, is the task of the next chapter.

Notes

1 Conant, *My Several Lives*, p. 91.
2 Charles D. Biebel, "Politics, Pedagogues, and Statesmanship: James B. Conant and the Public Schools, 1933-1948" (PhD dissertation, University of Wisconsin, Madison, 1971), p. 51.
3 Conant, *My Several Lives*, p. 112.
4 Ibid., pp. 114–15.
5 Smith, *The Harvard Century*, p. 69.
6 "Report of the President of Harvard College and Reports of Departments for 1932-33," *Official Register of Harvard University* XXI (February 5, 1934): 6; hereafter cited as Presidential Report with the year of the report indicated.
7 Hershberg, *James B. Conant*, chapter 1.
8 Smith, *The Harvard Century*, p. 109.
9 As quoted in Ibid., p. 101.

62   *Scholarly Leadership in Higher Education*

10 Morton Keller and Phyllis Keller, *Making Harvard Modern: The Rise of America's University* (New York: Oxford University Press, 2007). The subtitle of the Kellers's several chapters' account of Conant's presidency is "The Meritocratic University 1933–1953." It should be noted that meritocracy was a term that was unfamiliar to Conant, even if he embodied its essence in his presidential plans and actions. Of course, meritocracy spoke both to the modernization and the nationalization of Harvard.

11 Presidential Report, 1932–3, p. 8.

12 As quoted in Smith, *The Harvard* Century, p. 101.

13 Ibid., 112.

14 Keller and Keller, *Making Harvard Modern*, p. 33.

15 Conant, Presidential Report, 1932–33, pp. 8, 9.

16 For the increases in high school enrollment in the twentieth century, see Wayne Urban and Jennings Wagoner, *American Education: A History* (New York: Routledge, 2014), p. 179 Also see Conant, *My Several Lives*, p. 135.

17 Ibid., chapter 12, "The National Scholarships."

18 Ibid., p. 131. Conant's positive view of standardized testing was long-lasting, as will be seen in the subsequent chapters.

19 Ibid., p. 132.

20 Presidential Report for 1938–39, pp. 24, 25, 7, 8.

21 We will consider Chauncey in a later discussion of the Educational Testing Service.

22 VM, "The New Tests in Practice" (August 28, 1934), James Bryant Conant Presidential Papers, Box 29, Folder Education, General, 1934–1935; hereafter cited as Presidential Papers.

23 W. S. Learned to Conant (February 21, 1939), Presidential Papers, Box 129, Folder Carnegie Foundation, 1938–1939. While Chauncey was unable to arrange a release from his administrative duties for this work, he managed to find a capable graduate student to do it, under his supervision.

24 By the mid-1940s, Conant was advocating scholarships for all professional schools, including graduate schools of arts and sciences, suggesting a nationwide examination as the major vehicle for the selection process. See Presidential Report for 1945–46, pp. 10–11.

25 Henry Chauncey and Henry S. Dyer, "Estimating Graduate School Success … at Harvard University" (January 15, 1940), Presidential Papers, Box 151, Folder Carnegie Foundation, 1939–40.

26 Ben D. Wood to President James B. Conant (December 14, 1937). Carnegie Foundation for the Advancement of Teaching Papers, Series II, Box 154, Folder 4, Butler Library, Columbia University; hereafter cited as CFAT Papers.

27 Presidential Report for 1951–52, p. 18.

28 Keller and Keller, *Making Harvard Modern*, pp. 47–48.

The Harvard Presidency in the 1930s 63

29 The issue of anti-Semitism in admissions at Harvard, and sister institutions like Princeton and Yale, is discussed in a number of sources. For example, see Harold Wechsler, *The Qualified Student: A History of Selective College Admissions in America* (New York: John Wiley, 1977); and Marcia Graham Synnott, *The Half-Opened Door: Discrimination and Admissions at Harvard, Yale, and Princeton, 1900–1930* (Westport, CT: Greenwood Press, 1874). Most recently, see Jerome Karabel, *The Chosen: The Hidden History of Admission and Exclusion at Harvard, Yale, and Princeton* (New York: Houghton Mifflin, 2005). Lowell and the proposed quota for Jews are discussed on pp. 86–109.

30 Keller and Keller, *Making Harvard Modern*, pp. 47–49.

31 Karabel, *The Chosen*, pp. 172–74.

32 Presidential Report for 1932–33, pp. 7, 8.

33 Ibid., p. 12.

34 Smith, *The Harvard Century*, p. 115.

35 Ibid., pp. 97, 83.

36 Keller and Keller, *Making Harvard Modern*, p. 64.

37 Presidential Report for 1934–35, p. 9.

38 Presidential Report for 1938–39, p. 19.

39 Presidential Report for 1934–35, p. 9.

40 Ibid., pp. 10–11.

41 Letter from President Conant About the New University Professorships at Harvard (May 28, 1935), Carnegie Corporation of New York Papers, Series IIIA, Box 121, Folder 4, Butler Library, Columbia University; hereafter cited as Carnegie Corporation Papers.

42 Ibid.

43 Keller and Keller, *Making Harvard Modern*, p. 25. On the actions of the Visiting Committee for the Economics Department in the mid-1930s, see Presidential Report for 1935–36, pp. 13–14.

44 Presidential Report, 1932–33, p. 14.

45 Conant, *My Several Lives*, p. 157.

46 Ibid., pp. 160–61.

47 Ibid., pp. 162–63.

48 The Special Committee Appointed by the President of Harvard University, Report on the Terminating Appointments of Dr. J. R. Walsh and Dr. A. R. Sweezey (May 24, 1938), Presidential Papers, Box 145, Folder Walsh-Sweezey.

49 Ibid., James B. Conant to the Board of Overseers (June 1, 1938).

50 Conant, *My Several Lives*, p. 167.

51 Ibid., pp. 169–71; quotation, p. 170.

52 Presidential Report for 1934–35; quotations, pp. 13 (my emphasis), 14.

53 Keller and Keller, *Making Harvard Modern*, p. 24.

54 Ibid., p. 65.

55 Presidential Report for 1946–47, p. 8.

56 Presidential Report for 1947–48, p. 6.

57 Ibid.

58 Keller and Keller, *Making Harvard Modern*, p. 145.

59 Ibid., 145–48; quotation, 146.

60 Smith, *The Harvard Century*, p. 110.

61 Keller and Keller, *Making Harvard Modern*, p. 143.

62 Smith, *The Harvard Century*, p. 108.

63 Marybeth Smith and I have dealt with the issue of Nazi influence at the Harvard tercentenary, and in some of Conant's other activities, in "Much Ado about Something: James Bryant Conant, Harvard University, and Nazi Germany in the 1930s," *Paedagogica Historica* 51 (February–April, 2015): 152–65.

64 Keller and Keller, *Making Harvard Modern*, pp. 155–58; quotation, p. 158.

65 Ibid., p. 158.

66 Ibid., p. 60.

67 Ibid., pp. 59–60.

68 Ibid., p. 41.

69 Presidential Report for 1934–35, p. 16.

70 Presidential Report for 1938–39, p. 29.

71 Presidential Report for 1950–51, p. 18.

72 Smith, *The Harvard Century*, p. 110. Smith's source for this was an interview with a Harvard College administrator.

73 Keller and Keller, *Making Harvard Modern*, pp. 124–26.

74 Smith, *The Harvard Century*, p. 185.

75 Presidential Report for 1951–52, p. 35.

76 Conant, *My Several Lives*, p. 151.

77 Ibid., p. 653.

78 Ibid., p. 655.

79 Ibid.

80 Ibid., p. 656.

81 Ibid.

82 Ibid.

83 Ibid., pp. 657–58.

84 Keller and Keller, *Making Harvard Modern*, pp. 130–32.

85 Presidential Report for 1936–37, p. 25.

86 James Bryant Conant, *The Education of American Teachers* (New York: McGraw-Hill, 1963), pp. 1, 2.

87 Presidential Report for 1934–35, pp. 25–26.

88 Conant, *My Several Lives*, p. 186.

89 Ibid., p. 15.

The Harvard Presidency in the 1930s 65

90 J. B. C., Memorandum on the School of Education (November 2, 1933), Presidential Papers, Box 6, Folder Education: Graduate School Dean, 1933–34.

91 Presidential Report for 1937–38, pp. 5–12; quotations, pp. 10, 11.

92 Ibid.; quotations, pp. 13, 14.

93 Conant, *My Several Lives*, p. 182.

94 On the difficulties this created with at least one faculty member, see Truman L. Kelly to J. B. Conant (September 29, 1939) and Conant to Kelly (October 4, 1939); Presidential Papers, Box 154, Folder Education: Graduate School of 1939–40.

95 Arthur G. Powell, *The Uncertain Profession: Harvard and the Search for Educational Authority* (Cambridge, MA: Harvard University Press, 1980).

96 Presidential Report for 1937–38, p. 14.

97 Presidential Report for 1935–36, pp. 7, 8.

98 Ibid., p. 9.

99 I. Bernard Cohen, "George Sarton," *Isis* 48 (September, 1957): 286–300; and James B. Conant, "George Sarton and Harvard University," Ibid., pp. 301–305.

100 Cohen, "George Sarton," p. 296.

101 Conant, "George Sarton and Harvard University," p. 304.

102 Presidential Report, 1935–36, p. 9.

103 Ibid., pp. 11, 12.

104 Presidential Report for 1936–37, pp. 23, 25.

105 Presidential Report for 1939–40, pp. 18, 19; quotation p. 18 (my emphasis).

106 Presidential Report for 1938–39, pp. 22, 23.

107 Presidential Report for 1936–37, p. 22.

108 Presidential Report for 1938–39, pp. 19, 21; Presidential Report for 1937–38, p. 27.

3

The Second World War, the Cold War, and the Nationalization of Harvard

Harvard University, like most American universities, experienced substantial changes after the onset of the Second World War. One of these changes at Harvard was that the president became much less directly involved on campus as he gradually, and then more fully, entered into the Second World War work for the federal government. The Manhattan Project and Conant's other war work, which was not directly related to the welfare of Harvard, or any other education issue, will not be dealt with here. His work for the federal government did, however, occupy a considerable amount of Conant's time and effort for several years and took him away from campus for a long portion of those years. The war itself also had significant direct effects and indirect effects on Harvard, which will be of interest in this chapter. Of particular interest throughout this period was Conant's ambivalence about the impact of war-related activities, especially the influence of the federal government, on Harvard.

The aftermath of the war proved central to continuing the largely successful development of Harvard University begun under Conant in the 1930s. That development continued his priorities of the first decade of his presidency—student and faculty excellence, initiatives in general education, and moving Harvard to the forefront of national affairs. Conant's emergence as a major proponent of a Cold War suspicion and competition with the Soviet Union punctuated the last five years of his presidency.

The most significant federal impact on Harvard came through the GI Bill, passed in 1944 before the formal end of hostilities. This presented Harvard, and Conant, with an opportunity and a challenge. The university benefited financially in large part from the presence of returning veterans who came on campus with full federal funding, but Conant worried about the academic quality of the students who came with that support. The GI Bill also increased the influence of the federal government on campus through the federal financial subsidization of the student veterans. As always, federal funds came either with strings or with a fear of strings so manifest that institutions acted carefully not to antagonize their federal benefactor. Additionally, the provision of federal funds to support faculty research, largely in the sciences, meant more federal influence and institutional fear of that influence, especially by Conant at Harvard. In spite of that fear, an increased federal presence on university campuses, especially through federal funding of research and allied activities, was a significant factor in the nationalization of Harvard University and other American research universities after the Second World War. Conant frequently agonized over the threat, as well as the benevolence that accompanied it, both of which came from the federal government.

The developing Cold War conflict with the Soviet Union in the late 1940s influenced Conant profoundly and anti-communism threatened Harvard and other campuses. The threat came through politically motivated searches for subversive influence on campuses that had intended, and unintended, consequences. Conant was the quintessential Cold warrior and his pursuit of containing the Soviets meant problems for him as a leader of a presumably nonpartisan university. In fact, Conant's penchant for addressing larger political and social problems often created conflict over issues of academic freedom with individuals and groups on campus who did not see the world through his eyes. Thus, he dealt with adversaries on and off campus. These conflicts will be examined here in some detail. While he was usually generous personally in dealing with opponents in such conflicts, they often made life politically uncomfortable for him and threatened on-campus relations with students and faculty and off-campus relations with alumni and government.

In spite of the upheavals of the world war and the Cold War, we will show that Harvard proceeded in the 1940s and early 1950s in many respects along the lines established in the first decade of Conant's presidency. He maintained his commitment to student diversity, as long as it was undertaken to seek the best academically qualified students. He also persisted in his quest for faculty excellence and prominence and his pursuit of interdepartmental and interdisciplinary initiatives. And there were a few such successful initiatives in this decade that Conant would proudly point to as indicative of his attempts to improve Harvard. Not coincidentally, one of these initiatives, the Russian Research Center, represented a move to make Harvard influential internationally, to go along with its increasing national prominence.

In the postwar years, as in the early years of his presidency, Conant continued to be interested in the Graduate School of Education. He pursued its development

The Second World War, the Cold War, and the Nationalization of Harvard   69

as an academically sound and innovative body and also as an effective agent for the improvement of the public schools. This initiative, as will be shown, testified to Conant's increasing interest and commitment to public education. One of the ways he illustrated this commitment was through the publication of two books on education in the late 1940s and early 1950s. This interest and these publications, however, ran the risk of alienating significant portions of the Harvard community.

The Second World War

The influence of the Second World War on Harvard University and on other universities was enormous. As the war developed, military manpower requirements meant a shrinking pool of students eligible to enroll, and a diminishing of faculty and administrator numbers, caused by those who left to join the armed forces or to pursue one or another aspect of war-related research or administration. Campuses like Harvard were opened up, in varying degrees, to the presence of war-related training and other activities. The experience of the First World War, however, when campuses were almost turned over to the federal government's Student Army Training Corps (SATC) made several administrators, including Conant, careful about the nature and extent of federal influence on campus.[1] In spite of this caution, the federal largesse that accompanied the acceptance of the federal presence on campuses, as well as the patriotic impulses that swept the campuses once war was officially declared, made the federal government a major partner in campus activities. This was true at Harvard as well as at most other universities large and developed enough to be seen as desirable settings for war involvement of one kind or another by the federal government.

Conant had been an open advocate of war preparedness long before the official entry of the United States into the Second World War. His 1939–40 presidential report, for example, began with a discussion of the impact of what he called the coming national emergency. He discussed the needs of the federal government in an impending conflict against a background of academic institutions' need to protect their integrity.

> To discover ways and means of making effective use of a university as an auxiliary to the national government during a period of intense preparation for war is relatively easy. The difficulty is to avoid jettisoning, in the process, ideals, hopes, ambitions, projects which in the long run may be as essential to the welfare of the country as the immediate contribution for which the sacrifice is made.[2]

Conant added that the task of the university was "the choice and the guardianship of eternal and spiritual values" but noted that "in these days it cannot be proclaimed too loudly." More specifically related to curriculum, he discussed how teaching science, mathematics, and foreign languages during a war had widespread lay support, but teaching humanities, something in which he had been interested since the dawn of his presidency, was much more likely to be contested. He added that "with the general trend toward more emphasis on utilitarian education and with the increased stress laid on the so-called vital problems of the day, the academic guardians of the eternal values in art and literature need all the support they can possibly receive."[3]

One year later, with war clouds much more directly on the horizon, he did not retreat from his statements above but stated flatly, "It is for war, therefore, and not for peace that we must now lay our immediate educational plans." Harvard's plans included the expansion of the Reserve Officers Training Corps (ROTC) program through which enrolled students were given some military education and training in preparation for their commission as officers. Additionally, a draft age of twenty that looked likely to be reduced in the near future meant special arrangements to accelerate the completion of academic work by enrolled college students to allow them to graduate before entering the military. Conant noted that enrollment in the School of Medicine, a critical need area for the war effort, also required acceleration and that the School of Public Health would have to play an important role in studying immediately war-related topics such as communicable diseases. Student enrollment in several of the other professional schools was severely restricted by the need for military manpower, he added, meaning financial problems for those parts of the university that needed to be addressed. Also, given the impending war, faculty were put on a twelve-month employment calendar, facilitating more year-round instruction and protecting their pay. Even more importantly, Conant mentioned, several Harvard faculty members had begun to undertake defense work; this included administrative work of various kinds in Washington, work on leave with the military forces, research work in the sciences, and work on educational programs connected with the national defense. Further, some facilities of the university were being placed at the disposal of the federal government.[4]

In contrast to the situation of the late 1930s, when most students and many faculty members opposed what they considered Conant's warmongering, most of Harvard was clearly on board by 1941 with the plans to be involved in the war effort. Conant remarked that the faculty had formed an "American Defense— Harvard Group" that had a membership of 1,300 and well over 200 working

The Second World War, the Cold War, and the Nationalization of Harvard 71

on one or another committee. Again, however, as he had previously, he ended the discussion with a warning that many people worried that the liberal arts college tradition, at Harvard and elsewhere, would be "extinguished by the technological demands of war." He concluded that the "danger is real and we do well to recognize it."[5] Yet he could not move beyond recognition to any kind of specific recommendation for action.

One year later, now in wartime, Conant noted that the federal Manpower Commission Policy meant that all able-bodied students were to be involved in the war effort and added that Harvard was in agreement with this policy and priority. What it meant for the curriculum was that the army's need for young soldiers, the army's and navy's need for engineers, and the industrial need for the technically educated personnel to aid in the war effort all had to be heeded. Wartime manpower needs meant that there were fewer students in the university, and those few were studying more technical things, a situation that did not bode well for the liberal arts. Conant, however, did not support those who proposed that there be numbers of students set aside to study social sciences and humanities. His position on this issue was that the "liberal arts will survive this war" and that the future for the liberal arts was not one of extinction but of a period of slow growth and evolution. The future of the liberal arts would depend, he speculated, on the imagination of the faculty. He added another qualification about the primacy of war work in education when he noted that while today we "are at the moment concerned with the first stages of the transition from peace to war," he added that at "some later and happier time we shall be concerned with a reversal of the process."[6] Needless to say, that reversal promised more favorable prospects for the humanities and social sciences than did wartime conditions.

By the end of the first few years of the war, the negative consequences for Harvard enrollment were quite clear. The total civilian enrollment at Harvard for the 1942–43 academic year, consisting of foreign students, those physically unfit for service, and those deferred to finish their studies, was 1,829, compared to a prewar enrollment of 8,078. The total enrollment drop was not so stark, however, since army and navy enrollment was 3,166 and other military programs increased the total military and naval enrollment at Harvard to well over 5,000. The instructional facilities were being used in a variety of ways to facilitate army and navy training programs. Again, Conant juxtaposed discussion of the necessary military presence on campus with traditional concerns. He remarked that Harvard "must continue to give every assistance to the national government in . . . prosecuting the war with unmitigated vigor." He added, however, that we "must endeavor to keep unbroken in every field . . . our scholarly and teaching effort. We must plan for the days of peace to come." He concluded this discussion by noting that it had become clear recently that "Harvard could both carry out her pledge of placing all her resources at the disposal of the government and still preserve intact the continuity of our varied academic undertakings."[7] Conant was walking an academic tightrope, making sure that the university was totally on board with the government priorities in the time of national emergency while taking whatever steps he could, many if not most of them rhetorical steps, to remind the university community that the wartime set of priorities was temporary, though total. He wanted to make sure that more traditional academic concerns and interests would not be forgotten.

Conant referred to his own personal situation in regard to war work when he told readers of his presidential report for 1942–43 that his work as chairman of the National Defense Research Committee had required his absence from the campus for a large portion of each week. He added that only "effective and cooperative staff work" made the situation manageable.[8] The arrangements that were made to allow for Conant's absence from campus were, at least initially, controversial. He began his work with the National Defense Research Council (NDRC), at the invitation of his friend Vannevar Bush, in June of 1940. The NDRC was a scientific research committee that worked with the White House to prepare scientifically and technologically for America's defense effort. Later in that year, after Franklin Roosevelt's election to a third term, Conant accepted a presidential invitation to coordinate the scientific communities on both sides of the Atlantic in their opposition to the Nazis. Conant eagerly accepted this invitation and spent a good bit of the next few months on two trips to England. According to one historian of Harvard, from that point on, Conant "would be caught up in bigger issues than university governance."[9]

As Conant himself continued to spend significant time away from campus, on federal work, including the Manhattan Project, his absence became controversial with some advocating that he give up his office in order to pursue his war work. He heeded the concern of some on the Harvard Corporation that at the least he needed to do something to alleviate the situation. In particular, one suggestion was to appoint a top-flight person as deputy president to mind the campus in the president's absence.[10] Eschewing any title like that, Conant instead established officially in 1944 the position of provost of the university. To acknowledge the primacy of academic priorities, and priorities that were long-term Harvard priorities, the provost selected was the dean of the Faculty of Arts and Sciences.[11]

Paul Buck, an American historian who had published a landmark history of Reconstruction in the late 1930s,[12] was Conant's choice as provost. The two

The Second World War, the Cold War, and the Nationalization of Harvard 73

worked well together both before and after the establishment of the position of provost. Buck was loyal to Conant in every way and anticipated much of Conant's thinking on any number of issues. He was dean of the Faculty of Arts and Sciences and, as we will see in the next chapter, worked hard on the general education report of the Harvard Committee that institutionalized Conant's ideas on general education. The Buck appointment was successful, both administratively and politically, allowing Conant to at least respond that someone was in charge during his frequent and lengthy absences from campus. Given all his duties, Conant was frequently gone from Cambridge for extended periods. Further, even in periods not characterized by long absences, he usually spent about half of the workweek in Washington and the other half in Cambridge. Given this situation, his relationship with Buck, and its acceptance on campus, became crucial to the successful continuance of his administration.

Conant also cut his presidential salary substantially when he started working in Washington, again in an effort to at least recognize the legitimacy of concerns over his absence from campus. And after Pearl Harbor, he undertook further changes to help him in administering the campus. He relied on Paul Buck, as well as on the treasurer of Harvard, William Claflin and a senior Harvard Corporation fellow, Charles Coolidge, to keep the campus running during his increasingly long absences.[13] While these efforts proved successful in keeping the campus going during the war, they also resulted in some harm to the president. Conant thought, at the end of his presidency, that he "had become too remote from the faculty."[14] The war, as we will see later in this chapter, was not the only thing that came between Conant and Harvard faculty, however.

The Second World War, then, brought James Bryant Conant a new set of responsibilities that reached far beyond the Harvard campus. Yet, he managed to stay in touch with what was going on at the campus and to allay most fears that he was dilatory in his conduct of his office. His astute statements balancing war priorities with campus traditions, though weighted toward the former, testified to his ability to deal with issues and commitments that could easily have provoked enormous difficulties.

As the Second World War progressed, Conant's attention turned to postwar planning. Here he had to contend with something for which he had no great love, the Servicemen's Readjustment Act of 1944 or GI Bill. As on many issues, Conant thought long and hard about the education of returning veterans from the Second World War. His views, however, were quite different from those that were institutionalized in the GI Bill. He discussed the education of veterans well before the act was passed by Congress, and his discussion was animated by his long-standing concern for education of the academically best qualified students and also by his fear of the federal government. He accurately predicted that the returning veterans would be quite different from the college students prior to the war, especially in their interest in education in the professional schools. This interest indicated the advent of a no-nonsense, utilitarian approach to higher education that contrasted greatly with the hijinks of college students before the conflict and, potentially, with the concerns of a liberal education. More ominously, Conant worried that the government plans for financing veterans' education, which provided funding for all who had served, did nothing to indicate how to select those who would be admitted to the professional schools. One way to alleviate the situation would be to allow veterans' programs to be administered through the states. Conant felt that state control of veterans' education allowed for various solutions to the problem of selectivity, the virtue that any decentralist administrative arrangement provided over a centralized, federal government management system.[15] Of course, the problem was that the veterans had served their nation more than individual states, and thus the argument for a national system of veterans' education was formidable. In any case, Conant's state control scheme was never implemented.

Conant, ever conscious of the need for the best students on his campus, feared that Harvard, and other prestigious institutions, would be inundated by veterans of questionable intellectual qualifications. Speaking shortly after passage of the GI Bill, he criticized it for lack of a selective feature. He remarked that the generous funding provisions were fine, but that if the bill were not modified the risk was that the least capable veterans would be "flooding the facilities for advanced education in the United States."[16] Conant's sentiments were widely publicized, even printed in an army newspaper. Many servicemen were alienated by Conant's open desire for selectivity. One wrote him, "The general consensus seems to be that you are perfectly willing to make the smart people smarter, and of course those that are so unfortunate not to be equipped with an ample amount of that gray matter might just as well stay that way."[17]

Interestingly, the GI Bill proved to be much more of a boon to Harvard than a threat, increasing the diversity of its student body in the immediate postwar years economically, ethnically, and in intellectual outlook to a degree greater than anything that Conant's national scholarships had accomplished.[18] The GI Bill aided Conant's push for a meritocratic Harvard, rather than obstructed it, as he had feared. The Harvard graduate and professional schools were especially strengthened by the caliber of student who came to them with GI Bill funding. While Conant never admitted his error in fearing for the quality of student

The Second World War, the Cold War, and the Nationalization of Harvard 75

admitted through the GI Bill, at least at Harvard, he cooperated enthusiastically in making provision for the new graduate and professional students. A commons area for graduate students opened on the campus in the fall of 1950, surrounded by residence halls for graduate students, all designed by the noted architect and Harvard faculty member Walter Gropius.[19]

Other Administrative Issues and Academic Concerns

A focus on the changes on campus that came in reaction to the war should not lead to the conclusion that there was great discontinuity in the Conant administration in its twenty years of stewardship. In fact, in many ways the two decades of his presidency reflected much continuity in Conant's work, including his ambivalence about the federal role in higher education.

First, in terms of finances, the second decade of Conant's presidency was like the first in many ways. Conant was never a profligate spender, and his relative penury served Harvard in good stead as the institution and its president navigated through wartime and postwar time, each of which presented different financial challenges. The Second World War meant severe downward pressures on the number of students enrolled at Harvard, and accommodation to a different type of student as military-related students replaced most of the normal undergraduates. The federal government supported military students and military studies, at Harvard and elsewhere, but Conant was always watchful that the federal dollar not be accompanied by federal control of campus life. He adjusted the term of faculty appointments to mesh with the new circumstances, thereby maintaining a modicum of faculty morale in a situation where a lack of change might have meant economic penalties for faculty members. He also managed to survive the outside employment of several faculty members in the war effort, not just in the sciences but also in the professional schools and social sciences.

As Conant's Second World War–related work for the federal government developed, beginning with the National Defense Research Committee, Harvard benefited directly in federal grant support. In discussing NDRC grants, one account noted that Harvard received a total of $31 million in support, exceeded in amount only by the Massachusetts Institute of Technology and the California Institute of Technology.[20] However, in spite of his work for the federal government, Conant was not a completely willing recipient of federal funds for his institution. This was true especially in the postwar period, when federal research funds, mostly in the sciences, became available through grants from new federal agencies. Almost immediately after the end of the Second World War, Conant indicated his strong preference for quasi-independent bodies to provide federal funds through grant competitions, over individual universities doing research directly for the federal government, and secretly as well. He also advocated support from agencies such as the Departments of Commerce, Labor, or Agriculture for research in the social sciences.[21] The fundamental condition that Conant favored in federal grant work at Harvard was that only those grants would be accepted, which would provide for public dissemination of their results.

As the proposed National Science Foundation (NSF) moved closer to approval by Congress in the late 1940s, Conant accepted that agency as an institutionalization of the federal government's willingness to help universities. Once again, however, he stated a caveat. Up to this point, he remarked, centralization of control over university activities had not been a problem; he added that, however, "the question of whether or not in the long run the vital autonomy of a university might be sacrificed in the search for funds must be examined with all candor." Centralization through federal involvement, for Conant, threatened the diversity of universities, a great source of their strength. While federal funds were important for support of some programs, they were to be accepted only if they did not threaten the autonomy of those programs. One way, he thought, to ensure such autonomy was for universities to seek private funding, as well as government support. Harvard, he remarked, was taking concrete steps to seek private dollars. He announced the creation of a Committee on Plans and Development to help seek private funds and the appointment of a high-level university staff member to take charge of those efforts.[22] He also announced that several of the professional schools, and the Graduate School of Arts and Sciences, had federated their efforts for fundraising, a notable change for Conant's Harvard, which had been highly decentralized, with the separate schools and colleges "on their own" financially.

Conant's concern over possible negative consequences from federal research funding continued through the closing years of his presidency. In his penultimate presidential report, in a climate increasingly dominated by the Cold War and the Korean conflict, Conant reiterated his fundamental concerns. He stated that there was general agreement, in spite of the war in Korea, that "only in a few special instances is it necessary to call on the universities to establish secret laboratories and recruit scientists from other institutions." He added that at "Harvard we have no such laboratories" and that no secret research had been done with one exception, a study done by the

The Second World War, the Cold War, and the Nationalization of Harvard   77

Harvard Business School for the Defense Department. He also noted that even if mobilization of universities were to occur because of the Korean conflict, "we must keep our universities active as scholarly centers." Conant remarked emphatically that all programs at Harvard, except for ROTC, were for purposes of peace not war.[23]

At the end of the Second World War, Conant had indicated quickly that he intended to restore the emphases of Harvard he had established in the 1930s, including the stress on attracting the best students and faculty. In terms of student recruitment, Conant moved quickly to reinstate prewar priorities at Harvard. He continued to advocate his national scholarship plan for Harvard, noting in 1946 that in order to keep opportunity available to the talented, "Harvard and like institutions would be well advised to increase the number and size of their scholarships." He also advocated federally funded scholarships to help many students to enroll in other higher education institutions.[24] In his final report before leaving the Harvard presidency, he concluded that the National Scholarship Program had been designed to increase the number of highly qualified students from the South and the West. It had not succeeded as much as he wanted it to, but it could be more successful with the cooperation of alumni and alumni groups. That cooperation, however, ran the risk of being turned into a "vast recruitment of football players." He concluded that in "no single matter can the alumni of the Eastern colleges perform a greater service for their own institutions and for the future of higher education than by balancing the spirit of rivalry in athletics with an insistence that each college be judged primarily by its services to the nation as an educational institution."[25]

Conant's final presidential report also summarized his accomplishments in faculty personnel policies. He recounted his efforts to reform faculty promotion and tenure policies in the 1930s and the political backlash they had created. Progress in obtaining the best faculty available was impeded by the war, as well as by a need for more endowment income to facilitate the process. The implementation in the early 1940s of an ad hoc committee for each permanent appointment had been a large step toward recruitment of the very best scholars for Harvard. Each committee was made up of departmental or school representation plus outside scholars appointed by the president. Each committee was also chaired by the president, thereby ensuring that the process would yield the strongest candidates available and, in turn, that the president could take each nomination to the boards for final approval confident in the quality of the selection process. Conant paused to include in this final report, words that characterized his approach to Harvard from his first year as president. For the

78   *Scholarly Leadership in Higher Education*

successful operation of Harvard, the three necessary conditions were "solvency, a student body of high quality, and an outstanding faculty."[26]

One notable episode during Conant's administration marked it, though at least for Conant unwittingly, as a relative pioneer in the education of women at the major American universities. In the first years of the war, when students were becoming increasingly scarce and some faculty were being deployed for war work, Harvard hit upon a way to keep employment of its faculty much more regular than it might have been. A June 1943 agreement was reached between Harvard and Radcliffe College, the women's college attached, though indirectly, to Harvard. According to the agreement, Harvard's Faculty of Arts and Sciences took over official responsibility for the instruction of Radcliffe College students.[27] Prior to the agreement, instruction at Radcliffe had been given by Harvard faculty, most often as an overload to supplement their salary, and without any organizational commitment to do anything but teach classes. The official agreement that ended the haphazardness of the existing situation was a landmark along the way to eventual coeducation at Harvard. While the initial agreement provided for separate classes for Radcliffe and Harvard students, especially at the freshman and sophomore levels, the realities of what has now come to be called enrollment management rather quickly led to a system of *de facto* coeducation. While it took the Harvard faculty, administration, and governing boards several years to bring policy in line with practice, coeducation at Harvard was a reality and then a policy instituted under the Conant administration. Conant, who had no daughters, had no great interest in coeducation, but the situation impelled him in that direction, in spite of his lack of personal fervor or commitment to the issue.[28]

Academically, like in his approach to student and faculty quality, Conant often stressed issues and concerns in the postwar years that were similar to those he had raised and discussed in his first ten years. For example, new development in the social sciences, which he advocated frequently in the first decade, was acted on in the second. The Department of Social Relations was created in 1946, a body that brought together work done in the Department of Sociology and related areas of study in anthropology and social psychology. Conant also initiated a Laboratory of Social Relations, a research arm of the new department, and persuaded the Carnegie Corporation to make a five-year grant of $125,000 to get it started "as a center for fundamental research." The announcement of the grant noted that services of the faculty involved in the new laboratory were in heavy demand from defense programs, a situation that threatened the fundamental research in the social sciences that was needed. The grant ensured

The Second World War, the Cold War, and the Nationalization of Harvard 79

that Harvard would keep its priorities intact as "one of the few institutions which has kept its government commitment to a minimum in order that it may pursue fundamental research problems as vigorously as possible."[29]

One eminent faculty member of the Department of Social Relations, David Riesman, described it as a research and teaching enterprise that attracted very good students and served as a model of attempted, though incomplete, interdisciplinary integration. The scholars initially involved in the new department were the sociologists, the cultural anthropologists who were overshadowed in their own department by physical anthropologists, and the social psychologists who represented the less behavioral and less quantitative wing of psychology. Conant's official announcement of the new department described its makeup as follows: "With the traditional subject matter of Sociology and Social Ethics, it unites that portion of psychological science that treats the individual within the social system, and that portion of anthropological science relevant to an understanding of culture and the working of social systems."[30] Riesman judged the department to have been successful at the undergraduate level as a field of concentration and even more effective at the doctoral level. Its doctoral graduates, according to Riesman, were notably successful as researchers, teachers, and "often as administrators." Intellectual compatibility between cultural anthropology and psychoanalytic psychology created some of the most innovative and interesting work in the Department of Social Relations, again according to Riesman. He noted that the same qualities of intellectual innovation that characterized the Department of Social Relations were not always present in the more traditional academic departments and that the existence of interdisciplinary areas like social relations meant that some in the departments, those who refused to join any new groups, were protected in their sometimes flat-footed opposition to innovation.[31]

One other notable innovation of the Conant presidency in the social sciences was the creation of the Russian Research Center. Established in the late 1940s, as the Cold War was heating up, the Russian Research Center, like the Social Relations Laboratory, received funding from the Carnegie Corporation. Conant's ties to the Carnegie Corporation were deep and long-standing. In addition to funding for the two innovations just described, we will show in the next chapter that he also had garnered Carnegie funding for the general education program and, more particularly, for his own work in developing science education courses in general education.[32] The Russian Research Center was important in developing Harvard's reach into international affairs and relations, at the

80   *Scholarly Leadership in Higher Education*

same time that the university had become increasingly prominent as a national institution under Conant.

The Russian Research Center and the Department of Social Relations epitomized Conant's efforts toward improving Harvard in the second decade of his administration. Through these entities, and through others, he continued the development of Harvard that he had begun in the first decade of his administration. Of course, the war and development of postwar federal government programs also contributed substantially to that process. It seems fair to say that by the end of Conant's second decade as president, Harvard was without a doubt one of the leading universities, arguably the leading university, in the nation. It was far more advanced in graduate studies than it had been when he took on the presidency and increasingly playing a role in national, and international, affairs.

The Cold War, Internationalization, and Academic Freedom

While Conant was enthusiastic about the Russian Research Center and its work, one episode in its early history raised the issue of academic freedom, an increasingly important concern as the Cold War developed. Shortly after creation of the Russian Research Center, a young Russian historian, H. Stuart Hughes, left the State Department for a position in the center. Hughes was quite active politically in Henry Wallace's left-wing 1948 presidential campaign. This activity drew interest from the Carnegie Corporation, which wanted it to cease. When Hughes withdrew from the Wallace campaign, over an intellectual dispute he had with the candidate, Carnegie was not satisfied. It still pressed for Hughes to withdraw from the center, presumably because of his left-wing politics. After discussion with Provost Paul Buck about the avenues a young scholar needed to pursue to achieve his place at Harvard and in the larger scholarly world, Hughes resigned his position at the Russian Research Center to assume an assistant professorship in Russian history. Hughes himself never discussed the incident as an assault on his academic freedom, but more than one study of the events has questioned the political interference in the university's affairs. While accounts of this episode did not mention any direct involvement by President Conant, his close relationship with his provost and with the Carnegie Corporation suggested that he was aware of the situation and not dissatisfied with the final outcome.[33]

In fully describing Conant's position on censorship and academic freedom, the first thing to be noted is that he always paid homage to the freedom of

The Second World War, the Cold War, and the Nationalization of Harvard   81

university professors to research and teach without external restrictions. This is a consistent theme in his writings and official actions from the beginning of his presidency, as illustrated by his stated opposition to a teachers' oath passed by the Massachusetts legislature in 1935. In discussing the oath, he remarked, "Those who understand the true nature of the functions of an institution of higher education have always stood firm in their support of the principle of free inquiry."[34] As the Second World War approached, he acknowledged the universities' need to sacrifice in order to serve the national government but followed the acknowledgment with the following: "The difficulty is to avoid jettisoning . . . ideals . . . which in the long run may be as essential to the welfare of the country as the immediate contribution for which the sacrifice is made."[35] During the war, he frequently mentioned that a major goal of the war was the preservation of political freedom, on campus and off.[36]

As the Cold War developed in the late 1940s and the Korean War began in the early 1950s, Conant again combined his devotion to the national interest with a defense of intellectual dissent, at Harvard and elsewhere. As Senator Joseph McCarthy increased his attention to communists on campus, Conant reacted defensively, trying to protect Harvard against McCarthy and other "redbaiters." He defended John Kenneth Galbraith, liberal member of the economics department, against a politically oriented move from some Harvard board members to deny him tenure in the late 1940s. Earlier in the decade, he had defended the appointment of Harvard faculty member Granville Hicks, a politically radical literary critic, as an adviser to a new program in American civilization. Similarly, he later defended Harvard scientists who had spoken out for Julius and Ethel Rosenberg, scientists who were accused of divulging secrets to the Soviet Union. And finally, he supported Harvard-educated diplomat Alger Hiss against charges of providing secrets to the Soviets.[37] In perhaps the most flat-footed statement of opposition to those vilifying Harvard as a seedbed for communists and other radicals, Conant remarked that there were "no known adherents to the Party on our staff and I do not believe that there are any disguised communists either." Perhaps anticipating the cries of disbelief from readers to this assertion, he added, "But even if there were, the damage that would be done to the spirit of an academic community by an investigation by the University aimed at finding a crypto-communist would be far greater than any conceivable harm such a person might do."[38]

In spite of these pronouncements, several scholars of the period in which Conant served as Harvard president have not seen him as a principled defender of dissent and the academic freedom which should have protected that dissent. Ellen

82   *Scholarly Leadership in Higher Education*

Schrecker, for example, in a volume on the spinelessness of university administrators in their dealings with the McCarthy committee investigating communists on campus, exhibited a jaundiced view of Conant. She initially reiterated Conant's position opposing campus investigations of subversives. But she went on to quote at length a qualifier to this commitment. Conant noted that in the period of a Cold War, "I do not believe that the usual rules as to political parties [that is the notion that political party membership for professors was to be protected] apply to the Communist Party." For Conant, because of the conspiratorial and deceitful activities of the Communist Party, "card-holding members of the Communist Party are out of bounds as members of the teaching profession."[39] This is certainly an opinion in tension with, if not in opposition to, the statements in the preceding paragraph about the damage done to a university by an investigation. Yet, the two are not necessarily contradictory and, in a sense, reveal a man struggling both with his own personal opinions and the responsibilities of a university president.

Schrecker's criticism of Conant was magnified a few years later in a full-scale indictment of American universities and their relations with intelligence agencies in the federal government during the Cold War. Most notable here was the Federal Bureau of Investigation (FBI) that, under its Director J. Edgar Hoover, was intent on purging American universities of communists and other subversives between 1945 and 1955. Sigmund Diamond indicated his thesis in the title of his book, *The Compromised Campus*, and its subtitle, "The Collaboration of Universities with the Intelligence Community." Diamond reported that he had obtained his PhD in history at Harvard in 1955 and then took an administrative position at the university, offered to him by then dean of arts and sciences, McGeorge Bundy. A year later, Bundy offered Diamond a second position, one that included teaching duties. The offer was subsequently withdrawn, however, after Bundy discussed with Diamond whether or not he, Diamond, had been associated with the Communist Party and, further, what Diamond might say about his activities with the party if called on to testify by the FBI or a congressional committee. Diamond's answer, which was that he would testify about his own activities but would refuse to name names of other involved in them, was deemed unsatisfactory. Bundy withdrew the offer of employment.[40] Diamond's book was a response to that action and an indictment, mainly of Harvard and Yale, for their cooperation with the FBI and other federal entities and agencies in ways that clearly violated the spirit of academic freedom and the obligation of universities to protect that freedom.

Conant was gone from Harvard by the time that Diamond received his PhD and gained employment, so he is not the direct target of Diamond's ire.

The Second World War, the Cold War, and the Nationalization of Harvard   83

The long attack on Harvard launched by Diamond, however, using mainly FBI files obtained through Freedom of Information Act requests, contained several particulars about Conant's actions. Most egregious for Diamond, as for Schrecker, was Conant's "staunch" anti-communism.[41] This, combined with his seemingly inconsistent statements about the primacy of protecting academic freedom and not allowing communists to teach, led Diamond to indict Conant as a collaborator with the FBI in its persecution and prosecution of communists on the Harvard faculty. Diamond's book is long and detailed, dealing also at some length with the cooperation of the Harvard Russian Research Center with the FBI, though not saying anything specifically about Conant in this regard.

What then can we finally say about the commitment of James Bryant Conant as president of Harvard University to the principle of academic freedom? First, it should be noted that Conant was an ardent defender of academic freedom rhetorically. His commitment to the principle was frequently stated and elaborated on. Second, his actions in regard to Harvard faculty members were usually taken to be in conformity with the defense of academic freedom. In cases where he was charged with inconsistency in his actions, such as the Walsh-Sweezey affair in the 1930s or the statements he made regarding communists not being allowed to teach in the late 1940s, his own explanations ranged from ones that were defensible (in the 1930s case) to ones that were seemingly indefensible (in the statement about communists). As president of the most notable university in the United States, with a faculty, a student body, and alumni that held the full range of political opinions from the extreme right wing to the radical left wing, Conant did the best he could to appease his various constituencies at the same time he sought to uphold the long-standing principles of academic freedom and free inquiry that he himself espoused. His actions taken in regard to communists were tinged with his own visceral opposition to communism and his vigorous role as a Cold War partisan.[42]

The Graduate School of Education

Another instance of continuity between the Conant administration in its first and second decade was his support for the Graduate School of Education. Conant's appointment of Francis T. Spaulding as dean of the School of Education in 1940 meant that he had in the leadership of that school a dean that he respected greatly and from whom he learned a great deal.[43] In announcing the appointment of Spaulding as dean, Conant noted that new faculty appointments were also to be made in the School of Education in the areas of educational psychology

84   *Scholarly Leadership in Higher Education*

and educational administration. The latter area, a special interest of Spaulding, was marked for future development in the school. Work in educational administration was to be undertaken in cooperation with the Littauer School of Public Administration, another favorite entity of Conant. Using Littauer to help educate school administrators would allow the work of economists, law experts, and municipal government specialists to inform and complement the work of educators. Products of the new program, according to Conant, would be "educational statesmen" as well as educational administrators.[44]

The Second World War intervened here, however, as it did in the rest of Harvard University, and the Graduate School of Education suffered both from loss of students and of faculty to the war effort. Spaulding himself left campus early in 1942 to join the US Army as an officer in its Information and Education Division. Spaulding's appointment as dean continued until late 1945, though the school had an acting dean in his absence. Spaulding returned briefly to the Harvard Graduate School of Education in 1945, leaving officially in 1946 to assume the position of commissioner of education in the state of New York.[45] His departure was disappointing, but not surprising, to Conant who tried hard to keep Spaulding in Cambridge. Conant had kept in touch with Spaulding during the latter's service in the Second World War and would stay in contact with Spaulding after his departure in 1946. In the final analysis, the financial and political attraction of the commissionership in New York was too strong, especially when compared to the relative weakness of the Graduate School of Education on the Harvard campus, in spite of Conant's support.[46]

After the end of the Second World War and the departure of Spaulding, Conant continued to be greatly interested in the Graduate School of Education. He announced that it would keep its stress on the education of school administrators and would keep training teachers in cooperation with the Faculty of Arts and Sciences. He added that he wanted to hire a new dean when funds became available, and that the school was to be "strengthened by recruiting from certain of the social sciences men of the first rank who are eager to direct their attention to the study of education as a social process."[47] Conant wanted the newly oriented Graduate School of Education to cooperate with sociologists, anthropologists, and social psychologists from the recently established Department of Social Relations, and with the Business School, in research and in the education of school administrators. The Graduate School of Education in its search for new faculty targeted younger men who had practical experiences in industry and the schools, as well as scientists "who were directing their attention to the behavior of man as a social animal." These two groups would combine to help direct the

The Second World War, the Cold War, and the Nationalization of Harvard   85

public schools to achievement of their historic goals of democratic education. "Indeed, their efforts might be decisive in insuring that this nation continue as a strong, vigorous, and united body of free men." More modestly, Conant proclaimed that soon "Harvard would be in a position to play a highly important role in improving secondary education in the United States."[48]

In fact, Conant was deeply committed to his efforts to improve the Graduate School of Education. In his autobiography, he referred to the events of the late 1940s as "the Second Rescue of the School of Education."[49] However, things did not proceed initially as he expected. Conant had difficulty both in obtaining grant funds for the Graduate School of Education and in persuading a noted social scientist to take on the role as leader of the school. He labored for several years on both of these issues before finally deciding that no eminent social scientist would take on the deanship. He then decided to turn internally to Harvard for the new dean of the Graduate School of Education. Conant's choice was a rather obscure, at least to educators in and out of Harvard, assistant dean of Harvard College named Francis Keppel. Keppel was young and energetic but lacked any graduate degree and had never been involved in any capacity in a public school. Conant recounted that he chose Keppel with the approval of, and maybe even at the suggestion of, former dean Spaulding, who had worked with Keppel in the army during the Second World War.[50]

Keppel was unqualified by education and experience for the deanship, but he had a decent record as an administrator at Harvard and support from other administrators on the campus. When he became dean, Conant made a special effort to introduce Keppel to school administrators from around the country, mainly through contacts in the American Association of School Administrators (AASA), the professional association of school administrators. One slogan that Conant used in explaining why Keppel had been selected was that "education is too important to be left solely to educators."[51] Plausible perhaps at face value, the slogan also rationalized Conant's effort to sell an obviously unqualified dean to American educational leaders. Conant obtained a $300,000 grant from the Carnegie Corporation for the Graduate School of Education, a grant that was given with the understanding that its objective was to aid the school in increasing the number of social scientists on the faculty. The Carnegie grant was remarkable in its lack of specifications, an indication that, as Keppel remarked later, the foundation was funding the ideas and plans of Conant, not any specific design or program that it had in mind.[52] Keppel in turn pledged to carry out Conant's desire to bring social scientists into the faculty in the Harvard Graduate School of Education. And he was generally successful in this effort.

86   *Scholarly Leadership in Higher Education*

This entire episode, however, seemed to contradict Conant's devotion to hiring the best qualified individual for any academic position. In terms of objective academic qualifications or accomplishments, as already noted, Keppel was severely lacking. He had other, nonacademic qualifications, however, personal and familial connections and contacts, that made him, and the Graduate School of Education, attractive to potential funders over the course of his deanship. Francis Keppel was the son of Frederick Keppel, who had been the chief executive officer of the Carnegie Corporation of New York. And Conant was intimately involved in many Carnegie projects during the entire time of his presidency. Further, Conant was aware of the younger Keppel's presence on the Harvard campus, as a student and then as a neophyte administrator, in the 1930s and 1940s. In fact, in the late 1930s, Conant corresponded with Frederick Keppel about his son's career and prospects at Harvard.[53] Frederick Keppel retired from Carnegie in 1941, but Conant continued to cultivate his contacts at the Carnegie Corporation and to serve in various capacities on different corporation boards and projects. When Conant got the money for the Graduate School of Education in the late 1940s, the grant was administered directly by the new dean, Francis Keppel. The younger Keppel had personal ties to the officer at the corporation who was responsible for the grant, Charles Dollard. The two had been longtime friends and their friendship boded well for the success of the Carnegie funds in energizing the Graduate School of Education.[54]

One hesitates to make too much out of this one episode of personal and familial connections. As we will see in the next chapters, however, Conant was incredibly successful in receiving Carnegie funding and in deciding who else might receive such funding. His personal influence was enormous, too enormous to justify solely on grounds of his intellectual qualifications and achievements. Conant used Carnegie money, and money from other philanthropic foundations, in pursuit of his major objectives for Harvard University, improvement in student and faculty qualifications, creation of timely new centers and schools, and various initiatives that transcended departmental boundaries. Yet one is hard-pressed not to see Conant's easy *entre* to Carnegie dollars, and his actions in appointing a marginally qualified dean such as Francis Keppel, as severely at odds with his other notions of merit for students and faculty at Harvard.

Public Education

In tandem with his support for the Graduate School of Education, Conant continued, actually intensified to a considerable extent, his interest in the

The Second World War, the Cold War, and the Nationalization of Harvard   87

American secondary school. The high school, and all the public schools, became increasingly important for Conant in the 1940s and 1950s as bulwarks of American democracy in a world engaged in a Cold and not so Cold War (in Korea) with communism.

As early as 1935, less than two years after his inauguration, Conant was discussing the secondary school but mainly in its relation to the college. This article was published initially in *School and Society*, a periodical circulated mainly among the ranks of professional educators, school administrators, and the professors of education who trained them. But it was quickly excerpted in the *Bulletin of the American Association of University Professors*, which had an audience of faculty and administrators in the nation's colleges and universities. Conant here acknowledged the importance of a college education for the increasing numbers who, in the era of the expanding New Deal, were entering public service and public administration. While such leaders were not necessarily philosophers, Conant wanted to make sure that they had both great intellectual ability and postgraduate training. This approach, however, was added to the larger task of civic education of all students, particularly in the high schools. He summed up his argument as follows: "The schools and colleges have a large task before them to provide the best possible education for the mass of their students. They have an equal responsibility to the country to select the future cultural leaders as young as possible, finance them if necessary, and provide a school and college education on which they can build."[55]

In his 1940 coauthored book on the high school and the college with Francis Spaulding, the first two chapters, written by Conant, focused mainly on school-college relations. The third chapter in that book, written by Spaulding, represented a set of ideas and analyses that, if not new to Conant, were not the usual things he considered in his own writing.[56] Spaulding's chapter discussed the secondary schools and their role in operating for the public good. These institutions were charged with the education of all students and also with identifying talent and abilities and guiding the ambitions of students. All students needed education for membership in a democratic society, as well as to be equipped to take their proper place on the ladder of opportunity. The place on the ladder, however, unlike in education for democratic citizenship, was different for each student. Recognizing that difference meant seeking out and planning for the academically able students, the artistically inclined, and the crafts oriented. Not only should the intellect be nourished in the high school but also the eye or the ear and the manual abilities. In addition to learning from the printed page, the intuitive judgments of students interested in practical affairs needed to be stressed. This was a tall order for the high school, and the nonintellectual aspects were topics on which Conant had not spent much time or attention. Thus, in looking at the high school, as discussed by Francis Spaulding, Conant was learning about the nonacademic but real educational goals and needs of students.[57]

Spaulding was initiating the Harvard chemist-turned president into the extra academic but important considerations that occupied the attention of most American educators, particularly public school administrators. Their agenda, in large part a kind of progressive educational orientation, would occupy a considerable amount of Conant's attention for the next three decades. While this version of progressive education never embraced the child-centered pedagogy that fascinated many educators, it did try to address the variety of talents and interests of the students who increasingly were coming to the American high school, particularly the American public high school. This type of progressive education, perhaps best described as "social efficiency progressivism," was what Conant learned from Francis Spaulding and what captivated much of his educational energy and attention for the rest of his life.[58] Advocating social mobility through identifying and sponsoring talent with minimal regard for economic wealth or social status and serving the nonacademically talented in ways that provided them with the chance at social and economic success were two challenges that Conant and Spaulding tried to address in 1940. They remained as challenges for Conant throughout the rest of his life. These challenges certainly took him well beyond the issues and debates ongoing in Harvard Yard and potentially exposed him to criticism on campus for his off-campus interests.

By the middle of the 1940s, Conant was addressing public education by name and beginning to discern the version of the public high school, the comprehensive high school, which he would defend for the rest of his life. It was very different from the academic school that he himself had experienced at Roxbury Latin and the high school that most of his faculty at Harvard knew. It resembled greatly the high school that many American public school educators were in the process of developing. Conant addressed this institution, and its relation to academics like himself and to professional educators, in a speech in December at Teachers College, Columbia University. He was here speaking directly to the concerns of the intellectual leaders of the American public school.

This speech, titled "A Truce Among Educators," showed how far Conant had come on the road to educational progressivism and away from the purely academic approach to secondary education that had animated the creation of his MAT program for high school teachers at Harvard. The truce that Conant

The Second World War, the Cold War, and the Nationalization of Harvard   89

sought was between university academics, or as he called them the professors of arts and science, and professional educators. The former needed to understand that the necessary alteration of the American high school to meet the demands of its increasingly diverse student body meant that the days of old when a high school graduate could be presumed to have mastered some set of prescribed academic content or gained certain academic skills were gone. The latter group, the professional educators, for Conant, needed to meet the needs of the new groups of students but without the total abandonment of academic concerns in the high school. This could be accomplished through policies that recognized the importance of intellectual achievement and the need for the identification and development of academic talent that should accompany the diversification of the curriculum necessarily undertaken to meet the new groups of students. Conant desired this preservation of an academic emphasis without a segregation of the academically oriented students that "might turn the boys and girls in question into either prigs or academic snobs." For Conant, the colleges and universities would have to abandon their admission requirements that called for specific content mastery in the high schools while the educators should be willing to identify scholastic aptitude in their students without necessarily relating that to specific subject matter. If these two objectives were realized, the result would be that "if the college can no longer count on adequate training in special skills it may know better than ever before that it is choosing potential brains."[59]

Thus, while Conant called for a truce among academics and educators, he addressed mainly the latter group. Educators were told that their approach to the high school, which necessitated a diminution of academic studies to meet the needs of new groups of students, was understandable and defensible. What they needed to do, however, was to acknowledge that academic study was not obsolete but rather in need of some degree of preservation alongside of the new emphases. The key, for Conant, was the identification of what he called "scholastic aptitude" for the college bound. Identifying this aptitude was to be accomplished, as Conant had advocated in the 1930s at Harvard, through standardized testing.

Conant returned to Teachers College one year after his "truce" speech to give a series of lectures in November of 1945. In these lectures, he fleshed out his view of the challenges to American education presented by what he called the structure of American society. Conant laid out his specific view of the existing American social structure and how education could and should be used to address, and alter, that social structure.[60] In the first of three lectures, Conant outlined his

90   *Scholarly Leadership in Higher Education*

view of American society in the mid-twentieth century. He summarized that view in a lengthy, italicized statement:

> *One of the highly significant ideals of the American nation has been equality of opportunity. This ideal implies on the one hand a relatively fluid social structure changing from generation to generation, and on the other mutual respect between different vocational and economic groups; in short, a minimum emphasis on class distinctions. It is of the utmost significance for our future that belief in this ideal is strengthened and that we move each year nearer to its realization in our practice. In our modern industrialized society, national educational policy largely determines the future of our social structure. In the last fifty years educational forces have been at work which have tended to stratify the American nation. On the other hand, a vast instrument of American democracy has been created by the extension of universal education to the high school stage. If we so desire, this instrument can restore a high degree of fluidity to our social and economic life; we can make available for the national welfare reservoirs of potential talent now untapped. Furthermore, education can inculcate the social and political ideals necessary for the development of a free and harmonious people operating an economic system based on private ownership and the profit motive but committed to the ideals of social justice. The nearer we approach through education to our avowed goal of equality of opportunity (which, however, admittedly can never be reached) and the better our schools teach and practice the basic tenets of American democracy, the more chance there is for personal liberty as we know it to continue in these United States.*[61]

Having stated his ideal, Conant spent the rest of his first lecture discussing how a rigid social structure conflicted with it. Heredity was one pillar of such rigidity. American society for Conant, through its schools, particularly its high schools, was in a position to combat the stultification inherent in a hereditary social structure. Ostensibly good secondary schools existed in private settings as well as in wealthy American suburbs. The goal, for Conant, was not to break up those schools but to improve the schools in cities and rural areas to the point that they would produce students who could compete successfully with the graduates of the established academic secondary schools, private and public.

Conant frequently provided a radical cast to what he was saying. At times, he spoke of haves and have-nots, or owners-managers and workers, or the politically and economically powerful and the rest of society. Struggle between these groups was where, for Conant, the "real social dynamite of this century" resided.[62] Yet, in his plan to defuse that social dynamite through the democratization of education, he revealed a fairly orthodox belief in mobility achieved not through

The Second World War, the Cold War, and the Nationalization of Harvard   91

social or political conflict but through individual educational achievement. He remarked that fluidity of the social structure was the desirable situation and added that in achieving that aim "public education is of prime importance."[63] He spent a considerable amount of space elaborating the American belief in equality of opportunity, its historical and political base, and positioning his view in the middle of a dispute between holders of hereditary privilege and advocates of socialism. While establishing a society with genuine equality of opportunity immediately required changes in employment practices and in inheritance taxes, along with changes in educational arrangements, he discussed mainly the educational concern in this document, given the limits of time and space for his ideas, the setting in which he was speaking, and the audience he was addressing. Of course, he had not developed any ideas on how to change employment practices and, if he had, they likely would have been less appealing to a general audience, or an audience of educators, than his educational proposals. Similarly, his ideas about taxing income and wealth, if publicized outside of the context in which they were delivered, would likely have caused controversy he did not want.

After a digression in which he argued that American society had become more stratified since the 1870s, Conant proceeded to the important point he wanted to make: that public education could enhance the possibility of a more fluid, more democratic society. That did not mean that this was what was happening. Invoking social scientific studies such as *Who Shall Be Educated*, Conant argued that education was too often contributing to the social stratification he detested, rather than combating it.[64] To change things, educational opportunity needed to be equalized through its extension in areas where it was lacking such as rural settings, towns, and cities. Doing this, however, required federal intervention, since rural areas and small towns were quite often poor and also economically stratified and often featured political structures and taxation policies that enhanced the stratification. Only the federal government had the financial ability and the political power to intervene educationally on behalf of the economically marginalized elements of American society.[65]

Conant's delivery of these ideas at Teachers College, one year after he had called for a truce among educators in the same location, indicated how far he was traveling down the road to educational analysis and advocacy that ventured away from the concerns of colleges and universities. He wanted college and university personnel to recognize that their approach to education, stressing traditional academic disciplines and studies, was appropriate for higher education but not for the high schools that had a far larger and much more intellectually and

92   *Scholarly Leadership in Higher Education*

socially diverse student body. For the school people, and those who trained them, he tried to foster an understanding that, in addition to their genuinely difficult job of educating all the students who came to them, they needed to take on the task of identifying and nurturing intellectual talent. The search for talent was important especially in places where it might not be expected to be found. Identifying the talented from unlikely backgrounds and settings was an exceptionally important task. Guidance and counseling were one way to deal with the issue of talent. Another, and equally important concern for Conant, was the standardized testing that would identify that talent. Relationships among these priorities were something that Conant would spend much of his time on in publications in the rest of the 1940s and early 1950s.

Two Books on Education

Conant published two books on education between 1948 and 1952 that built on his ideas of earlier in the 1940s and continued to sketch out a role for public education in the changing world that it inhabited. *Education in a Divided World* was published by the Harvard University Press in 1948. It is a sizable volume in comparison to most of Conant's published works, over 230 pages of text. Conant indicated in his prefatory material that the book was intended to be a reworking of his lectures at Teachers College. The extended size of *Education in a Divided World*, in relation to the size of his Teachers College lectures, indicated that something had intervened since the earlier publication.[66]

Conant identified that something in the preliminary pages. He noted that *Education in a Divided World* differed from the earlier works because international challenges had intervened. Specifically, Conant meant the Cold War then beginning between the United States and the Soviet Union. The dispute, debate, or conflict with the Soviet Union was more ideological for Conant than it was military. He had three rather lengthy chapters on the Cold War, one early in his volume that described the contours of the conflict, a second chapter specifically on communism and the challenge it presented to the United States and other Western countries, and a third concluding the book, which addressed changes needed to wage the Cold War effectively in areas such as the draft and the economy. In each of these chapters, he voiced his belief that there would not be military conflict between the United States and the Soviet Union. Rather, he declared that the ensuing ten years would be a period of an armed truce between the two powers, followed by an ideologically divided world

The Second World War, the Cold War, and the Nationalization of Harvard   93

for the next several decades. Though he was a stout anti-communist, he noted that those who saw the Soviets like the Nazis as an overwhelmingly military rival were wrong. Unlike the Nazis, the Soviets represented "an ideological and political thrust supported by military means."[67] The ideological battle with the Soviets would be lengthy and highly contested.

Conant wrote his book as an initial guide to what was necessary to conduct such a battle. On the first page of the book he indicated that it was specifically about the free elementary and secondary schools, which were "the sinews of our society." He added that they represented an important manifestation of American democratic ideals and that, therefore, "The strength of this republic is . . . intimately connected with the success or failure of public education."[68]

The rest of *Education in a Divided World*, with one exception, basically restated points made in the Teachers College lectures. The one exceptional chapter was entitled "Education for a Career," and it followed the chapter on general education. Conant's focus here was much more pointed than career, occupational, or vocational education, however. The main focus of this chapter was education for the gifted, a theme not likely to have been highly welcomed at Teachers College, the hotbed of equality-focused educational progressivism. Conant's audience here, however, was not progressives or teacher educators. Rather, it was teachers and school administrators and perhaps even the general public, and he wanted to alert that public to the need for the preservation and development of the talented, particularly in public schools. He nodded favorably to a Common Learnings course, which had been developed by educators as a staple of general education in the high school for all students.[69] But then, he went on to address the problem of the education of the brilliant students, adding that most educational commentators misunderstood the significance of this issue. He defended the approaches to secondary education taken in the public high schools, acknowledged that they might disadvantage gifted students by diminishing the attention they received, but decried those who saw this as the ruin of secondary education. What he advocated was the identification of students gifted in mathematics and science, just as the gifted were identified in art, and the provision of opportunities for those students to practice their gifts. He admonished that a particular curriculum was not necessarily an answer for the gifted but, rather, what was needed was a stimulation of general intellectual interests, an understanding that book learning was relevant to the problems of the day, and the inculcation of habits appropriate for serious intellectual work. Good teaching in a variety of curricula might get at these criteria in different ways. He chastised arts and science faculties for simply bemoaning the end of the

94   *Scholarly Leadership in Higher Education*

traditional curriculum, rather than for trying to find ways to educate teachers to identify the gifted and support their development within the existing high school.[70]

Five years elapsed between Conant's *Education in a Divided World* and the publication of a second volume, *Education and Liberty* in 1953. That book, based on lectures given at the University of California early in 1952, was mostly continuous with his earlier educational writings. Its title spoke to Conant's approval of the political and educational ideas of Thomas Jefferson. The continuity with his earlier volume on education was well illustrated in the subtitle of the 1953 volume, "The Role of the Schools in a Modern Democracy." In the first chapter of the book, "The Anglo-Saxon Tradition," Conant compared educational provision and organization in the United States with that in four "other" British countries: England, Scotland, Australia, and New Zealand. In a finding not surprising to anyone familiar with his earlier work, Conant described the other four nations as wanting in their approach to secondary and higher education compared to the United States. Their shortcomings, though they were less prominent in Scotland and New Zealand than in England and Australia, lay in two directions. The secondary schools in all four nations enrolled a lesser percentage of the age-eligible student body than in the United States, and the curriculum in the secondary school and the university sector was narrow. Secondary schools, especially in Australia, featured an almost completely academic curriculum. This dominance characterized both the private, religious secondary schools and the academically competitive state secondary schools that existed. Few, if any, secondary schools featured a diversified curriculum in which either technical education or general education was a concern. Conant had a similar criticism of Australian universities. They were narrow and specialist, leaving little if any room for the general education of their students or for any technical studies.

Another quality that the Australian and English systems of secondary and higher education shared, for Conant, was that they were class-oriented systems that educated the children of the upper classes and ignored, especially in the private sector, the children of everyone else. He had made a similar point about the German secondary schools in *Education in a Divided World* five years earlier; the secondary schools in Germany constituted a dual system, academic and university preparation for the established classes and vocational studies in separate institutions for the other social strata. Thus, Australia and England, like Germany, were perpetuating a class system of education through their secondary schools and their universities. This system was flawed seriously in that it denied opportunity to those in the nonelite social classes who had academic talent. This class system was exceptionally inappropriate in a Cold War climate, much more intense in 1952 because of the Korean War than it had been in 1948. Soviet communists trumpeted their system as an egalitarian system that appealed to all classes. Only in the American public schools, where all classes attended and opportunities were being increasingly extended to the lower classes to excel educationally, was the class character of education being diminished, if not obliterated.[71]

The second chapter of *Education and Liberty* compared and contrasted the American liberal arts college with higher education in the four countries referenced in the first chapter. Here again, the contrast was significant in two ways: the number of students, both in raw numbers and as a percent of the age group eligible for entry, was significantly higher in the American colleges and universities than in the universities of the other nations. Also, the general education focus of the curriculum in American colleges was in stark contrast to the specialist focus in the universities elsewhere. Conant made clear his approval of the American pattern as more democratic than what existed in the other nations. American colleges had as part of their curriculum studies that addressed citizenship in the modern world. The other nations were too busy turning out specialists of all kinds to worry about this issue.[72]

The final chapter of *Education and Liberty* turned to Conant's recommendations for the future. The first four recommendations dealt with American colleges and advocated no expansion of four-year college student numbers or academic programs. This was a long-standing aspect of Conant's meritocratic vision for US higher education, a vision that saw an increase in qualified college and university students from whatever background and a corresponding decrease in marginally qualified students, again whatever their background. Other recommendations involved transforming all four-year colleges into institutions with high standards that would prepare students for studies leading to the various professions and making two-year colleges provide general and advanced technical education for the many other students who desired it.

Recommendations for secondary education included expanding junior and senior high school programs to meet the needs of the diverse students who were enrolling in them, adhering to the principle of a comprehensive high school (one that had both a common core of studies and a differentiation of special programs for different groups of students), the expansion of work experience programs in high schools and in two-year colleges, and the provision of more scholarships for high school graduates to institutions of higher education (but only for those

96   *Scholarly Leadership in Higher Education*

graduates who had academic potential). Finally, he advocated the expansion of general education for all students in high schools and in higher education, for those destined for manual work, those likely to enter business, and those bound for the professions.[73]

Conant was not naïve about the class character of American education. Beefing up the colleges academically, a new emphasis on two-year colleges, and the comprehensive high schools were all devices by which he thought equality of opportunity might be improved. Especially important was the comprehensive public high school, one that served multiple and general educational purposes rather than just academic preparatory study for higher education. He stressed the duty of the public high school to identify and serve the academically gifted as well as the other groups of students who were demanding other than academic courses. Conant found private secondary schools that were largely preparing affluent students for college were unsatisfactory, both on social class and on curricular grounds. Only in truly comprehensive high schools would the needs of American society for an education devoted both to social mobility and to democratic citizenship be served.[74]

Education and Liberty was a curious book in one respect. The three lectures that were originally delivered by Conant constituted eighty-seven pages of text. The notes added prior to publication provided almost as many pages, sixty-one. These notes contain Conant's description of the major controversy that resulted from the lectures. In discussing private education in the final chapter of *Education and Liberty*, Conant took on the topic of private secondary schools, religious or nonreligious. He argued, initially, that private secondary education was clearly established in the United States and that private religious schools were equally established, in accord with the Supreme Court ruling in the *Pierce* case of the 1920s, which had declared unconstitutional an Oregon law requiring attendance at only public schools.[75] He had no desire to abolish either private schools or private religious schools. His position, however, was that there should be no government support of private schools, religious or nonreligious. His commitment was to public schools, particularly the comprehensive public high school, and financial support for that institution was his paramount concern. This put him in conflict particularly with Catholic schools that had sought and were still seeking various forms of government support for their schools. Conant made sure that his opposition to government support for Catholic schools would be heard by more than the listeners to his lectures or the readers of their published version. He read his remarks on religious schools to a professional group of school administrators and had them published in the *Harvard Alumni*

Bulletin (April 19, 1952) and in the *Saturday Review* (May 3, 1952).[76] Conant's position opposing government aid to private schools put him in direct conflict with Cardinal Richard Cushing of the Catholic Archdiocese of Boston, who condemned Conant as an opponent of Catholicism.[77] Conant made no direct reply to Cushing, or others who were critical of his position, preferring to restate his own position as often as necessary to reiterate his support for public schools as the chief defense of democracy in an age fraught with conflict over its meaning.

Education and Liberty, then, became a sort of manifesto for Conant in defense of the public school, particularly the comprehensive public high school, as the essential institution for American democracy immersed in a Cold War ideological conflict. While it broke no new ground in Conant's ideas, repeating many that had been offered before, some as long as nearly twenty years earlier, it put Conant firmly in the public eye as a defender of public schools and an opponent of all those who sought to siphon money away from them for other educational arrangements. This point of view endeared Conant to the educators of the National Education Association (NEA) and the AASA.[78] It also associated him, wrongly in his own mind, with the anti-Catholicism of groups formally organized to protect or advance non-denominationalism and/or secularism in American life. It put Conant in the public arena in the midst of a highly charged political and ideological debate over religion and alienated him from several religious groups, most particularly the Roman Catholic Church. As we have seen earlier, Conant as Harvard president had to contend with the city fathers of Cambridge, a city with a distinct Irish-Catholic character in its politics and government. It is not that this dispute over support for Catholic schools put him in an untenable position but rather that it increased his involvement in extra-Harvard affairs to the point that it seemed almost to make his presidency an ancillary part of his life, rather than the core of his existence. Harvard itself had no great affinity for the Catholicism that was prominent in Boston and Cambridge. On the other hand, for the Harvard president to become embroiled in a public dispute over an issue unrelated to Harvard with the cardinal archbishop of Boston was not "good form," to say the least.

Conclusion

Conant's involvement with public school matters, and the resulting controversy with the archbishop of Boston, was a prime example of the president straying from Harvard's interests and priorities in his discussion of affairs outside of Harvard. While his devotion to national defense had taken him away from the presidency for several years during the Second World War, his activities were performed during a national emergency and his absence from campus was tolerated, if not always applauded. As we have seen, the postwar years brought more and more interest and involvement in public education for Conant. While education and education policy were not unrelated to Harvard, his embrace of the public schools was much further removed from Harvard and its day-to-day concerns or even from its long-range priorities. Such activity increasingly threatened the success of his presidency. Yet he became more and more involved in public school advocacy in spite of these dangers.

This straying from a Harvard-centric agenda will be a theme in our next two chapters. In general education, the topic of our next chapter and an area that was directly and intimately related to Harvard College, Conant and his university assumed a leadership role in a national discussion of a crucial issue in higher education. Conant used his teaching of a new course in the reformed general education curriculum to reestablish himself as a meaningful colleague to his faculty peers and a thoughtful student of his and the efforts of others. He also managed, however, through his discussions of the issues and publications related to the topic to take his involvement far away from campus. And in developing his reputation as an analyst and commentator on public education and other public affairs, the topic of Chapter 5, Conant managed to spend a great deal of time and take a number of positions that were increasingly controversial on his campus. The controversy eventually resulted in his decision to leave Harvard in late 1952.

Notes

1 Jonathan Frankel, "The Ivory Boot Camp," *Harvard Magazine* 94 (September–October, 1991): 71–74. For the larger influence of the First World War on campuses, see Carol S. Gruber, *Mars and Minerva: World War I and the Uses of the Higher Learning in America* (Baton Rouge, LA: Louisiana State University Press, 1976).

2 Presidential Report for 1939–1940, p. 6.

3 Ibid., p. 10. The similarity between this situation and the contemporary love affair between higher education and the STEM disciplines is obvious. Similarly, the threatened situation of the humanities in both periods is worthy of note.

4 Presidential Report for 1940–41, pp. 8–21; quotation, p. 8.

The Second World War, the Cold War, and the Nationalization of Harvard   99

5 Ibid., pp. 23, 24.

6 Presidential Report for 1941–42, pp. 8–11; quotation, p. 11; p. 19.

7 Presidential Report for 1942–43, pp. 5–7, 9.

8 Ibid.

9 Smith, *The Harvard Century*, pp. 145–46; quotation, p. 146.

10 Keller and Keller, *Making Harvard Modern,* p. 136.

11 Presidential Report for 1944–45, p. 17.

12 Paul H. Buck, *The Road to Reunion: 1865-1900* (Boston: Little Brown and Company, 1937).

13 Smith, *The Harvard Century*, pp. 152–53.

14 As quoted in Keller and Keller, *Making Harvard Modern*, p. 136.

15 Presidential Report for 1942–43, pp. 12–16.

16 Presidential Report for 1943–44, pp. 10–12; quotation, p. 11.

17 As quoted in Keller and Keller, *Making Harvard Modern*, p. 30.

18 Smith, *The Harvard Century*, p. 168.

19 Keller and Keller, *Making Harvard Modern*, p. 112.

20 Ibid., p. 163.

21 Presidential Report for 1945–46, p. 13.

22 Presidential Report for 1947–48, pp. 9–12; quotations, pp. 9, 21.

23 Presidential Report for 1950–51, pp. 8, 9, 24–25.

24 Presidential Report for 1948–49, pp. 18, 19.

25 Presidential Report for 1951–52, p. 18.

26 Ibid., p. 14.

27 Presidential Report for 1942–43, pp. 18, 19.

28 Conant, *My Several Lives*, pp. 374–83.

29 Harvard University Grant of $125,000 for Research in Social Relations (n.d.), Carnegie Corporation Papers, Series IIIA, Box 163, Folder 4.

30 Presidential Report for 1945–46, p. 19.

31 Seymour Martin Lipset and David Riesman, *Education and Politics at Harvard: Two Essays Prepared for the Carnegie Commission on Higher Education* (New York: McGraw-Hill, 1975), pp. 315, 349.

32 Office of the President, Record of Interview, DCJ (Devereaux C. Josephs) and President James B. Conant (March 24, 1948), Carnegie Corporation Papers, Series IIIA, Box 121, Folder 2.

33 Lipset and Riesman, *Education and Politics at Harvard,* pp. 184–85 and Smith, *The Harvard Century*, p. 184. The Carnegie position was to avoid political controversy in the institutions that it supported.

34 Presidential Report for 1935–36, p. 13.

35 Presidential Report for 1939–40, p. 6.

36 For one example, see James B. Conant, "How Can a Democratic Nation Fight a War and Still Stay Free," *School and Society* 54 (October 18, 1941): 313–15.

100   *Scholarly Leadership in Higher Education*

37 Smith, *The Harvard Century*, pp. 133, 174–75, 180.

38 James B. Conant, "Academic Independence," *AAUP Bulletin* 38 (Winter, 1952–53): 517–19; quotation, p. 519; also see Press Release, Harvard University (June 23, 1949), Presidential Papers, Box 338, Folder Communism.

39 Ellen Schrecker, *No Ivory Tower: McCarthyism and the Universities* (New York: Oxford University Press, 1986), p. 111. Conant's quotation in Schrecker is taken from an article in the *Harvard Crimson* (June 23, 1949). Schrecker's major criticism of Conant appears to have been for his virulent, "almost violent" (p. 183) anti-communism, rather than for particular actions taken against communist academics at Harvard or elsewhere. We will see in a later chapter that Conant's stricture against employing Communist teachers first surfaced in a report by the Educational Policies Commission of the National Education Association, a group on which he served frequently in the 1940s and 1950s.

40 Sigmund Diamond, *Compromised Campus: The Collaboration of Universities with the Intelligence Community, 1945-1955* (New York: Oxford University Press, 1992), p. 3.

41 Ibid., p. 111.

42 To find a convincing consistency in all of those actions is extremely difficult. We will consider this issue again in a later chapter when we discuss his relations with the National Education Association.

43 In fact, Conant and Spaulding coedited a book in 1940. See James B. Conant and Francis T. Spaulding, eds., *Education for a Classless Society* (Cambridge, MA: Harvard University Graduate School of Education, 1940).

44 Presidential Report for 1939–40, p. 24.

45 "Frances Trow Spaulding, 1896-1950, Dean, 1940-1945," http://www.gse.harvard. edu/about/history/deans/spaulding.

46 Powell, *The Uncertain Profession*, pp. 200–30.

47 Presidential Report for 1946–47, p. 19.

48 Ibid., p. 20.

49 Conant, *My Several Lives*, chapter 29.

50 Ibid., p. 394.

51 "Francis Keppel, 1916? 1990," Center for Higher Education Support Services (nd); http://www.chessconsulting.org/financialaid/keppel/html.

52 "Francis Keppel," Carnegie Corporation Project, Oral History Research Office, Columbia University (1967), esp. pp. 39–53. For a comprehensive account of Carnegie educational philanthropy, see Ellen C. Lagemann, *Private Power for the Public Good: A History of the Carnegie Foundation for the Advancement of Teaching* (Middletown, CT: Wesleyan University Press, 1983).

53 F. P. Keppel to James B. Conant (January 25, 1938), Presidential Papers, Box 104, Folder Carnegie Corporation, 1937–1938.

The Second World War, the Cold War, and the Nationalization of Harvard   101

54 "Francis Keppel," Carnegie Oral History Project, p. 53.

55 James B. Conant, "Function of the School and College in Educating for Social and Cultural Leadership," *Bulletin of the American Association of University Professors* 21 (April, 1935): 329–31; quotation, p. 331. Also see *School and Society* 41 (January 5, 1935): 1–7.

56 Conant and Spaulding, *Education for a Classless Society.*

57 Ibid., chapter 3.

58 For the classic account of social efficiency progressivism in the high school, see Edward A. Krug, *The Shaping of the American High School: 1890-1920* (New York: Harper and Row, 1961).

59 This quotation is taken from the publication of Conant's speech in a periodical for high school principals. See Conant, "A Truce among Educators," *NASSP* (National Association of Secondary School Principals) *Bulletin* (January, 1945): 1–8; quotations, p. 8. This article is available electronically at http://bul.sagepub.com/content/29/127/3.citation.

60 James Bryant Conant, "Public Education and the Structure of American Society," *Teachers College Record* 47 (December, 1941): 145–92.

61 Ibid., p. 147.

62 Ibid., P. 148. Conant would use the phrase "social dynamite" some fifteen years later in describing poor urban communities, particularly minority race communities. He seemed then to have forgotten that he had used the phrase here.

63 Ibid., p. 151.

64 Ibid., p. 158. See W. Lloyd Warner, Robert J. Havighurst, and Martin B. Loeb, *Who Shall Be Educated: The Challenge of Unequal Opportunity* (New York: Harper and Brothers, 1944).

65 Conant here reflected the program of the NEA seeking federal aid for American public schools.

66 James Bryant Conant, *Education in a Divided World* (Cambridge: Harvard University Press, 1938); and Conant, "Public Education and the Structure of American Society."

67 Conant, *Education in a Divided World*, pp. 1–3, 211–18; quotation p. 218.

68 Ibid., p. 1.

69 In a later chapter, we will discuss Conant's work on the Educational Policies Commission. One of their reports, a 1944 document called *Education for All American Youth*, had advocated a Common Learnings course for all high school students as a core of their education for citizenship.

70 Conant, *Education in a Divided World*, chapter 8, "Education for a Career."

71 Compare *Education and Liberty*, chapter 1, with the discussion of Germany and the United States in *Education in a Divided World* on pp. 62–65.

72 Conant, *Education and Liberty*, chapter 2.

73 The particulars of Conant's general education program will be discussed in the next chapter.

74 Conant, *Education and Liberty,* chapter 3.

75 *Pierce v. Society of Sisters* 268 US 510 (1925).

76 Conant saw this issue as still important twenty years later when he published his speech to the American Association of School Administrators as an Appendix to his autobiography. See "Unity and Diversity in Secondary Education: Address before a meeting of the American Association of School Administrators, Boston, Massachusetts" (April 7, 1952); in *My Several Lives,* pp. 665–70.

77 Ibid., p. 467.

78 We will say more about his relationship with these two groups in a later chapter.

4

General Education:
An Increasing Priority

Conant's presidency, as we have seen, was characterized throughout by his commitment to improving the caliber of the Harvard student body and the faculty. Also noticeable during his presidency was the emergence of Harvard as a national, perhaps even *the* national, leader in higher education and as an increasingly influential player in international relations. This chapter takes a decidedly different focus, concentrating on Conant's views on and participation in general education reform, at Harvard and outside of Harvard. It shows how Conant extended his ideas about history of science and cultural history in the 1930s further to a consideration of the importance of the historical approach as an essential part of liberal or general education. General education for Conant meant the liberal education offerings at Harvard College in studies outside of a student's chosen concentration and similar studies at other colleges and universities. It also meant the same type of education, that is, nonspecialist and nonvocational education, at other institutions such as two-year colleges and high schools. Any distinction between general education and liberal education, then, for Conant, was not qualitative; rather, general education was a larger category within which liberal education at Harvard College and other higher education institutions was a subcategory. At Harvard, liberal education was within the purview of Harvard College and the Faculty of Arts and Sciences who handled most of the instruction in the college.

As early as 1935, Conant had identified a main problem for liberal education when he discussed "great obstacles to stimulating teaching and imaginative research." The first of these obstacles was "the present division of the faculty into a multitude of special departments which have all too little contact with each other—a result of the rapid and tremendous growth of our universities which has paralleled and reflected the increase in our organized knowledge." He went on to add that while much of this specialized development was good, "more might be accomplished in our universities if the various fields of knowledge could be brought into close contact."[1] Conant's development of university professorships was one way to break down departmental barriers. Within the curriculum, particularly the undergraduate curriculum, the place to counter the negative effects of narrow specialization was in the provisions for liberal education.

Conant's 1930s efforts to create a program in history of science had involved both a new doctoral program and an undergraduate course, the latter designed specifically for those not in the sciences. That latter effort was clearly within the universe of liberal education. Similarly, Conant's unsuccessful efforts in devising studies in cultural history for all Harvard students were geared directly to the purposes of a liberal education at Harvard, one that liberated students from the narrow concerns of intellectual specialization. And like in the history of science course for undergraduates, the target was not students who majored in history but "rather a suggestion to the non-historian. Here is a vitally important aspect of his liberal education which he might at least start developing during his college years." Conant added that general or liberal education was not the kind of thing that could be got at through tests of specific knowledge. "I should reject all informational tests . . . as indicative of the effectiveness of our general education. Whether a liberal education has been a success or failure should be measured by the student's breadth of vision fifteen or twenty years after graduation." And he became even more dramatic when he noted that there was a need for students to be inculcated with that "educational virus which alone maintains its potency throughout life—the virus of a self-perpetuating liberal education."[2] And it was not just at in higher education that general education was important. In advocating his reading list in cultural history for those outside of Harvard, he remarked, "The importance of a knowledge of American civilization to every citizen is evident."[3]

The longer he served as president, the more comfortable Conant became in seeing the relationship of his views on liberal education to the priorities of his predecessor, Abbott Lawrence Lowell. Near the end of the fifth year of his presidency, in discussing how to counter the effects of narrow specialization, he noted, "If we arrange the details of student life in such a way that . . . all lunch and dine together day after day, then the most powerful of forces making for a liberal education are set at work." He concluded that this was exactly what the House Plan of President Lowell had accomplished.[4] Then, in further discussion of the House Plan, he contrasted its positive effects with the "unsatisfactory conditions in most of our graduate schools." Specifically, he remarked that "the trend of professional education in the last quarter century has been toward what might

General Education: An Increasing Priority   105

be designated as academic nationalism." One antidote to this nationalism could result from having one or two houses for graduate and professional students. Such a development "might make an important contribution toward liberalizing the graduate work of this University."[5]

Lowell's curricular solution for the revival of Harvard College was the institution of a system of concentration and distribution of courses, that is, what might be called studies in a major and in nonmajor courses required of all students. But here again, problems persisted. Conant had noted in the late 1930s that the fields of concentration were too often "those in which a student in the Graduate School of Arts and Sciences may study in order to obtain a Ph.D." He argued that to these fields "others might be added, broader in scope, which would be particularly valuable to those who wished to relate their courses to later study in professional schools or even to executive work in government, industry, or commerce." In a word, the concentrations had to be liberalized to avoid replicating academic disciplinary concerns that were largely unrelated to life other than that within a discipline.[6]

At the end of the 1930s, the president continued to express his dissatisfaction with the situation. In 1939, he reiterated his idea that departmental autonomy, essential at the graduate level, was not a necessary feature of undergraduate education. He added that tentative "explorations toward breaking down departmental lines for undergraduate concentration are being explored by committees." He concluded that "the faults of the Harvard system today may be roughly summarized as the penetration into the college of university functions." Conant worried, though not with any real expectation of a successful outcome, about the narrowness of doctoral programs. He thought that it "was at least worth discussing whether the candidates for the Ph.D. should not be required to keep alive at least some minor interest in the broad general fields of culture, entirely apart from their specialty."[7]

The president by this time, however, had acquired a powerful ally in critiquing undergraduate education at Harvard, the Harvard College student body itself. A report from a Student Council Committee in 1939 noted "the failure of Harvard College to provide an intelligible and broad view of the main areas of learning." This clearly pointed to student acknowledgment of a need for reform of liberal education. Additionally, the same report "criticized the present system of concentration as leading too often to narrow specialization."[8] With the attention of the student body now drawn to the debilities in Harvard's approach to liberal education, the president had another strong voice in looking seriously at how the situation might be addressed.[9] Alas, before this effort could bear fruit, the onset

106 *Scholarly Leadership in Higher Education*

of the Second World War precluded meaningful and wide-ranging discussion of liberal education.

Yet by the middle of the next decade, Harvard had produced a wide-ranging report on general and liberal education that was to be read and discussed throughout the nation. In his autobiography, Conant recounted the genesis of the Harvard Committee appointed in 1943 to work on the idea of a general education in a discussion with Paul Buck about academic war work: "The idea occurred to us that if the scientists could take time off from their research interests and normal duties to do applied research for the government, why could not a group of professors devote themselves to drawing up plans for education in the postwar world?"[10] This statement revealed that, for Conant and many of his faculty, the problem of general education was as formidable an area of study as anything related to national defense.

Conant's interest in general education was quickly challenged as not whole-hearted shortly after he had appointed the Harvard faculty committee to study general education. He had a conversation with W. H. Cowley, then president of Hamilton College, a small liberal arts college in upstate New York. Cowley accused Conant of being a research university president basically uninterested in liberal education. When Conant responded that he had just appointed a committee to study the subject, Cowley replied that appointing a committee was not really much of a meaningful step. He challenged Conant to support this committee as he would support a research project in the sciences, with funds. Conant took up that challenge and returned to campus to obtain $60,000 from the Harvard Corporation to support the endeavor.[11] In essence, then, Conant was putting his money where his mouth was and the committee was given resources sufficient to produce a thorough, and convincing, report.

Conant wrote a substantial introduction to the published version of the Harvard Committee on General Education report in which he reiterated a good bit of his own thinking about the importance of the topic. Among other things, he explained that the term "general education" was used instead of liberal education because the report was to consider the "problem at both the school and the college level." He went on to discuss the meaning of the term when he noted, "The heart of the problem of a general education is the continuance of the liberal and humane tradition. Neither the mere acquisition of information nor the development of special skills and talents can give the broad basis of understanding which is essential if our civilization is to be preserved."[12]

The president, then, was seeking the understanding that would underlie effective, democratic, citizenship in the modern world. Such understanding was

General Education: An Increasing Priority   107

needed especially at the secondary school level for the majority of students who would not be going on to college. And it was also essential at the college level to counter the tendency in higher education to emphasize special, or specialized, education in preference to general education. And Conant also argued that general education was a priority beyond formal education, whether secondary or higher education. He remarked that a distinct possibility in the postwar world was "an enormous expansion of so-called adult education" and added that such an expansion should include both "general and vocational work." Thus, for Conant, general education dealt with all those things not covered in specialized education, in education for work, or in preparatory education for graduate or professional school; and general education was just as important as, or perhaps more important than, these other curricular emphases.[13]

In regard to Harvard, Conant restated in his Introduction to the Harvard Committee Report his long-standing interest in how to create larger understandings than those that were communicated through a field of concentration for undergraduates or a specialized major field in a professional or graduate school. The notion of a free society in the title of the report testified to the significance that the term had attained in the climate of a world war being fought in defense of freedom against totalitarian states such as Nazi Germany, Fascist Italy, and Japan. Conant clearly thought that the report should, and did, speak to the issues of effective and thoughtful citizenship in the United States and indicated this explicitly when he responded negatively to a 1943 proposal to establish a Center for Education in Citizenship from a School of Education professor. Conant explained his response by noting that he did not want to proceed on this topic until hearing from the Committee on General Education.[14]

Conant indicated much about the nature of his interest in general education, at and beyond Harvard College, through the individuals appointed to the committee. It consisted of twelve members: nine came from the Faculty of Arts and Sciences including the dean, and soon to be provost, Paul H. Buck, and individuals from biology, classics, English, government, history (three members, one of whom was the dean and another who was the president of Radcliffe College), philosophy, and zoology. Additionally, three individuals were from the area of education, two faculty members from Harvard and a third representative, a two-year college president who came to Harvard specifically to be on the committee.[15] The makeup of the committee thus was another indication that the report would move beyond Harvard College in its analysis and recommendations. The two-year college person and the education faculty members guaranteed that two-year colleges and high schools were to be part of the reach of the committee. The wide academic representation on the committee also allowed Conant to be true to his long-stated preferences for interdisciplinarity and interdepartmentalism.[16]

The report's ideas were congruent with much of what Conant had written about the topics of general and liberal education before the committee was established. The Letter of Transmittal to President Conant that prefaced the report spoke positively of the committee's relationship to the president. It opened noting that the president's instructions to the committee "were as expansive as its [The Committee on General Education in a Free Society] name was long." It then acknowledged the broad reach of its charge: "We were urged to consider the problem of a general education in both the school and the college." Further, in keeping with Conant's focus on the high school as well as on higher education, and on the large majority of high school students who were not college bound, the report noted, "We were cautioned that the general education of each generation in the high schools was vastly more important than that of the comparatively small minority who attend our four-year colleges." The letter acknowledged that it was not so much the contents of general education that were in question but rather "what is new in this century in the United States is their application to a system of universal education." The committee had considered "the vast field of American educational experience in quest of a concept of general education that would have validity for the free society which we cherish." Success in this larger effort would also guarantee success in identifying the contribution that discussion of general education at Harvard "could make to American democracy."[17]

At the end of the letter of transmittal, the committee outlined its committed agreement to the theme enunciated by President Conant in announcing the effort. "The primary concern of American education today is not the development of the appreciations of the 'good life' in young gentlemen. . . . It is the infusion of the liberal and humane tradition into our entire educational system. Our purpose is to cultivate in the largest possible number of our future citizens an appreciation of both the responsibilities and the benefits which come to them because they are Americans and free." The committee concluded that the concept of general education as presented by the president "is the imperative need of the American educational system. It alone can give cohesion to our efforts and guide the contribution of our youth to the nation's future."[18]

Of course, the total output of a committee of twelve individuals had to be different from the ideas of the person who appointed them. And this committee met weekly for two years, discussed its ideas with university colleagues and people outside of the university, hired consultants to come and meet with the

General Education: An Increasing Priority   109

group, and utilized subcommittees and conferences within and outside of the committee in pursuit of its report. And yet, even this discussion of the complexity and wide reach of the task yielded a conclusion that echoed the ideas of the president. "It should not go unmentioned that twelve men, whose ideas and scholarly interest lie in some phases of *special* education, could by . . . process of intimate study achieve so common an understanding of the basic philosophy and content of *general* education."[19]

Conant acted on his interest in liberal education by volunteering to teach a course in the new program. A close look at that course and several publications that ensued from it allow us to see a university president who was intimately involved in a significant educational problem on his campus and who built on that involvement to extend his interest on liberal education, especially in the sciences, into larger American intellectual circles. Before looking at that phenomenon, however, a discussion of the Harvard Report on general education itself is in order.

The Report

The Harvard Report itself consisted of six chapters, three that laid out the problems and issues conceptually and three that applied the conception of general education to the secondary schools, to Harvard College, and to the larger community, respectively. The ensuing discussion of the body of the report shows that it stressed several themes that Conant dealt with, before, during, and after its publication.

The introductory chapter discussed the United States, noting the growth of formal schooling in the nation, the relation to and impact on that growth of social change, the particular case of the phenomenal growth of the high school, and the tensions raised as it encompassed students of more diverse backgrounds. It also considered the sometime conflicting approaches associated with Thomas Jefferson and Andrew Jackson toward merit and equality, respectively, and the search for a sense of unity to encompass, if not solve, the tensions and contradictions of those two orientations that were then confronting American education and society. Discussion of the strengths and weaknesses of religion, Western culture, problem-focused (as opposed to discipline-based) studies, and science and scientific outlook or method as unifying themes ended the chapter. None of the themes, according to the committee, provided a satisfactory solution to the issue of identifying the general concerns or issues or studies that should unify the nation.

110   *Scholarly Leadership in Higher Education*

The second chapter discussed the Western educational heritage, the difference between general and special (specialized) education which it located in the approach or method taken not in content, an identification of the three areas of knowledge in the contemporary world (science, social science, and humanities), and the traits and characteristics of mind to be fostered through general education. Effective thinking, communication of thought, the ability to make relevant judgments, and the ability to discriminate among values and value choices were identified as the appropriate attributes of general education. Finally, the ideal good citizen was discussed with special attention paid not only to the virtues of open-mindedness but also to the limits of a mind that was so open that it found it hard to make real and relevant distinctions or judgments.

The third chapter was titled "Problems of Diversity." The meaning of diversity for the Harvard Committee, however, had little if anything to do with ethnic or cultural diversity, staples of twenty-first-century discussions. The kinds of diversity that were important to the committee were also important to President Conant, as he had looked to diversify the Harvard student body. For the Harvard Committee, diversity meant basically two things: differences based on intellectual abilities and differences based on social and economic backgrounds. And the committee, like Conant, was intent on making sure that the differences in ability were to be much less dependent on social and economic factors than they had been. Much of the chapter was spent on trying to figure out how to find the most talented students intellectually, whatever their place in the social structure.

Standardized testing, long favored by Conant as a means to this end, was also endorsed by the committee. It noted that testing facilitated policies that precluded, or at least diminished, the possibility that differences in the social structure were the same thing as differences in the opportunity structure. Much space was devoted to how to induce academically able students from middle- or lower-class backgrounds to go on to higher education. The importance of teachers, guidance counselors, and parent education was all discussed in that regard.

Yet the committee made it clear that it was not interested in general education that would be identical for all students, whatever their academic or economic backgrounds. Rather, diversity in background and aspirations of students meant a differentiation in what they would study, in high school or in college; and this differentiation also meant a difference in the general education experiences to which they would be exposed. For the committee general education, whatever group was being instructed, involved understandings and attitudes more

General Education: An Increasing Priority   111

than it involved particular content. So, the committee tried simultaneously to differentiate the general education curriculum according to student ability and interest but not to make that differentiation mean a less challenging experience for any group of students. A section of the third chapter got at this issue when it noted that general education was seeking "Utility Conditioned by Difference."[20] The specific problem addressed here was "how can general education be so adapted to different ages and, above all, differing abilities and outlooks, that it can appeal deeply to each, yet remain in goal and essential teaching the same for all." And the answer to the problem, the committee added, "is the key to anything like complete democracy."[21]

For the committee, "general education does represent a force in the curriculum, and ultimately in society, which is not in the main competitive." This meant that general education was, if anything, more important than specialized education. The reason for this priority was due to its social imperative. "The very idea of a common body of training and knowledge means that everyone, irrespective of his bent, owes a duty to his general sharing in the culture and to his membership in society." Acknowledging this social participation by all had to be done at the same time real differences in student preferences in studies were also acknowledged. The outcome of both of these recognitions for the committee came in an American society "made up of myriad smaller societies representing between them all of the arts and insights, all the duties and self-dedications, of civilized men."[22] Thus, the Harvard Committee acknowledged here the pluralistic nature of its vision of American society and of the general educational experiences appropriate to that society.

The fourth, fifth, and sixth chapters of the Harvard Report addressed general education in the secondary schools, in Harvard College, and in the community, respectively. Our major concern here is James Bryant Conant's Harvard University, so we will leave the Harvard chapter for extended discussion in the next section. As we have seen, however, both the secondary school and adult education were of great interest to Conant. Thus, it is no surprise that they were of interest to the committee. A brief account of their treatment of these two topics follows.

The chapter in the Harvard Committee report on the secondary schools was the longest in the book, exceeding in number of pages even the chapter on Harvard itself. The bulk of the chapter involved extended discussions of the high school curriculum in the areas of the humanities, the social studies, and mathematics and the natural sciences. In the first of these discussions, the committee opted for literature as a core concern of humanities instruction in

112   *Scholarly Leadership in Higher Education*

the secondary school but refused to be overly specific in making prescriptions for what was to be studied. It was specific, however, on what was to be avoided in this instruction, including too much stress on facts, too much emphasis on literary history, strained correlations with social studies, too much technical analysis, and "overly didactic lessons in behavior resulting from study of a work." Just as problematic as these dangers were superficial reading with no context or import addressed, avoidance of critical terms and appraisals when students were ready for them, and an irresponsible "attitude to the implications of what is being read."[23]

Other specific suggestions about things to avoid or to embrace were followed by a general statement about teaching all aspects of English. "As a whole it aims to secure the maximum freedom for the teacher compatible with a coherent and reasonable order." Then the committee went on to qualify that generalization with a statement that "there is no doubt that this freedom should be carefully guarded."[24] Other aspects of language studies such as reading and composition were discussed but with a rather curious combination of detailed specifics and then generalities that almost seemed like trivialities. The ensuing discussion of foreign languages was similarly broad and nonprescriptive.

The treatment of the social studies began with a few paragraphs on the elementary and middle schools, advocating topics and activities at each level that were consciously chosen with the realities of the high school curriculum in mind. European and general history were being shorted in the amount of time spent, according to the committee, and American history was a subject to which too many students were overexposed in their school careers. In all studies of history, the committee recommended that the method of "uniform coverage" was to be avoided. Rather, any particular focus could yield positive results if the students were meaningfully engaged with the group(s) being studied and the contributions they had made. Courses in the nature of contemporary society and in problems of American life were also discussed, again with admonitions to be appropriately realistic in coverage but also to avoid being too particularistic to the point that generalizations were eschewed. The committee cautioned against excessive chauvinism in social studies, advocated well-trained teachers, and cautioned against outside restrictions on the enterprise.

The discussion of science was more pointed and, at least to this reader, more interesting and convincing than the English and social studies treatments. It started with a definition of science, particularly as implemented in general education. Science was defined as a "primarily distinct type of intellectual enterprise, involving highly restricted aspects of reality and prepared . . . to make particular types of contributions to general education." The contributions included "a persistent effort toward precision" as evidenced in things like exact definition and measurement.[25] Experiment and direct experience in the laboratory or the field were also identified as characteristic of science studies as was critical appraisal of evidence gathered in those arenas. Of course, measurement involved mathematics and the relationships between the measurement and what was being measured were points of discussion. Specific elaborations of these points in chemistry, biology, and the physical sciences were then offered.

A comparison of science as general education and as special education ensued in which the former was indicated as encompassing "things not primarily for their own sake, but as they fit into an integrated intellectual structure."[26] General education science instruction was described as broad in scope, comparative of the sciences with each other, and stressing science's relations with its own past as well as with the rest of society. Alas, for the committee, these were the areas that were too often slighted in science courses in the secondary school by teachers who were intent on covering all the material in a particular science course syllabus. Similarly, science teachers were seen as too enamored with experiment and the scientific method. In general education, the point of science teaching was not to idolize or internalize the scientific method. Rather, the goal was to illustrate how scientists were engaged in problem solving and how, often, the problem was solved by analysis as much as by experiment, by critical thinking about a problem as opposed to the rote method.

A final section of the chapter devoted to education and the human being brought in a completely new concern. The issue addressed here was the intellectual level of the high school curriculum for various groups of students. Attempts to substitute activities for abstract instruction for some were considered but rejected as a final answer. The committee was prepared to accept the need to customize the curriculum for groups of students but not to abandon subject matter as a need in whatever customization occurred. Two concluding paragraphs cautioned against an excessively bookish education on the one hand and a too practical and specific approach on the other. The committee opted for a middle road, holding that education was fundamentally a rational enterprise but one that used reason to address life. Thus, relevance, which was discussed often in the preceding pages of the report, was again offered as a guide to how reason and rationality were to be employed in the secondary schools in pursuit of a good life.[27]

The final chapter on general education in the community was the least specific in content of any chapter in the report. This reflected the reality that the whole area of adult education was much less studied than the secondary school or higher education. The brevity of the committee's treatment of the topic illustrated this reality. It described the educational difficulties encountered in the Civilian Conservation Corps and the National Youth Administration, cornerstones of the work-study approach that had characterized the New Deal efforts in adult education. The failure in both programs was to offer a meaningful educational experience for the adults involved. Lack of understanding of adult learning was offered as an explanation for these failures, as well as a caution to be noted in any contemporary efforts. Brief discussions of new media such as radio and television ensued, with indications that they might solve the problem, though offering no specific ways in which that could happen. Like the committee, Conant was enamored with media such as radio, though he, like they, did not understand enough to make meaningful recommendations educationally.

One is hesitant to be too critical of the chapter on community education, especially since it had little in the way of meaningful secondary literature to rely on. Such was not the case for the chapter on secondary education, where the available sources were many and varied. The two chapters disappointed any reader looking for insight as to how general education in the secondary school and in the community might be improved in specific ways. In contrast, the chapter on general education in a collegiate setting, which was placed between the secondary and community education discussions, was on a topic that this particular committee was ready to analyze convincingly.

General Education in Harvard College

In discussing the recent evolution of Harvard College, the committee paid homage to the diversification of the Harvard student body, geographically and economically, in the recent past. It then mentioned the increasing public school background of Harvard freshmen and the diversity of curricula taken in high school, which this phenomenon represented. This allowed the committee to give specific, positive mention of the National Scholarship plan of President Conant. Also given positive review was the use of the Scholastic Aptitude Test (SAT) and a few achievement tests as excellent indicators of student ability and as vehicles for the successful diversification, which it celebrated. A description of the existing curriculum for freshmen at Harvard ensued, where students chose from a number of optional, available courses for the freshman year. After students chose a concentration, additional courses outside of the concentration

General Education: An Increasing Priority   115

were added to represent a distribution of studies that constituted a general education. In discussing the concentration chosen by students, the committee noted the rigor often present in many of the concentrations and the enrollment of undergraduates with graduate students in many courses in the various concentrations as an illustration of that rigor. General education at Harvard was, on the one hand, characterized by vagueness and, on the other hand, by the tendency of distribution courses used in general education not to be designed for that purpose but rather as introductory or ancillary courses to a concentration.[28]

Given this rigor in concentration and the vagueness of the distribution requirements, the committee concluded that there "has been ... no very substantial intellectual experience common to all Harvard students."[29] The committee's answer to the problem began with a recommendation for the establishment of separate courses devoted to general education in place of introductory courses in various specializations that claimed to address the issue. The point was that not all, or even many, introductory courses provided general education. Courses crafted to meet the objective of a general education were necessary and should be carefully designed and offered, perhaps experimentally at the beginning of the effort. In terms of the amount of time to be devoted to general education, the committee recommended that of the sixteen courses completed by the typical Harvard College student over his undergraduate career, six should be in general education. Three of the six, the more basic courses that might have considerable numbers of students, should be taken in the first two undergraduate years and three more general education courses, involving different topics and methods of study than those characteristic in the basic courses, should be taken in the junior and senior years. The committee also recommended that the English composition requirement be eliminated in favor of a distinct writing emphasis in all the basic general education courses.

The committee then discussed general education offerings in three areas, humanities, social sciences, and science and mathematics. Each student would have to take one course in each of three areas, with three additional courses chosen outside of the student's area of concentration. Returning to the three basic courses to be taken early, in the humanities, the committee recommended a required course for all students, entitled "Great Texts of Literature." The course was not to be a survey but a deep study of selected texts and the selection would vary from section to section of the course offered. Examples of possibilities for inclusion in this course included "Homer, one or two of the Greek tragedies, Plato, the Bible, Virgil, Dante, Shakespeare, Milton, Tolstoy."[30] These were simply examples of possible authors, not mandatory authors for study. The committee added that the level of intensity it envisioned for the study of texts in this course meant that the number of texts selected in a given course should be relatively small, certainly less than eight. Lectures and discussion sessions were recommended by the committee for this course, with the former being less frequent than the latter and geared to setting up the issues to be discussed. The additional general education courses in the humanities were not specified, though the committee discussed possibilities and principles of selection for courses in the areas of literature, philosophy, the fine arts, and music. Notably absent was study in foreign languages.

In the social sciences, the committee recommended that a course in "Western Thought and Institutions" be the basic requirement. Again, as in the humanities required course, comprehensive, chronological coverage like that undertaken in typical survey courses was not recommended. Rather selection should be undertaken of areas or issues to be studied in some depth. Greek or Roman classics were recommended for study as was the Reformation, the time and setting where reason and tolerance became part of the Western tradition. Again, specific authors were recommended, such as "Aquinas, Machiavelli, Luther, Bodin, Locke, Montesquieu, Rousseau, Adam Smith, Bentham and Mill."[31] Whatever authors or texts were chosen, the committee prescribed that the readings be contextualized historically and socially, as well as considered in depth for their content and presentation. The committee also recommended the possibility of cross-referencing and comparison between this course and the required literature course.

The committee engaged in extensive discussion of other courses in the social sciences and recommended a course in American democracy, involving the study of issues raised in texts such as de Tocqueville's *Democracy in America*, Bryce's *The American Commonwealth*, and Myrdal's recently published *The American Dilemma*. The Myrdal work considered the race issue that was beginning to come to the fore in American society. Since the committee was confident that the social science faculty members in Harvard College would propose numerous other courses for inclusion as general education options, it offered only one more recommendation for consideration, a course in human relations. It recommended that student numbers be kept small if the course were to fulfill the expectations expressed by students and understood as necessary by the committee.

In considering the sciences, the committee did not recommend one required general education course but suggested a choice between two courses, one in physical science and one in the biological sciences, which were to be offered at

General Education: An Increasing Priority   117

the first-year level. Care was needed in developing these courses so that they avoided the specialist tendency that pervaded all introductory courses in the sciences. A fundamental issue for general education in science was that many of the topics or issues to be studied were not necessarily of great interest to the practicing scientist, or even to the student majoring in science. Presenting these topics or issues in the context in which they occurred, where they were of great controversy and absorbing concern, fulfilled the objectives of general education in the sciences quite convincingly. The committee concluded, "The historical development of the subjects considered in our courses, therefore, should occupy an important place in their design."[32] Thus, general education courses in science would be far different from the normal courses, emphasizing much more the concerns about the philosophy and history of the sciences than speaking to the consideration and solution of contemporary scientific problems. These recommendations echoed wholeheartedly the views of President Conant who had supported establishing a history of science graduate program and a history of science course for nonscientists in the 1930s.

A final particular included in this chapter was the recommendation for a Standing Committee on General Education to be appointed by the president to administer the general education curriculum. The committee would be responsible for the encouragement and approval of courses that met general education requirements and would also be responsible for the appointment of faculty to teach those courses. A separate general education faculty was not envisioned, but choosing faculty carefully to teach general education courses and making sure that the teaching of those courses was valued were priority concerns. And, of course, they were concerns that were in possible, if not inevitable, conflict with the priorities of disciplinary, research-oriented faculty.

Reaction to the Harvard Committee report was diverse and not all that unpredictable. An academic reviewer in a foreign language journal lamented the lack of inclusion of foreign language studies in general education, both in the high school and at Harvard. It should be noted that foreign language and mathematics, two subject areas that were excluded by the committee from the proposed Harvard general education curriculum, were not represented on the committee. While the review in a foreign language journal might be seen as a sort of special pleading on behalf of one of the groups left out, the critique of social science in general education as lacking an international dimension seemed more detached, that is, less partisan and thus more formidable.[33]

A review in *The Clearing House*, a journal circulated primarily to professional educators in the elementary and high schools, was also quite predictable.

The author concentrated on the committee's devotion to classics, ignoring the committee's refusal to identify any book as necessary to be treated and its indication that whatever the text, the way it was taught was of primary importance. This review argued that general education, or citizenship education, was a laudable goal but, at least for the high schools, a goal that required much more than the intellectual work discussed in the report, no matter how varied that work.[34]

A review in *The Journal of Higher Education* was basically favorable, though not uncritical. The reviewer pointed out that the report, which consciously rejected "survey" courses as appropriate for general education, often described the courses it thought desirable in ways that seemed not easily distinguished from survey courses. The reviewer also cautioned against wholesale adoption of recommendations for Harvard College by liberal arts colleges in other settings with distinctly different configurations of students and faculty. This review did note that with this report, Harvard was seeking to repair the damage to general education on its campus that had been done through the elective system. Finally, the reviewer endorsed the goal of providing "a common cultural experience" for Harvard students and for all Americans through general education. Also provided was a rather flat-footed approval of how recommendations for higher education might simply be adapted to the secondary schools and, though not stated, at least implied also for community education. The review's final two sentences portrayed sentiments that should have heartened the committee and President Conant. "The deep moral tone which characterizes the whole report and the emphasis on the need of character training add a much needed note to American education. This report should not be read, it should be studied."[35]

The general education program recommended by the committee was successfully approved by the Harvard College faculty, with only minor modifications of the original proposals. Conant noted after a year or two of implementation that the general education courses had "solved" the problem of the inadequacies of the distribution requirement in the college curriculum, which had been to take four courses outside of a student's field of concentration. Each student was now required to take three basic courses, one each in humanities, social science, and natural science in his freshman and sophomore years. Additionally, three other courses were to be taken outside of a student's concentration in his junior and senior years. These courses did not necessarily have to be general education courses but, if they were not, they needed to be chosen to fulfill a general education purpose for the student. Courses in general education developed to meet this second requirement included the following:

General Education: An Increasing Priority   119

"Classics of the Christian Tradition," "Art in Man's Environment," "Human Relations," "Interpretations of American Institutions," "The Impact of Science on Modern Life," and "Organic Evolution."[36] Conant's participation in teaching one of the new general education courses in science helped the entire program to develop successfully. And he frequently reiterated the most basic objective of the general education requirement that it looked "first of all to a student's life as a responsible human being and a citizen." Such an objective was not easily measured or evaluated, and its realization was not likely to surface for many years after a student's education. In fact, it was an illustration of what Conant referred to as the "old cliché that 'education is what is left after all that had been learnt is forgotten.'"[37]

President Conant stressed the importance of general education to him, and to Harvard, in a variety of ways. He described the tentative nature of specific course requirements and the need to innovate, experiment, and evaluate different aspects of the program. Two years after publication of the committee report, he noted that it would take a few more years to decide if it were worthwhile to proceed with the new program. If that were to happen, then there would be a need to hire new faculty for the general education courses with salaries "assured from the income of a special fund."[38] And one year after that he included a long discussion of general education in his presidential report. He noted that the committee now in charge of general education recommended that the requirements of the 1945 report should be extended to all students in Harvard College and that the faculty discussion showed them to be in overwhelming agreement. He added that new courses in general education, in addition to the basic courses in science, social science, and the humanities, were being developed. Among the latest offerings were "Classics of the Christian Tradition, Art in Man's Environment, Human Relations, Interpretations of American Institutions, The Impact of Science on Modern Life, and Organic Evolution." He also noted that Harvard University had rich resources to draw on in developing general education courses and that these courses were not the property of any academic department. He then discussed the immediate political relevance of general education in its look at a student's life "as a responsible human being and as a citizen." This was particularly important in the current Cold War climate. While the criteria for specialized education such as in engineering might be similar in both Cold War political systems, "the general education must be miles apart." He explained that "as the impact of Party orthodoxy on biological investigation in Russia demonstrates, the basic presuppositions of a society affect even technical and scientific work."[39]

The discussion of the issues raised in *General Education in a Free Society* was spirited and long-lasting. The volume itself brought Harvard into the forefront of consideration of academic issues that clearly had larger social repercussions. It thrust Harvard into a leadership role in a larger educational arena than the natural science research in which Harvard and other large research universities also excelled. Conant got what he wanted in the area of general education, and it remained an arena for academic excellence at Harvard even after he left.

Conant himself found a variety of ways to reinforce his belief in general education and the intellectual innovation that it represented. In the midst of the renaissance of general education on campus sparked by the 1945 committee report, he founded a second version of the shop club, the interdisciplinary discussion group in which he had participated as a young faculty member in the 1920. This version met a few times a year and it involved "those on the college faculty—scientists, social scientists, and humanists—who participated in the General Education teaching program." According to one of the members, this "allowed the civilizing experience of discussion with Jerome Bruner, Harry Levin, Ernst May, Henry Murray, Talcott Parsons, David Riesman, Paul Tillich, George Wald, Morton White, and others."[40] Tillich, a famed theologian, came to Harvard shortly after Conant left campus for good. Tillich was brought to be one of the university professors established by Conant. Tillich chose to teach, not in the Divinity School, however, his likely home, but in the general education program. Tillich's teaching choice indicated that general education was still exceptionally important, at least to some of the leading scholars on the campus, after Conant was no longer present.[41]

In his final report before leaving the Harvard presidency, Conant again discussed general education at some length. He noted that it needed a second report, one that described and evaluated what had so far been accomplished. Restating his regard for individual faculty who were willing to cross-disciplinary boundaries and his suspicion of departments as too rigid defenders of those boundaries, he concluded, "If the program ever comes to be regarded as the property of a group of departments, its effectiveness will disappear."[42] And as president, he had taken steps to hire instructors specifically for general education courses and not necessarily through departmental structures or involvement.

The point of this lengthy discussion is not that Conant, or his faculty committee, had the final answers to the makeup of liberal or general education. It is that, rather, Harvard University, under the leadership of President Conant, addressed one of the major educational problems of the mid-twentieth-century world, the development of intelligent citizens for a democratic society. Further, the issue was considered in its widest context, outside of Harvard as well as inside of Harvard and even outside the world of formal educational institutions. It represented an intellectual depth in President Conant and a broad reach of the Harvard faculty committee that seemed, and still seems, unusual for both a university administrator and his faculty.

President Conant and General Education in the Sciences

The previous discussion alluded to the compatibility between many of Conant's ideas and those of the Harvard Committee. Conant himself testified to this compatibility but saw it more as a case of him being influenced by them than vice versa. This seems a bit too modest to one who has studied both Conant's views and the committee's report. Whether the direction of influence went between committee and president or was reversed, and of course either of these would be an oversimplification, there is no question that Conant saw the committee's recommendations for Harvard College as exceptionally important.

Perhaps the best illustration of this importance for Conant was that he offered to develop and teach one of the first-year general education courses in natural science, an offer that was quickly accepted by the then reconstituted committee. He had noted in 1936 that a course in the history of science, "in which various phases of development of science were thoroughly explored might serve as an introduction for non-scientists to the methods of science."[43] Not quite a decade later, Conant was announced as the developer of the Natural Science 4 course. He described his actions as a way of indicating his clear endorsement of the new general education curriculum. Additionally, he had at least two other motives: he noted that his actions were related to a long-held desire to "demonstrate a way of presenting science to laymen" and he remarked that given all that had taken him away from campus for war work, the course offering was "positive proof that I could stay in Cambridge and devote myself to an educational task."[44]

Coincident with Conant's return to campus from war work, he also recommitted himself to academic publishing. He published two volumes on his development and teaching of Natural Science 4 and also had the actual syllabi of his and other natural science courses published, one at a time, and, subsequently, in a compendium.[45] The Yale University Press and the Harvard University Press were the publishers of these volumes, a testimony to the scholarly quality of the enterprises but also likely a nod to the power of the Harvard University presidency. Whatever the particular explanations for the publications, these volumes testified to Conant's desire while president to maintain a strong publication record, even if it was not in his discipline of chemistry. These publications all testified to the unwillingness of the president to discard his professional adherence to the sciences, at the same time he was trying to explain the importance of science to nonscientists. His use of studies grounded in the history of science testified to his long-standing interest in historical studies, not for their own sake but for the larger intellectual and social benefit, or general educational purpose, that they offered.

The prime objective of Conant's general education science course was to provide students with an understanding of science that showed its relation with fields other than science. Understanding experiments and related developments in science provided a sound grounding for understanding current problems and issues that required scientific knowledge. Teaching science to nonscientists was difficult but not an impossible task. The use of the human drama often involved in scientific discovery was helpful to the effort. Conant described the method he used as emphasizing the "detail of the historical development of a new concept or scheme" in which the description emphasized "both the human agency and the scientific progress, or lack of progress, which came as a result of that agency." He thought that understanding science would become part of a student's larger intellectual stance, one that related scientific development to intellectual and cultural history.[46]

Conant described his course as a study of the tactics and strategy of science, an area for which intelligent nonscientists had "no feel."[47] Further, this lack of feel for the topic was made worse by some in the natural and social sciences who argued that "modern science as training the mind to be an exact and impartial analysis of facts is an education specially fitted to promote sound citizenship." For Conant, this analysis could not have been more wrongheaded. It "put the scientist on a pedestal because he is an impartial inquirer," a judgment that would "misunderstand the situation entirely." In fact, in the early stages of the development of many sciences, according to Conant, "prejudice and vanity proved stumbling blocks to progress." Early scientists often stumbled through on their way to a discovery, hampered by poor formulations, prejudices, and misleading generalization. While more recently the professionalization of science had alleviated this situation a bit, there was no reason to put any absolute trust in the scientific method or in scientists. He noted, "My observations lead me to conclude that as human beings, scientific investigators are statistically distributed over the whole spectrum of human folly and wisdom much as other men." He concluded that to "claim that the study of science is the best

General Education: An Increasing Priority   123

education for young men who aspire to become impartial analysts of human affairs is to put forward a very dubious educational hypothesis at best."[48] Any notion of science as the ultimate way to human improvement was deeply flawed, according to Conant. The flaw came from seeing and studying science logically, or philosophically, or theoretically, seeking generalizations that would hold, or at least sought to hold, in all situations. Conant's approach to science was not philosophical, but historical, that is empirical, a consideration of science as it actually developed. He thought that such a study of science led not only to an appreciation of its accomplishments but also to their contextualization in ways that would also expose the foibles of science and scientists as well as the accidents and other unplanned factors related to scientific discovery.

Conant advocated study of particular cases in the history of science. The cases he developed were chosen specifically to illustrate the uneven development of science, the human factors that influenced this process, and the role of chance and other unexplained or unexplainable factors in the development. He relied on early cases in the history of science for study in his course, rather than more recent ones, because of their ease of accessibility to nonscientists. The cases that he chose did not require technical knowledge or skills to be understood by the student. Using cases also meant that the general education science course taught by Conant used a popular methodology, the case method, which became prominent in the Harvard Law School in the 1890s and became a core approach in the Harvard Business School in the twentieth century.[49]

Conant's cases, in addition to stressing the particularity of individual discoveries and the fallibility of science, emphasized two other factors not prominent in science teaching. The first was the inclusion of the practical knowledge and concerns involved in scientific discoveries, an emphasis downplayed in science courses that sought to illustrate the growth of science itself. The mundane and the practical, for Conant and his cases, were every bit as important as the theoretical in explaining scientific discovery. Additionally, he remarked that he would direct attention to "the less spectacular and the less known advances in the sciences," since more "can be learned from their study than from the few famous sweeping generalizations which in their time gathered up so much of the past and illumined the future so brightly."[50] The initial publication of the specific cases in Conant's course discussed three cases. The first was Robert Boyle's experiments in pneumatics, the second discussed the "Overthrow of the Phlogiston Theory," and the third dealt with early developments in the concepts of "Temperature and Heat." In each case, as one reviewer noted, emphasis was placed on "the methodological aspects of the research and the influence of social factors on the development of physical science." The reviewer concluded that the approach to these cases held "great promise," especially if new cases were added that involved the biological as well as the physical sciences and the social sciences also. Such additions would "help dispel the misconception that scientific rigor is an exclusive possession of the physical sciences, and that scientific progress is an exclusive contribution of these same sciences."[51]

Conant certainly must have been pleased by this review, though he himself was just a bit more reticent than the reviewer to expand on the value of his cases as an approach to work in other fields. Conant was not, however, averse to discussing the social sciences himself, in the context of explanations of his course development in general education. He thought that the learning about the sciences that students took away from his course would be helpful in a larger effort. Specifically, he noted, "We need to lay the basis for a better discussion of the ways in which rational methods may be applied to the study and solution of human problems."[52] In an exchange with a Harvard sociologist about the applicability of natural science to social science, he remained a skeptic. While he thought that there certainly had been advances in statistics, demography, and psychological testing, the advances were "empirical, not theoretical." Further, he thought that the sociologist's recommendation to concentrate Harvard's work in pure social science research was one with which he strongly disagreed. According to Conant, echoing a point made about the natural sciences in his course, "Only from practical problems can material come that will advance your science."[53]

We will have some final things to say about Conant and general education in our last chapter evaluating his leadership. Before that, however, it is important to note here that Conant took his general education in science activities beyond Harvard, to a wider audience that might be described as a general readership, in the publication of two books on science in the early 1950s. The two books, published in 1951 and 1952, respectively, followed the publications by Conant about the general education science courses he and other scientists taught because of the general education reform at Harvard.[54] The first of the two later volumes, *Science and Common Sense* (1951), was originally intended to be a second edition of a small book detailing Conant's work on his general education course, *On Understanding Science*, published in 1947. Both books were published by Yale University Press, and Conant in a preface to the 1951 volume described it not as an update but as "a much larger book on the methods of science for the general reader." In the first chapter, he noted that "this is a citizen's guide to the methods of experimental science . . . addressed to the intelligent citizen who,

General Education: An Increasing Priority 125

as a voter may, to an increasing extent, be interested in congressional action on scientific matters."[55]

Conant, as he had done before, critiqued those who believed that a rigorous, quantitative, laboratory approach would yield benefits attributed to the "scientific method" used in the natural sciences. Conant's critique was twofold. In the first place, there was no single scientific method, based on measurement or experiments, which resulted in scientific progress and accomplishments. Rather, close attention to past progress in the sciences showed that advances were halting, based on observation, intuition, and criticism, and on speculative reasoning and deduction, all of which were related to practical concerns advanced by nonscientists such as artisans and agriculturists. Both of these latter groups were focused on the solution of practical problems. Conant's main point, as foreshadowed in the words "common sense" in the title of this book, was that science and common sense were intimately related to each other. Rather than privilege the experimental scientist as an expert whose word should be granted an authorized status in public discourse, Conant demurred. He used the physical science cases he had used in his Harvard course and added to them cases from biology and geology to argue his thesis. The most important point for the layman in all of the cases was that the "great working hypotheses in the past have often originated in the minds of the pioneers as a result of mental processes which can best be described by such words as 'inspired guess,' 'intuitive hunch,' or 'brilliant flash of imagination.'"[56]

None of this was to doubt the technical attributes of scientists, but Conant also wanted to make sure that readers understood that whatever the technical qualifications or expertise of scientists in any field, they were not the sole, or even the most important, arbiters of scientific progress. He phrased his point this way: "In following my exposition of the methods of experimental science by using examples from the past, the reader must be asked to become as much of a skeptic about scientific explanations as he can." He followed this by noting, "Experimental science can be thought of as an activity which increases the adequacy of the concept and conceptual schemes which are related to certain types of perception and which lead to certain types of activities; *it is one extension of common sense.*"[57]

Laypeople, for Conant, should not be intimidated by science but, rather, were to come to appreciate scientific advance and also to understand the many extrascientific attributes of that advance. Conant was attempting to demystify science for lay readers often beset by scientists who pontificated about the complicated character of their work and who sought, through that complication,

126 *Scholarly Leadership in Higher Education*

to set themselves on a pedestal of expertise apart from the layman. It was easy to show science as an extension of common sense historically, since the early discoveries were not shrouded in technical complexities. But, for Conant, even in the increasingly complex science of the twentieth century, the relationship of science to common sense should not be ignored. He opined, "We start with the historic connection between common sense and science and follow these implications to the aspects of modern science (which are manifold) where the relation has hardly changed in this century." The contingency of scientific accomplishment was important to Conant, as was its dependence on chance occurrences and the careful observation of those occurrences.[58]

Conant insisted on contingency, intuition, deduction, and other extra-experimental concerns and qualities because he was trying to get the layman to become involved in discussions of science and its practical uses, exceedingly important concerns in the middle of the twentieth century. Conant viewed science as a dynamic enterprise rather than as some static and progressive accumulation of knowledge. He offered his own view of science as a corrective to those who saw it as progressive and technically intimidating to the layman. For Conant, "Science is an interconnected series of concepts and conceptual schemes that have developed as a result of experimentation and observation and are fruitful of further experimentation and observations. In this definition the emphasis in on the word 'fruitful.' *Science is a speculative enterprise.*"[59]

And Conant intended that his main skeptical points about the natural sciences be applied also, just as rigorously, to the social sciences and their impact on social affairs. Conant was a believer in the social sciences and greatly interested in what they might contribute to social welfare. He was not, however, one who looked to the existing social sciences for direction in social affairs. He thought that they could "benefit social organization and welfare, but not as easily as natural sciences impact economy and warfare." He added that one "should have no illusion that basic national issues can be handled by any group of social scientists in the way that problems of design of bridges and machines can be treated by engineers. Policy questions must be resolved, in the future as in the past, by governmental officials, business executives, and labor leaders; they cannot be handed over to scientific experts to find an answer which is 'right.'" Policy decisions, for Conant, also needed to be informed by the insights of historians who added to the consideration of present policy the conduct and outcome of past policies and by social philosophers who helped historians and social scientists to interpret the meaning of their work. Conant was not dismissive of the social sciences. He noted that they could be helpful in social policy, particularly in consideration of

General Education: An Increasing Priority   127

the "types of problems where one can hope for help form the social psychologist, sociologist, and anthropologist," namely those involving "human relations and those conflicts among individuals and groups which have been so much intensified by the conditions of modern life."[60]

Most important for Conant was that natural science, and social science, be open to scrutiny by the larger American public. The context for this concern was the burgeoning Cold War, made much warmer through the conflict in Korea, which was between competing social systems of communism and democracy. In this situation, it was imperative that scientific progress would be impeded "if the general public fails to understand the significance of free publication and discussion."[61] For Conant, it was that discussion and publication of science and social science that distinguished democracy from communism. That distinction could not afford to be ignored or downplayed in any fashion if democracy, the American version of which Conant fervently admired, were to be preserved.

In spite of Conant's intention to have his ideas on science applied to the social sciences, and disseminated to a general lay audience, the reviews of *Science and Common Sense* came largely from within the scientific community. One, by a noted botanist who also worked in the history of science, saw Conant's work as largely, and correctly, an endorsement of a true liberal education as the way for a layperson to begin to understand and participate in public affairs.[62] A second review, written by an affiliate of the Zoological Laboratory at Yale, endorsed Conant's declaration that there was no such thing as a single scientific method as well as his nuanced discussion of the role of quantification and measurement in science. The reviewer also approved of Conant's desire to distinguish scientific concepts from experiments and other aspects of empirical/experimental science but added that scientists themselves were not always aware of this distinction. This review also applauded Conant's rigorous views of the limitations of the contributions that science and scientists make to human affairs.[63]

Two other reviews of *Science and Common Sense*, one in a higher education journal and the other in a sociology journal, gave some evidence that he was reaching an academic audience outside of the sciences, though not the lay audience he desired. The brief review of Conant's book in *The Journal of Higher Education* was headed with the words "Helpful Reorientation." The reviewer went on to stress Conant's view of science as a speculative enterprise and concluded by noting that the last two chapters dealt effectively with issues related to science and government and private industry. These matters were of special interest to university administrators, causing the reviewer to conclude with the following evaluation. "This book should have value for the general reader, but its major contribution will be in helping university educators to reorient scientific education into more fertile and effective modes of operation."[64] The reviewer in the sociological journal applauded Conant's inclusion of the social sciences, especially sociology, in his analysis. The reviewer hoped that the inclusion of social science was a sign that the social sciences might be able to overcome their recent exclusion by the National Science Foundation (NSF) from research support. He added that Conant had changed his mind on the social sciences "during the last four or five years."[65] Yet my analysis of Conant's ideas in the earlier chapters of this book questions, if it does not contradict, that conclusion. Conant, from the first decade of his presidency, was interested in both the history of science and history and the social sciences and moved in the second decade of that presidency to promote innovations in the social sciences such as the creation of the Department of Social Relations in an attempt to make Harvard a leader in social science research and teaching. Conant thus was widening the academic audience for his work in raising conceptual and practical concerns about both science and social science, though he was not necessarily reaching the lay audiences he expressly addressed in his volume.

A brief look at the book on science Conant produced one year later allows us to see if it had any better luck than the earlier volume in attracting a wider audience. *Modern Science and Modern Man* was the publication of four Bampton lectures delivered at Columbia University in a series devoted to religion, culture, and public life. The content of the lectures was compatible with, often identical to, Conant's earlier work on science. A fundamental objective, as in the earlier works, was to make people aware of the contingency of science and scientific activity, as well as the nature of scientific theory as more analogous to common sense than to some sort of set in stone formulation based on an objective scientific method. There were a few new wrinkles, or rather points of emphasis, in this volume that were not foregrounded as much in earlier volumes. These included recognition of the atomic age as a new setting for scientific activity and a setting in which the totally unscientific attribute of secrecy had come to pervade science, at least that part of science attached to the technological development of war weaponry. Conant was intent on exposing the threat of this development to democracy and of combating it with his analysis of science as contingent, open, subject to change, in short, possessing many characteristics associated with democratic life. He stated his own position clearly: "I do not like the atomic age or any of its consequences. To learn to adjust to these consequences with charity and sanity is the chief spiritual problem of our time."[66]

General Education: An Increasing Priority 129

Conant wanted to make sure that his readers and listeners understood that scientists were not above human concerns, not value free as proponents of scientific expertise and objectivity might proclaim. In his own words, "The notion that a scientist is a cool, impartial, detached individual is, of course, absurd." Rather, in approaching scientists who claimed general expertise, he noted, "First of all, a healthy skepticism is in order in listening to an expert, particularly an enthusiastic one."[67] He then went on to discuss the social sciences, much as he had done in *Science and Common Sense*, voicing his own support for the value of the social sciences but also stating his own preference for "the uncommitted investigator who has ideas, irrelevant as these ideas may seem to practical problems," over the deterministic prescriptions offered by many in the social sciences as guidance for social conduct.[68]

Conant's final lecture addressed directly the relation of science and spiritual values. He indicated here the political utility for him of the spiritual realm when he contrasted a science cognizant of values and spiritual concerns with the doctrine of dialectical materialism that Marxists used to indicate the completely deterministic outcome of their own view of the world, scientific in both the natural and social connotations of the concept. The problem with this all-encompassing worldview for Conant was that it failed to acknowledge "the idealistic side of human nature . . . to accommodate . . . not facts of science but facts of human history . . . unselfish ways in which human beings often act with compassion, love, friendliness, self-sacrifice." Conant posited the value of faith, in contrast to the objective determinism of science. He opined that when "the scientist steps out of his laboratory and takes part in activities other than research, as a man of action he has to believe."[69] He concluded his lectures not with an endorsement of religion but with the notion that a reduction was needed in the empiricism represented by both communist materialism and noncommunist believers in the primacy of objective science as a social salvation. In his own words, "A continued reduction in the degree of empiricism in our undertakings is both possible and of deep significance—this, in a few words, is the message that modern science brings to modern man."[70]

An important review of Conant's book appeared in a noted psychological journal. Edwin G. Boring of Harvard's psychology department reviewed Conant's volume, treating his president as not a president but a scholar and intellectual writing for a large audience of other scholars and intellectuals.[71] Boring noted in the review that psychology was hardly mentioned in the book but that psychologists would be well advised to pay attention to its argument. Boring stressed Conant's emphasis on a contingent, open science as an antidote to any brand of scientific determinism. He agreed with Conant that the accomplishments of science were partial and could not be anything but partial, leaving room for both the views of nonmainstream scientists about scientific accomplishments and the views of those in other areas than science. He also discussed Conant's endorsement of the social sciences, not for their wonderful accomplishments but for their intention, at their best, to try and help improve the state of society and its citizens. He closed with a reminder that Conant sought to use his limited and open view of science to counter dialectical materialism and added that Conant's view could also serve as an answer to the scientific determinism of Boring's behavioral scientist colleague in psychology at Harvard, B. F. Skinner.[72] While this part of the review alluded to an internal dispute at Harvard, in another sense, it also illustrated the eminence of Harvard's psychology department, encompassing the leaders of two views of psychology in distinct opposition to each other. Finally, it represented the result of the development of the social sciences at Harvard under Conant as well as the respect at least one of the eminent social scientists at Harvard paid to his president by taking his ideas seriously.

Conclusion

We see in Conant's publications on science for the layman an echoing of the Harvard Committee on General Education's foray into the secondary schools and adult education in its report. In neither case was the effort a major success, however. Harvard's impact on general education was mainly felt on its own campus and at other institutions of higher education. Conant's teaching of a general education course allowed him to act on his long-held beliefs about the importance of history as a part of liberal education and to be seen across campus as a fellow teacher by the faculty. Conant taking his interest in general education in science activities off the Harvard campus and into the wider world was again consistent with his intellectual orientations developed as Harvard president. As we have seen, and will see, this was not the only occasion in which Conant sought wider audiences for his work. In terms of general education in science, it seems fair to conclude that Conant indeed did take his views to a larger public than the Harvard university faculty, student, alumni, and donor communities. The authorship of reviews of Conant's two works in science for a more general audience shows, however, that it was more of a wider academic audience than Harvard that he reached, rather than an elusive general or lay public. Our next chapter looks more closely at Conant's off-campus activities to see if they too fell short of reaching a general audience and also to illumine the response to these activities by various Harvard constituencies.

Notes

1 Presidential Report, 1934–35, p. 9.

2 Presidential Report, 1935–36., pp. 12, 11, 10.

3 Ibid., p. 12.

4 Presidential Report, 1936–37, p. 19.

5 Ibid., pp. 22–23.

6 Presidential Report, 1937–38, p. 27.

7 Presidential Report, 1939–40, pp. 22, 23.

8 Presidential Report, 1938–39, p. 21.

9 On the student committee report of 1939 and student reaction to the faculty committee and its report, see Craig Kridel, "Student Participation in General Education Reform," *Journal of General Education* 35, no. 3 (1983): 154–64.

10 Conant, *My Several Lives*, p. 364.

11 Ibid., pp. 364–65.

12 "Introduction," in Report of the Harvard Committee, *General Education in a Free Society: With an introduction by James Bryant Conant* (Cambridge, MA: Harvard University Press, 1945), p. viii.

13 Presidential Report for 1941–42, p. 12.

14 Howard E. Wilson to Mr. Conant (May 27, 1943) and Conant to Wilson (June 1, 1943), Presidential Papers, Box 226, Folder Education, Graduate School of, 1942–43.

15 Committee names and affiliations can be found p. xv of the Harvard Report. Information regarding the third educator, Byron Hollinshead, can be found on p. xix.

16 The lack of high school representation on the committee was noticeable, though the representatives from the School of Education might have been expected to address that concern.

17 *General Education in a Free Society*, p. xiii.

18 Ibid., p. xv.

19 Ibid., p. xiv.

20 Ibid., p. 92.

21 Ibid., p. 93.

22 Ibid., pp. 97, 98.

23 Ibid., p. 111.

132   *Scholarly Leadership in Higher Education*

24 Ibid., p. 113.

25 Ibid., p. 151.

26 Ibid., p. 155.

27 Ibid., p. 176.

28 Ibid., pp. 177–91.

29 Ibid., p. 192.

30 Ibid., p. 207. The "Western" bias in this list was characteristic in both the literature
    and the social science required courses. Such "bias" is much clearer seventy years
    after the committee designed the general education curriculum. Surely wartime was
    one explanation for that bias as well as a lack of understanding and appreciation for
    non-Western cultures.

31 *General Education in a Free Society,* p. 216.

32 Ibid., p. 226.

33 Mario A. Pei, "Some Reflections on the Harvard Report," *The French Review* 19
    (January, 1946): 168–73.

34 Leon Mones, "Harvard Report: A Socially Important Education?" *The Clearing
    House* 20 (January, 1946): 262–66.

35 George B. Cutter, "A Book to Be Studied," *The Journal of Higher Education* 17
    (February, 1946): 109–10.

36 Presidential Report for 1948–49, pp. 8–13; course titles pp. 12, 13.

37 Ibid., p. 11.

38 Presidential Report, 1947–48, p. 12.

39 Presidential Report, 1948–49, pp. 9–12; quotations, pp. 11, 12.

40 Gerald Holton, *Thematic Origins of Scientific Thought* (Cambridge: Harvard
    University Press, 1973), pp. 41–42.

41 Lipset and Riesman, *Education and Politics at Harvard*, p. 354.

42 Presidential Report, 1951–52, p. 25.

43 Presidential Report, 1935–36, p. 9.

44 Conant, *My Several Lives*, p. 272.

45 James B. Conant, *On Understanding Science* [Dwight Harrington Tarry Foundation,
    Lectures on Religion in the Light of Science and Philosophy] (New Haven: Yale
    University Press, 1947); James Bryant Conant, *The Growth of the Experimental
    Sciences: An Experiment in General Education: Progress Report on the Use of the Case
    Method in Teaching the Principles of the Tactics and Strategy of Science* (Cambridge:
    Harvard University Press, 1949); and James Bryant Conant, general ed. and others,
    Harvard Case Histories in Experimental Science (Cambridge: Harvard University
    Press, 1957). For Conant's own course, see James Bryant Conant, *Harvard Case
    Histories in Experimental Science* (Cambridge: Harvard University Press, 1950).

46 Conant, *The Growth of the Experimental Sciences,* pp. 2, 4.

47 Conant, *On Understanding Science,* p. 12.

General Education: An Increasing Priority 133

48 Ibid., pp. 6, 10, 15.

49 https://hbx.hbs.edu/blog/post/the-history-of-the-case-study-at-harvard-business-school.

50 Conant, *On Understanding Science*, p. 21.

51 R. L. A., Review of *Harvard Case Histories in Experimental Science, Philosophy of Science* 20 (October, 1953), p. 346.

52 Conant, *On Understanding Science*, p. 5.

53 As quoted in Keller and Keller, *Making Harvard Modern*, p. 93.

54 These volumes are mentioned earlier in this chapter. See note 45.

55 James B. Conant, *Science and Common Sense* (New Haven: Yale University Press, 1951), pp. vi, 1.

56 Ibid., p. 48.

57 Ibid., pp. 31, 32, my emphasis.

58 Ibid., p. 27.

59 Ibid., p. 25, my emphasis.

60 Ibid., pp. 343, 344.

61 Ibid., p. 348.

62 Conway Zirkle, Review of *Science and Common Sense* by James B. Conant, *Isis* 42 (October, 1951): 268–71.

63 Jane Oppenheimer, Review of *Science and Common Sense* by James B. Conant, *The Quarterly Review of Biology* 26 (December, 1951): 364–66.

64 Ordway Tead, Review of *Science and Common Sense* by James B. Conant, *The Journal of Higher Education* 22 (November, 1951): 453–54.

65 Bernard Barber, Review of *Science and Common Sense* by James B. Conant, *American Sociological Review* 16 (October, 1951): 735–36; quotation, p. 736.

66 James B. Conant, *Modern Science and Modern Man* (New York: Columbia University Press, 1952), p. 6.

67 Ibid., p. 67.

68 Ibid., p. 78.

69 Ibid., p. 102.

70 Ibid., p. 111.

71 Edwin G. Boring, Review of *Modern Science and Modern Man* by James B. Conant, *The American Journal of Psychology* 67 (March, 1954): 192–94. The publication date is more than two years after Conant left the Harvard presidency, but one cannot know with certainty if Boring wrote it before or after Conant's departure.

72 Ibid., p. 194.

5

Extra-Harvard, 1933–52

While I have argued that James Bryant Conant was an often effective president who contributed to the national and international prominence of Harvard during his twenty-year presidency, I have also shown that there were clear limits to that effectiveness, among which were his long absences from campus during the Second World War to pursue his duties in the federal government defense efforts. The theme of absence from campus, however, was not only characteristic of the war years. Both before the Second World War and, more consequentially, in the years after, Conant pursued an often-dizzying array of activities tied, at best, indirectly to Harvard. The task of this chapter is to describe these activities, and how they fit, and did not fit, with Conant's Harvard presidential pursuits.

Our first concern will be Conant's publication record, particularly later in his presidency. He published a great deal during his presidential years, though not much in his academic field of chemistry. His publications encompassed three categories: the present and future of the university, science and science education, and public education, particularly the American high school. We have seen some of these publications in earlier chapters. Conant's published articles kept him, and his institution, in the public eye. Further, they were on topics, with the exception of the public high schools, that enhanced the national and international reputation of both President Conant and his institution. Yet there were significant issues for many at Harvard, as we have seen, in the president's views on issues such as religion in education and academic freedom.

Another issue that was controversial was Conant's devotion to standardized testing and his involvement with philanthropic foundations in pursuit of that enterprise. His long-lasting interest in this area, beginning in the 1930s, eventually culminated in the establishment of the Educational Testing Service (ETS). His role in founding, and starting, ETS, particularly through his pursuit of financial support for it from the Carnegie philanthropies, is of special interest. Though Conant's contact with Carnegie and other philanthropies frequently benefited Harvard directly through grants, it also often embroiled Conant in disputes over issues such as standardized testing that had little to do with Harvard's prosperity. His increasing involvement in such disputes and his recognition of how they distanced him from campus concerns are important considerations.

A similar tension, if not conflict, characterized Conant's increasing involvement in the 1940s and early 1950s with professional educational organizations concerned with elementary and secondary education, particularly public education. Conant's activities in the arena of public secondary education initially were directly related to Harvard's Graduate School of Education. As shown in the previous chapters, he consulted frequently with administrators and faculty from that school about the public high school. Ultimately, however, Conant's work on public education thrust him into a wider civic arena through a variety of interactions with the National Education Association (NEA), the leading advocacy group for public schools through the mid-twentieth century. This relationship embroiled Conant in policy debates that seemingly had little to do with Harvard, an institution that traditionally had stood distant from the public schools. Many on campus favored private schools and noticed and disagreed with Conant's advocacy of public schools. Others with little interest in private or public secondary education deplored the stance Conant took that endorsed disqualifying communists as members of the teaching profession as part of his work on an NEA committee. Still other NEA-related controversies over issues like religion and education that clearly interested Conant often put him at odds with Harvard constituencies that he had no need to offend. These activities did keep the president and the institution he represented firmly in the public's eye, a quality that simultaneously served Conant's desire for influence in domestic and foreign political and policy matters distant from Harvard, and made Harvard an institution more accessible and attractive to the American public.[1] Eventually, however, the increasing distance from Harvard concerns overtook the enhancement of Harvard's public image for both President Conant and for the university that he served.

Conant never looked back to Harvard after these developments, which led to his departure from the institution in 1952. He preferred to think of himself as the university president who, while in office, became the educational statesman that others called him, or the penetrating educational analyst that he thought himself to be.[2]

Publications

Conant had been prolific in publishing in his chosen field of chemistry before assuming the Harvard presidency in 1933, and he remained prolific, though not in chemistry, after assuming the presidency. A bibliography of Conant compiled in late 1950 listed 173 items published from 1933 to 1950. This averaged out to ten per year, a more than decent record for any full-time scholar, let alone for a full-time university administrator. There are several qualifiers to be noted in assessing Conant's output in these years, however. First, some of the items were printed presidential speeches to student or alumni groups. Others were speeches to civic and community groups interested in hearing from the president of Harvard University on a variety of topics. And over fifteen of them were annual president's reports written for the Board of Overseers, the members of the Harvard Corporation, and alumni and interested faculty. Those reports, which provide much of the documentation for this work, were carefully written, intended to be read by a much wider audience than the two governing lay boards of Harvard University that were the official recipients of the works. In 1946, Vannevar Bush described Conant's presidential reports as "oases, broad in conception, lofty in aspiration, sound and practical in application." They constituted, for Bush, not only a philosophy of education but also "a basis for Conant's leadership as a citizen and the explanation of the unselfishness with which he has devoted himself to public service."[3]

To fully contextualize Conant's publication record, it should also be noted that he had a direct line to several journals that seemed willing to publish whatever it was he wanted to have in print. He frequently published in Harvard journals of one kind or another, in *School and Society*, an educational periodical issued so frequently that it seemed at times more like a newsletter, and in popular journals such as the *Atlantic Monthly* and *Harper's*. These last two journals, obviously, were a way for Conant to seek the wider audience for his ideas that he wanted to reach. He also often published in newspapers and other popular sources such as Vital Speeches of the Day, all of which indicated that Conant was not interested in amassing a typical scholarly record of manuscripts in journals that were reviewed rigorously by one's academic peers.[4]

With all of these qualifiers taken into account, however, the number of Conant's published works is still quite impressive, especially for a sitting university president. And when one considers the number and breadth of the outside activities engaged in by that president, during the Second World War, but also before and after it, the publication record is even more formidable. To

138   *Scholarly Leadership in Higher Education*

establish its significance further, a look at the variety of subject areas Conant chose to address through publication of articles is in order.

First, Conant did not stop publishing in the sciences. For the first three or so years after becoming the president, he published articles in chemical journals obviously based on the work done in his laboratory before moving to administration. Additionally, he was a coauthor of high school and college chemistry textbooks that carried on in later editions into the 1940s and after. And, in the early 1940s, he published science-related articles on research in biochemistry and rubber resources, two subjects on which he was working for the federal government.[5] He also exerted considerable effort, including some publications, to improve the physics department at Harvard, involving himself in adding significantly to the department faculty.[6] He published work on science and scientists in more popular journals such as *Science* and *Popular Science Monthly*. As noted in Chapter 4, he was prolific in publishing accounts of what he taught in the general education science course he developed at Harvard, as well as what others taught in their general education science courses.

A second area of interest in Conant's publications in this period encompassed the problems and issues that challenged colleges and universities and their administration. Conant was seldom interested in the nuts and bolts of administering a college or university. Rather, he preferred to write and talk about issues such as academic and intellectual freedom, the mission of Harvard and other private universities (and also of public universities), liberal and/or general education, and the future of higher education. He had written about each of these topics on more than one occasion in the 1930s. As that decade drew to a close, he turned to topics such as education and the national defense, or education and freedom, in an effort to prepare those who read or listened to him for the coming American participation in the Second World War. As the war commenced, he began to discuss topics such as what the war required from colleges and universities, the mobilization of manpower in universities (a topic discussed in several articles), "The Role of a Liberal Arts College in a Total War,"[7] and science and the national welfare. As the war progressed, Conant turned his attention to the postwar period, anticipating an allied victory in the war and trying to discern the role of the university in the postwar world. He addressed topics in the 1940s such as the university and the state, atomic energy, and the place of research in national life. Still later in the decade, he discoursed on "College and the Spirit of the Times."[8] By 1950, he was calling for a new look at higher education, one in which he saw the burgeoning number of two-year colleges as a way to equalize educational opportunity in the United States.[9]

Extra-Harvard, 1933–52 139

This two-year college article was published in the *New York Times*, an obvious indicator that Conant was seeking a larger audience for his views than scholars or educators. He had exhibited this tendency as early as 1938, when he called attention to what he hoped was the future of American higher education in an article in *Harper's Magazine*. In this article, Conant discussed the aristocratic and the democratic strands in the history of American higher education and indicated the ways in which he thought that the democratic direction could be encouraged to develop. His ideas here were not new, such as the expansion of opportunity for higher education through scholarships to the academically able who lacked the financial wherewithal to attend a college or university. And in this article, twelve years before he advocated the two-year college in the *New York Times*, he was touting the junior college as the agency to expand educational opportunity for those who were less competitively able to achieve in higher education.[10]

In 1943, with the nation firmly engaged in the Second World War, Conant went far beyond the institutions of higher education and made an ideologically and politically controversial splash with his article in the *Atlantic Monthly* entitled "Wanted: American Radicals." The title of the article was meant to be, and was taken as, inflammatory. In it, Conant advocated the necessity of solving the issues of the domestic economy such as labor-management relations and the control and ownership of the tools of production (a phrase usually associated with Marxist ideas) if the United States were to take its place as a leading nation in the postwar world that was soon to come. To further this objective, Conant sought to introduce the voice of an authentic American radicalism into the ossified debates between political liberals and conservatives. This radicalism was not the statist radicalism of Europeans that also animated much of the American left wing but an authentic "American" radicalism, one that was indigenous to the United States, that recognized its roots in the ideas of Thomas Jefferson, Andrew Jackson, and Ralph Waldo Emerson, and was respectful of but not seduced by the ideas of Marx and Engels. For Conant, the American radical was a believer in equality, equality of opportunity not equality of rewards, and in decentralization, though a decentralization that understood the realities of modern industrial production. Increased governmental activity was a requisite of modern life for Conant and his new American radical understood this at the same time he was on the lookout for unnecessary state intrusion into the life of the populace. The American radical was a committed advocate of social mobility and an opponent of caste-like systems that advanced individuals on the basis of who they were or knew rather than on what they could do. Conant ended the article with an invocation of our "radical ancestors" in American life, whose ideas must be followed to "attack the problems of a stratified society, highly mechanized and forced to continue along the road of mass production."[11] In terms of ideas, there was much in this article that simply echoed Conant's earlier views about an intelligent, meritocratic society. But the conscious use of the word "radical" and the placement of the article in a popular magazine indicated that the Harvard president was intent on reaching a larger audience, using what many took to be sensationalist language to attract attention for his ideas. Needless to say, this article ruffled the feathers of many Harvard alumni and donors, who were bastions of the American establishment—social, economic, and political.

Still another topic that Conant addressed frequently in publications during his presidency was elementary and secondary education, particularly the public high school. As early as 1935, less than two years after his inauguration, Conant was discussing the secondary school in relation to the college. This article was published initially in *School and Society*, a periodical circulated mainly among the ranks of professional educators, school administrators, and the professors of education who trained them. But it was quickly excerpted in the *Bulletin of the American Association of University Professors*, which had a national audience of faculty and administrators in the nation's institutions of higher education. Conant here acknowledged the importance of a college education for the increasing numbers who, in the era of the expanding New Deal, were entering public service and public administration. While such leaders were not necessarily philosophers, Conant wanted to make sure that they had both great intellectual ability and postgraduate training. This approach, however, was added to the larger task of civic education of all students, particularly in the high schools. He summed up his argument as follows: "The schools and colleges have a large task before them to provide the best possible education for the mass of their students. They have an equal responsibility to the country to select the future cultural leaders as young as possible, finance them if necessary, and provide a school and college education on which they can build."[12]

In 1940, as we have seen, he coauthored a book on the high school and the college with Francis Spaulding of the Harvard Graduate School of Education.[13] One of Conant's two chapters in the book was his essay discussed above on the future of higher education, as published in *Harper's Magazine* two years earlier.[14] Conant's other chapter was entitled "Education for a Classless Society" and had been published in *The Atlantic* Monthly earlier in 1940. Again, Conant's radical language, a "classless society," was overlain on his meritocratic agenda for the reform of American society. Only by recognizing and rewarding academic talent, regardless of wealth or status, could American society truly prosper and realize the potential that lay within its populace.[15] For Conant, realizing this equality of opportunity was the key to advancing to a truly classless society, not a society of pure equality but one in which merit and achievement were rewarded and were the basis for social and economic advance.

We have already seen how the third chapter in the Conant/Spaulding volume, written by Spaulding, represented a set of ideas and analyses that, if not new to Conant, were not the usual things he considered in his own writing. Spaulding's chapter discussed the secondary schools and their role in operating for the public good. And this approach necessitated consideration of many things besides academic subjects. Thus, in looking at the high school, as discussed by Francis Spaulding, Conant was learning about the nonacademic but real educational goals and needs of students.[16]

By the middle of the 1940s, Conant was addressing public education by name and beginning to discern the specific version of the public high school, the "comprehensive" high school, which he would defend for the rest of his life. It was very different from the elite academic school that he himself had experienced and the private preparatory academies that provided the secondary education familiar to many, if not most, in the Harvard academic communities. The comprehensive high school was a major institutional priority of the public educators with whom Conant was becoming more and more involved. And one of Conant's major priorities within the comprehensive high school was the search for academic talent. As we have seen earlier, standardized tests were a major vehicle to use in the search.

Creating the Educational Testing Service

James B. Conant's romance with standardized tests had begun early in his presidency, in conjunction with his effort to diversify the Harvard College student body through the National Scholarship Program. Conant's desire to use the Scholastic Aptitude Test (SAT) at Harvard involved him in discussions and debates about various testing initiatives and programs in that decade. He was convinced then of the need for a single organization to take hold in a field in which several groups competed with each other for support from universities and other educational institutions. In spite of efforts from individuals associated with the Cooperative Test Service, the College Entrance Examination Board

142 *Scholarly Leadership in Higher Education*

(CEEB), the Educational Records Bureau, and the Carnegie Foundation for the Advancement of Teaching, the effort at consolidation was unsuccessful in the 1930s when it was first attempted.[17] The Second World War provided another occasion for consideration of the need for one testing service, but, again, the effort produced no results. As the war neared its end, still another round of discussions was initiated, mainly by individuals associated with the Carnegie philanthropic interests in New York. Conant was by then a prominent member of the board of directors of the Carnegie Corporation.[18]

In mid-January 1946, the president of the Carnegie Corporation expressed the need for consolidation of the various testing programs, as well as a ringing endorsement of the merits of standardized testing.

> Objective testing was one of the few good by-products of the first World War and as might have been expected, has been greatly advanced in both method and scope during the war just ended. It can be confidently predicted that this heightened interest in testing will be accompanied by a proliferation of commercial testing agencies operated for profit. The maintenance of a single, strong, non-profit agency which will be a touch-stone of quality and competence in this relatively new field becomes therefore a matter of deepest concern to every American educator.[19]

In April of 1946, the Carnegie interests set up a Committee on Testing, chaired by President Conant. Discussion between Conant and Oliver C. Carmichael, president of the Carnegie Foundation for the Advancement of Teaching, resulted in a committee roster containing the presidents of Cornell and Brown Universities; the presidents of the Universities of California, Cincinnati, Minnesota, and North Carolina; the commissioner of education of the State of New York (Conant's old Harvard colleague and collaborator Francis T. Spaulding); and a prominent school administrator from the City of Philadelphia.[20] A lengthy document circulated to the committee in August of 1946 discussed the issues involved and indicated that consolidation was a desirable outcome for the maintenance of high standards in the testing enterprise. Specifically, "untrustworthy commercial exploiters of tests" were a target of the committee that sought to contain this unsavory influence through the development of significant research on testing.[21] The committee met in September and made a recommendation, dated October 4, that the consolidation be instituted. The recommendation was a "preliminary" measure, not because of any hesitancy on the part of the committee about the value of consolidation but rather to "stimulate the fullest possible discussion of the practical means of arriving at the objective."[22]

Extra-Harvard, 1933–52   143

This discussion needed to involve the members of the several agencies to be consolidated, as well as interested individuals from state educational agencies, school systems, universities, and any other bodies that might employ the proposed agency or use its tests. Getting to a recommendation for consolidation was a relatively easy task but the actual consolidation of four or five agencies, and the involvement of groups such as the American Council on Education (ACE) in the negotiations, meant that the political situation surrounding any consolidation was extremely delicate.[23] The politics were complicated and the eventual resolution of the situation took an additional year.

The political situation on the Harvard campus as the new testing agency was being considered was also not conflict free. Conant had been committed to the creation of a centralized testing agency since the 1930s. In that decade, however, his devotion to standardized testing was not widely shared by the Harvard faculty. As a Harvard president who respected his faculty, he was bound to consider and heed that opposition. In the 1940s, however, the issue of consolidation of distant testing agencies was one that was not of great interest to the Harvard faculty. There were still elements of the Harvard academic community, however, that were opposed to consolidation. Among them was the director of the Office of Tests of the Harvard Faculty of Arts and Sciences. Paul Buck, dean of the Faculty of Arts and Sciences, passed on a letter to Conant that he had received from the director, Henry S. Dyer. In that letter, Dyer objected to a single central agency, in part on the grounds that it would become too powerful. When that happened, the agency would be unwilling to admit any error in its ways. Specifically, for Dyer, so "much money and so many reputations are involved that if tests turn out to be no good, evidence of the fact is almost certain to be suppressed, or else the criteria of goodness are themselves called in question." Dyer added that bigness tended to arbitrariness and that a large central staff, enamored with technical problems and issues, would lose sight of practical problems. Buck set up a meeting with Conant, Dyer, and Richard Gunmere, dean of admissions at Harvard who shared Dyer's concerns. The meeting gave Conant a chance to reassure the two administrators about the testing agency, especially in its relationship to Harvard College.[24]

No faculty member objected publicly to the testing body, an objection that might have provoked a formidable on campus challenge to its existence and with which Conant would have had to contend. Objections from administrative underlings like Dyer and Gunmere were less formidable, able to be handled with reassurances from the president to his subordinates that all would be well on campus. These reassurances came from Conant, the campus chief executive

144   *Scholarly Leadership in Higher Education*

who also was enormously influential in the testing community. Unlike in the 1930s, then, when faculty had objected to various standardized tests, in the immediate post–Second World War years, Conant had less formidable on-campus opposition to his testing dreams, dreams that were about to come true.

On December 21, 1947, the creation of the ETS was announced, with a vigorous nod given to the Conant-led committee's work in the process. Special mention was made of the committee's unanimous declaration noting that "sound basic research in educational measurement and human abilities on a scale necessary for continued advance in this field is dependent on a concentration of resources which can only be accomplished by the establishment of a cooperative testing commission." The initial statement of purpose for the new agency indicated that its goal was to develop examinations covering elementary grades to graduate school, particularly better intelligence and aptitude tests. Research on testing, in addition to test development, was to be a primary activity of the new agency, as was service to educational institutions at all levels of education. This service would involve college entrance exams and general exams for schools, colleges, professional schools, and graduate schools. The board of directors for ETS was to include three ex-officio members: Oliver C. Carmichael from the Carnegie Foundation for the Advancement of Teaching, Edward Noyes from Yale University representing the CEEB, and George F. Zook, president of the ACE. Additionally, the board included Conant, Arkansas senator J. W. Fulbright, the presidents of the University of Washington and Bryn Mawr College, the dean of Arts and Sciences at the University of Minnesota, the superintendent of the Chicago Schools who was also the president of the American Association of School Administrators (AASA), the principal of Scarsdale High School, and Commissioner of Education Francis T. Spaulding of the State of New York. The makeup of the board indicated some diversification beyond the traditional testing establishment. This diversity was represented by the K-12 school people and the Western and mid-Western public university administrators.[25] These interests were less committed to Conant's search for a new academic elite and more oriented toward a diversification of services to help achieve other objectives such as increasing educational opportunity for more Americans. The choice of Conant as chairman of the Board of ETS, as well as the selection of his old protégé Henry Chauncey as president of the new corporation indicated, however, that the search for a new academic elite through tests like the SAT would be a major, if not *the* major, enterprise of the new group.

Extra-Harvard, 1933–52   145

Financial support from the Carnegie interests was quite evident in the establishment of ETS. The initial capital assets of ETS were $1.2 million, 750 thousand of which came from Carnegie. The rest came from the assets of organizations that were being consolidated. ETS was expected to do well enough financially to sustain itself through income from this endowment and income from its testing services.[26] With the creation of ETS, Conant had gone some way toward achieving his dream of installing an academic meritocracy in American colleges and universities. Given this, and his confidence in Chauncey as one who would execute the realization of the dream, Conant could afford to take on a less forceful role in ETS, serving as a benign board presence and watching the fledgling organization develop along lines that he endorsed. He had plenty of other interests outside of ETS, and outside of Harvard, to occupy his time and effort in the 1940s and early 1950s, the most notable one being the encouragement of the comprehensive public high school. Most of this activity was undertaken in cooperation with the NEA.

The National Education Association and Allied Organizations

As his presidency evolved, James B. Conant became increasingly influential in national affairs: in science, in foreign policy, and in educational policy. The scientific authority he wielded in war-related affairs in the 1940s is well known. Just as importantly, Conant exerted influence in a variety of scientific associations in the immediate postwar years. As noted earlier, he was elected president of the American Association for the Advancement of Science in 1946. Additionally, he was involved in several scientific organizations related to atomic energy that advised the president on various aspects of postwar atomic policy. He also had served as a representative of the administration during the war in trying to establish a cooperative research relationship between the United States and the UK and near the end of the war between the United States and the Union of Soviet Socialist Republics (USSR). After the war, he turned down an invitation to head the Atomic Energy Commission, instead taking a position as a member of the commission. He was active in the creation of the National Science Foundation (NSF) in 1950, after several false starts in that direction that were impeded by congressional opposition. All of these activities, and the notable attention paid to Conant in articles about his work in places like *Time* magazine, made him a national figure, one who was spoken about on more than one occasion as a possible presidential candidate.[27]

Of special concern for this analysis, Conant increased his activities taken in relation to American public education, particularly the American high school, throughout the 1940s and into the 1950s. Conant's willingness to discuss, if not to embrace, the public schools was noted by the leadership of those schools, particularly as represented by the NEA and its subgroup devoted to educational administration, the AASA. In July of 1937, the AASA invited Conant to speak at its February–March 1938 meeting. The day after the invitation was offered, Conant was told by the dean of the Harvard University Graduate School of Education that the AASA "is the most powerful body of people in public education." Speaking to these leaders, according to the dean, would give Conant an opportunity to publicize his ideas about the future of America and American education. Refusing the invitation, on the other hand, might be taken as a sign of Harvard's indifference to public education. The dean also told Conant that the AASA president who had issued the invitation was a Harvard graduate and that for Conant to speak at the convention, which was to be in Boston, would be an occasion for a revival of Harvard influence in public education.[28] Conant went on to speak to the school administrators on one of his favorite themes, broadening educational opportunity to reach talented youth who were not from wealthy families or New England backgrounds. Conant recounted that when he gave the speech, one of the attendees alerted him to the coherence of his own views with those of Thomas Jefferson. From then on, Conant would cite Jefferson often in his speeches and articles.[29]

The leadership of the NEA was especially enthusiastic about cooperating with James Bryant Conant. Linking public education to the president of Harvard University was a worthy goal for the NEA. In 1940, Conant agreed to serve a four-year term on the Educational Policies Commission (EPC), a blue-ribbon body established originally in the 1930s to help the public schools survive the financial crisis caused by the Great Depression. His agreement to serve provided a boost to the prestige of the EPC, as it dealt with the issues of the coming war and education's role in it. The organization also served the desire of the Harvard president to reach those who led the elementary and high schools of the nation.[30] Membership on the EPC provided Conant with the opportunity to interact with, to learn from, and to teach the leading school administrators of American public education, especially of the public high schools.

The EPC met at least twice yearly for several days, a significant addition to Conant's busy schedule that involved Harvard presidential and governmental science leadership duties. Though he did not make every meeting, Conant was a faithful participant in the deliberations and decisions by the EPC, sending

Extra-Harvard, 1933–52 147

in his ideas and recommendations on the occasions that he could not make a committee meeting. Early on in his initial membership on the EPC, the years from 1940 to 1944, the group tried to water down the power of, if not to abolish, the federal educational agencies created by the New Deal—the Civilian Conservation Corps (CCC) and the National Youth Administration (NYA). The EPC and its parent body, the NEA, were not opposed to federal involvement in American education but sought federal financial aid to public schools, rather than the creation of independent federal educational agencies, as the proper vehicle for institutionalizing that involvement. Federal aid was a touchstone for the NEA/AASA/EPC leadership, and it was sought without any accompanying, intrusive political control. For the educators, the public schools were locally and state-controlled institutions, and their leaders sought financial support from the federal government but financial support with "no strings" attached. Federal aid was a theme that would characterize much of Conant's writing and thinking about American education in the 1940s and in subsequent decades and one that he had spoken about seldom, if ever, before becoming an EPC member.[31]

Another, and even more important, theme that pervaded the work of the EPC was discussion of the enormous changes that the public schools, particularly the public high schools, needed to undergo in order to reach effectively the burgeoning numbers of students who were enrolling in them. Those changes had been a prominent part of the educational plans of the American public-school leadership at least since 1918. In that year, a commission of the NEA published a report on the *Cardinal Principles of Secondary Education*, which added a host of purposes for the American high schools to the academic studies to which they had traditionally been devoted.[32] Included in these new principles were health, citizenship, vocational training, and psychological adjustment. The addition of so many new emphases to traditional academic studies indicated that the educators were interested in a profound change in the American high school curriculum, one that would allow that institution to serve the increasing numbers of students with different and often nonacademic backgrounds, interests, and abilities that were enrolling.

All of these new principles were featured in an educational report of the EPC published in 1944, entitled *Education for All American Youth*.[33] This report was the result of over two years of discussions, deliberations, and debates about the American high school by members of the EPC. Those debates, reported verbatim in bound volumes of the proceedings of the EPC, featured vigorous defense of academic studies by a minority of the membership and even more vigorous attacks on those studies as the sole determiner of what was to take

148 *Scholarly Leadership in Higher Education*

place in the American high school, by most of the members.[34] Conant was a sometime supporter of each side in this debate but could also see the merits of both arguments. His own major priority in the new high school was the maintenance of an academic education for gifted youth; but he also was sensitive to the need for differentiated curricular innovations for the youth who were not so academically talented but who were securely under the reach of the high school and in need of an education that would fit them for their futures. For these youth, vocational studies, citizenship studies, social adjustment activities, and health and physical education were all appropriate emphases.

The EPC was intent on showing how public education could meet the needs of all of postwar American society. To accomplish this, its 1944 report sketched an educational plan for two fictitious American high schools, one in Farmville and another in American City. The two settings acknowledged the differences in the challenges faced by rural and urban America and differed in the number and diversity of subjects and services that could be provided in each. Yet, the similarity between the high schools in the two settings far outweighed the differences. In both settings, the curriculum was to be heavily diversified to serve the variety of students who would enroll in the high school. What united the rural and urban versions of reform was their agreement on the objectives of the new secondary education. Those objectives were enunciated in the report as occupational preparation, citizenship education, the pursuit of happiness, intellectual curiosity and rational thinking, and a democratic ethic.[35]

Also, in both settings, the reach of the high school would be expanded to handle the needs of what was called the thirteenth and fourteenth grade, the two years of post-high school study that were envisioned for most American students, urban or rural. Whether in a community institute, as recommended for Farmville, or in an extension of the high school, as recommended for American City, the two additional years of secondary education overlapped with what much of the fledgling junior colleges were doing. Conant had endorsed the junior college, as well as the diversification of the high school curriculum before coming on to the EPC, and he learned more about the value of and arguments for both of these innovations through his discussions with other EPC members. He came to believe fervently in the priorities of the educators and spoke often of the value and importance of *Education for* All *American Youth* and what he learned from the educators in the discussions leading up to publication of that volume.[36]

Just as he was ending his first term on the EPC in late 1944, Conant sent the chief NEA staff officer of the group a list of sixty-five people who should receive a copy of the report along with personal cards from Conant himself, which he enclosed with the list. That list included members of the Harvard Corporation, the Harvard Board of Overseers, eleven Harvard administrators or faculty members, and fourteen presidents of New England colleges or universities.[37] This was an audience unlikely to normally receive, or be persuaded by, a report from a body sponsored by the leading advocate of public schools in the United States, no matter how prestigious its membership. Being a signatory member of the body, and including his personal card with the mailing of the report to this audience, Conant indicated to his fellow academic leaders that he had clearly been influenced by the professional educators and had at least partially embraced their agenda. Whether or not the recipients agreed with Conant was an issue he ignored.

Conant left the EPC when his term expired at the end of 1944 and was not involved in its final discussions of the relationship of its report, *Education for All American Youth*, to the Harvard Report, published at the same time and discussed earlier herein, *General Education in a Free Society*. The Harvard Report dealt with the high school but mainly by trying to find suitable approaches to education in the high school in the fields of the social sciences, natural sciences, and humanities. The EPC report, in marked contrast, ignored any traditional, disciplinary classification of academic material, instead recommending a core course or courses in "Common Learnings" that were to be problem-focused while they encompassed academic content from fields like English and history in pursuit of that focus. There was no provision in the EPC report for an academic teacher to be in charge of the core course. Instead, it was to be taught by someone versed in human development who could capitalize on the relationship between the course and the lives of the students who would take it.[38]

Conant never specifically discussed with the EPC any conflict between its report and the Harvard general education report. In fact, however, in lectures he gave at Teachers College late in 1945, he specifically stated that there was no conflict between the two reports. While he acknowledged that the two made different prescriptions for general education, he indicated that the differences were much more due to the audiences to be addressed by the reports than to any contradictions in their content.[39] This statement allowed for differences in content but refused to make anything more out of them than differences due to context.

A late April 1946 letter to Conant from the secretary of the EPC noted that the two reports were often seen as in conflict with each other. Citing an article in *Life* magazine, which had discussed significant opposition in the recommendations

150   *Scholarly Leadership in Higher Education*

of the two reports, the EPC official told Conant that the notion of a conflict had
not come from the EPC. Rather, the magazine had taken upon itself the idea
of comparing the two reports and seeing them as in serious conflict with each
other. While the two reports reflected "different experiences and points of view,"
the EPC staff officer, William G. Carr, remarked that it was "most inaccurate
to picture them as bitter rivals contending for public favor and professional
approval."[40] But, in many ways, it was hard to reconcile the distinctly different
language and focus in the two reports, as Conant had done. A close reading
of the two shows clear differences in approach, content, and staffing of general
education courses, and Conant's idea that the differences reflected context more
than content is not completely convincing. General academic fields like social
sciences, natural sciences, and humanities discussed in the Harvard Report
are still academic fields, a long way from one study called common learnings
featured in the EPC report in which any academic content that might be found
was to be suited to the developmental needs of students.

Conant replied to the EPC letter that he himself was chagrinned by the *Life*
article, though he agreed that perhaps calling attention to both reports could
outweigh any negative attention to either that might result from the article.
Conant added that he had no wish for such publicity to alienate him from the
educators in the EPC and added that he hoped that the EPC would continue
to be influenced by his own desire to achieve a "truce" between academics and
public school educators.[41]

No permanent, or even temporary, rupture appears to have occurred between
Conant and the EPC. In 1948, when the group was reconstituted by the NEA,
Conant was again invited to be a member.[42] He accepted another four-year term
and looked forward to working again with the educators on issues of educational
policy. And during this second term, Conant was elected as chief executive
officer of the EPC and worked hand in hand with its secretary, William G. Carr,
on the promotion of American public education. Conant was getting more and
more comfortable with the leadership of American public schools and seeing the
ways in which his own educational agenda meshed with theirs.

In the four years in which Conant served his second term on the EPC, 1948
to 1952, he was involved in the preparation of papers on issues such as Moral
and Spiritual Ideals in Education (1950). The argument in the paper Moral and
Spiritual Ideals in Education (1950) was that secular public schools could still play
a major role in the moral education of American youth. The political context for
this paper was the controversy over the separation of church and state in education
that had come to pit NEA and the public schools against private religious schools,

Extra-Harvard, 1933–52   151

particularly Roman Catholics and their schools.[43] Other topics considered by the group included international tensions, an obvious nod to the Cold War in which the United States was engaged and how the public schools should operate in regard to this conflict. In a lengthy note to the EPC secretary, Conant outlined his own philosophy of the Cold War, as developed in his book, *Education in a Divided World*.[44] He told the official that what was needed in the Cold War climate was "tough minded idealists" who could assess realistically the threat coming from the Soviet Union and move to combat that threat educationally and in other arenas.[45]

In perhaps the most notable, at least for Conant himself, of his accomplishments on the EPC, he was instrumental in the preparation and publication of a report on Education of the Gifted in 1951. In arranging for publication of that report, Conant was able to persuade the public school people on the EPC to acknowledge their responsibility to make special efforts in the education of the academically gifted and talented. He wanted to make sure that the report noted that the gifted, identified through standardized testing, were to be prepared for leadership positions in many aspects of American society—the judicial arena, politics, private business, the professions, and science and engineering—not just in the preparation of academic researchers and teachers. He also questioned some criticism of standardized testing made by Professor Allison Davis of the University of Chicago that tests tended to reify social class differences. Conant wanted to make sure that the tests were credited for doing what they did so well, predicting academic success in higher education, though in doing so other aspects relating to success could not be completely ignored. He stated that he was an amateur in the field of standardized testing and would defer to the views of genuine experts in the field if they disagreed with his own. The discussion of testing in the final version of the report paid homage both to Davis's concerns about tests and to Conant's desire that their validity in predicting academic success be recognized.[46]

Still another area in which Conant influenced the EPC was in its preparation of a report on Education and International Tensions, published in 1951. American involvement in the Korean conflict was fully underway as the report was being prepared and Conant had much to say about the conflict itself and the underlying tensions with the Soviet Union that had provoked it. Additionally, he spent much time discussing the various ways of producing the manpower needed to staff a military of close to a half million members and the impact that various ways of doing this would have on the nation's colleges and universities.[47]

In terms of this last topic, Conant had been initially reluctant to have the EPC, a public education group, say anything about issues such as military manpower that would directly affect higher education. He relented on this particular issue, however, but never quite brought himself to see the EPC in the same light as higher education organizations, at least insofar as determining policy in higher education. In a note to the NEA's chief executive officer in March of 1952, about the EPC's effectiveness, he remarked that the EPC "publications have had almost no effect on the group of educators with whom I come in contact and certainly none among the faculties of our colleges and universities outside of schools of education." He added that he had heard that EPC influence was considerable on public school administrators and in schools of education. He wanted to make sure, however, that his opposition to the NEA or its bodies entering the field of higher education was registered and understood by the EPC and the NEA. Specifically, he remarked, "I think the NEA is not set up to be a good representative organization for sponsoring statements about four-year colleges and universities."[48] Conant himself, however, felt free to work for the changes that he deemed worthy of support in both groups of educational institutions.

In addition to working with the EPC, Conant took several other steps that allied him more directly, and publicly, with the NEA. In May 1947, in the midst of the consideration of an NEA-supported federal aid to education bill in Congress, Conant spoke out publicly for the bill in a speech to the US Chamber of Commerce. When NEA executive secretary Willard Givens complimented Conant on his speech, Conant remarked that he had made the speech enthusiastically. He added, "It is rarely that one is in a position to support a specific bill with as much enthusiasm as I can put into my support of S. 472."[49] Less than a year later, Conant reiterated his support for the federal aid bill for education in a speech to the US Conference of Mayors. Additionally, he apprised the mayors of his other longtime educational priorities such as citizenship education, provision for the talented in public schools, and the importance of equality of opportunity through education.[50] Conant was in the midst of a flurry of public activity on behalf of federal aid to education, taken in explicit cooperation with the NEA hierarchy.

Perhaps Conant's most visible public activity on behalf of public education in the late 1940s was his leadership in the establishment of a national citizens' group in support of public education. Corresponding frequently with NEA officials about the fledgling group at least as early as 1946, Conant persuaded Harvard Corporation member Roy E. Larsen, the president of Time Incorporated, to head an Exploratory Committee for the establishment of a national group. Larsen became president of the National Citizens' Commission on the Public Schools when it was officially founded in May of 1949.[51] Conant

Extra-Harvard, 1933–52   153

corresponded frequently with Larsen about the commission and its support of
public education, particularly through policies such as federal aid to education.
He also was instrumental in obtaining financial support for the commission and
its activities from the Carnegie Corporation and gave a lengthy address at the
first official meeting of the national group in January of 1949. Conant spent a
remarkable amount of time and effort on the National Citizens' Commission,
through the end of the 1940s and into the early 1950s.

In spite of the effort, the National Citizens' Commission did not succeed in
galvanizing American public opinion in support of the public schools. Evidence
of the failure of the commission to ignite the public is found in the records of
the Carnegie Corporation, which tried to keep track of the bodies to which it
offered financial support. A report on a Conference on Citizenship sponsored
by the NEA and the National Commission that occurred in September of
1952 remarked, "Important people made inspirational speeches, all in broad
generalities, about the importance of active citizenship." In relating citizenship
to the public schools, the report noted, "The consensus, if any, seemed to
be that the schools should do a better job in teaching more democratically
and in providing opportunities at all grade levels for the practices of good
citizenship; . . . and more encouragement should be given to young adults to
participate in local civic affairs." The lack of enthusiasm by the philanthropy
for the organization was evident. The initial sentence in the report remarked,
"It is hard to report this conference." The penultimate paragraph concluded, "It
was understandably difficult to find much common background, information,
experience or current interests around which to organize a discussion of
citizenship."[52]

Conant and the NEA: An Evaluation

In 1952, some months before he would leave the Harvard presidency, Conant
expressed ambivalence about the NEA's EPC, the group to which he had devoted
so much of his time for the preceding four years. He noted that he judged from
hearsay evidence that it did have an impact on public school administrators and
concluded that such an impact would make an argument for its continuation.
He reiterated, however, his long-held position that the EPC was not a group to
sponsor statements about "four-year colleges and universities" and that, if that
caveat be acknowledged, he believed it was important for the NEA to continue
its backing of the EPC.[53]

One wonders how much of Conant's sentiments here were related to the controversy generated on the Harvard campus over the EPC statement that communists were not fit to teach. As a member of the EPC, Conant had to acknowledge this statement at the same time he tried to mollify opposition to it from students and faculty who saw it as a deep infringement on academic freedom. The obvious out for Conant would have been to note that colleges and universities were not the same as elementary and secondary schools and, therefore, prohibitions might be more appropriate in the latter settings than in the former. To his credit, he did not take this out, but neither did he come up with any real justification for firing communist university teachers. Like so many times in his presidency, he tried to quell the controversy by stating that no communists were on the Harvard faculty, a statement that he likely knew to be untrue.

Harvard faculty and students were not the only critics of Conant's increasingly serious relationship with the EPC, the NEA, and the public schools. In October of 1946, W. H. Cowley, then a professor of higher education at Stanford, but formerly president of Hamilton College in upstate New York, wrote a ten-page letter to Conant that took issue with the latter's argument in his recently published lectures at Teachers College.[54] The two had been discussing a variety of educational issues over the years, and this letter marked a sort of focal point in their discussions, a time in which Cowley expressed his dissent over the turn Conant's ideas had taken. The nub of Cowley's criticism was that Conant, who had long believed in the uncommon man, or gifted individual, and who had acted on that belief in implementing policies such as the national scholarships and university professorships at Harvard, had gone over to the side of those who believed in the priority of the common man as a focus for educational efforts. Cowley concentrated on the several places in Conant's lectures where he noted that the problem of the educational treatment of the common man was the major problem of twentieth-century education. Cowley opined that this was a priority that Conant had learned from those on the EPC with whom he cooperated in the preparation and publication of *Education for All American Youth*. Cowley supported his argument with a discussion of the attention paid, or rather not paid, to the gifted in the EPC report. He noted that there was no entry for the gifted in the index to *Education for All American Youth*, added that it gave less than a page of attention to special opportunities for the gifted, and compared this space unfavorably to the almost four pages devoted to "special services for the handicapped."[55]

Cowley believed that the major educational problem of the twentieth century was to provide equitable opportunities for both the common and the uncommon

Extra-Harvard, 1933–52 155

man. Conant, for Cowley, had gone too far over to the side of the common man and away from concern for the uncommon man, or gifted student. Cowley acknowledged that this was not completely true for Conant. One problem was, however, that Conant's concern for the gifted related mainly to the education of the scientifically gifted, a group that encompassed the experiences of Conant himself. This inclusion, particularly its personal dimension, guaranteed that Conant would always have an emotional stake in the education of the scientifically gifted, an interest that did not necessarily carry over into a consideration of the gifted in other areas. Cowley attributed this change in Conant away from the gifted to his being influenced by the educators on the EPC. Cowley added that this "has blotted out, I suggest, most of your interest in the uncommon man except the interest that grows from your own emotional concern for science."[56] Cowley believed that the consequences of this blotting out were disastrous for the future of the nation. He cautioned that "the leaders of educational opinion, like you, must not only direct the thinking of the nation in the need of providing for our gifted youth, but they must also stir up people's emotions, attitudes." Cowley concluded, "Along with many others I consider these youth to be the treasure-trove of the country. I also believe that if we fail to develop their capacities, our days as a great people are numbered."[57]

No letter of reply to Cowley from Conant is extant in the Conant papers. This may have been due to Conant's extremely heavy workload in all of his endeavors, or perhaps to his inability to craft a reply that acknowledged Cowley's criticisms and either accepted or responded to them in the same relatively critical spirit in which they were offered. Conant did, however, as already mentioned in this chapter, eventually get the EPC to publish a document on the Education of the Gifted. The relative lack of attention given to that document, by the EPC, the NEA, and the general public, however, suggests that perhaps the NEA leaders considered it a kind of intellectual payoff to Conant, one that was made in good faith but not with the enthusiasm or powerful commitment that they made to the education of the newer groups of students who were attending the public schools. Whatever the deeper meaning or intent of the EPC may have been, it seems fair to conclude that Cowley had identified a significant factor in Conant's intellectual development through the 1940s. He had at the least added a major concern for the more ordinary or less gifted student to his own intellectual arsenal and, though he did not let that commitment overshadow his own orientation toward the gifted completely, he associated himself with publications like *Education for All American Youth* that called it into question. Conant in taking on this kind of commitment or orientation seemed to distance

156   *Scholarly Leadership in Higher Education*

himself, to a considerable extent, from the problems and issues he confronted as the president of Harvard University. As the historically leading institution of American higher education, and one that had enhanced both its substance and reputation in relation to that status under his leadership, Harvard's priority was much more educational excellence than the educational equality or equity advocated by the NEA.

One cannot say that this issue was the straw that broke the proverbial camel's back in explaining Conant's decision to leave Harvard. Nor can one say that controversy like that between Conant and the archbishop of Boston over federal aid to Catholic schools, discussed in an earlier chapter, was decisive. What can be said is that these and other activities and issues indicated a rather clear rift between the Harvard president and many of the movers and shakers in Cambridge. This rift, though shrouded in formal politeness, had festered during the world war when Conant spent considerable time away from campus, intensified during the academic freedom communists on the faculty disputes of the late 1940s, and intensified further when many of the religionists on campus whom he had offended earlier in his presidency, as well as many private school supporters, were perturbed at what they considered his provocations in the tax support for Catholics school debate.

Leaving Harvard

While Conant's educational activities outside of Harvard caused considerable controversy on and off campus, he participated in other, more obviously political, activities that managed to pave the way for his exit. As we have seen earlier, he had become increasingly critical of the Soviet Union in the late 1940s, making it an underlying factor in explaining the title of his already discussed 1948 book, *Education in a Divided World*. The divided world consisted of communism and capitalism, or the Soviet Union and the United States, or freedom and collectivism—all formulations that Conant used in his political commentaries in this period. In 1951, shortly after the Korean War had broken out, he was presented with a political opportunity that he undertook with alacrity. Approached by a former Department of the Army official, Conant participated in the establishment of a citizens' committee not unlike that which he had helped the NEA create a few years earlier.

This new committee had nothing to do with education. Rather its concern was the world situation and America's participation in it. Conant, as we have

Extra-Harvard, 1933–52 157

seen, was a passionate cold warrior and in this situation needed little prodding to embrace the new group. In fact, Conant claimed to have been the author of the name of the new group: the Committee on the Present Danger. Of course, the danger was international communism as represented by the Soviet Union and a much more immediate danger since the inception of the Korean War. The new committee, however, was just as concerned with the communist threat in Europe as it was in the Korean conflict. The task of the committee was to communicate the seriousness of the threat to the American public and to encourage policies that recognized and dealt with it such as increased defense spending and a draft. Conant interacted with like-minded university presidents such as Dwight D. Eisenhower, then president of Columbia University, in pursuing the committee agenda. Some months later, Eisenhower left Columbia to assume control of the American military forces in Western Europe. Conant and the committee lauded this appointment and continued to agitate on behalf of an enhanced defense budget, cooperating closely with Eisenhower in the effort.[58] Within a year, Eisenhower had been elected president of the United States. He did not forget his close ally when it came to picking his diplomatic representatives.

Conant had turned down a diplomatic post in Germany early in 1951 when it had been offered by a democratic administration. Given controversies at Harvard over his various extra campus activities in support of public education, he came to have second thoughts about his refusal. When the incoming Eisenhower administration offered him the post of high commissioner to Germany, which would soon turn into an ambassadorship to the new nation of West Germany, he accepted with alacrity. Conant's own account of the Senate committee hearing on his nomination, as well as the Congressional Record verbatim account, reveals that his use of language like American radicals and a classless society, as well as his criticism of private schools, was as controversial in the larger political arena as it had been at Harvard. The Senate hearings featured attacks on Conant as a coddler of communists, as an anti-religion and anti-private school extremist, and as an advocate of inflammatory social change. Fortunately, the committee, controlled by establishment Republicans rather than by newly empowered right-wing conservatives in the party, approved his nomination by a large margin. The words of Senator Leverett Saltonstall, senior senator from Massachusetts, were quite influential in attaining approval. Saltonstall, a member of the Harvard Corporation for several years during Conant's presidency, though not a member of the foreign relations committee that was considering the nomination, came to the hearing to speak on Conant's behalf. In answer to allegations that Conant was a controversial figure, Saltonstall responded that any Harvard president worthy of the office was a controversial figure. His enthusiastic endorsement of Conant was acknowledged by the committee. Not quite as enthusiastic was the junior senator, recently elected, from the Bay State, John F. Kennedy. In acknowledgment both of Conant's qualifications and his questioning of aid to Catholic schools, the Irish-Catholic Kennedy stated that he was in favor of Conant's nomination to this diplomatic post, though he would not have approved him for the position of commissioner of education.[59]

Conant's goodbye to Harvard was not long or overly emotional. By the time of his acceptance of his new diplomatic position, he seemed to have drifted away from Harvard in the last several years; the drift may also have been reciprocated on the other side of the divide. Harvard may well have been ready for new leadership.

In his final official report to the Harvard community, he reiterated his presidency's classic themes: a sound and thrifty budget, a successful scholarship program that had strengthened the student body academically, and a series of faculty personnel policy changes that had greatly strengthened the faculty. He chastised the politics of right-wing Republicans such as Senator Joseph McCarthy of Wisconsin, mocking their characterization of Harvard and other campuses as subversive and defending those campuses as protectors of the intellectual freedom that was a necessity in a democratic society. He acknowledged success in a few of his interdisciplinary efforts such as the Master of Arts in Teaching (MAT), the Russian Research Center, and the Department of Social Relations. In spite of these accomplishments, he also acknowledged his larger failure to achieve the interdepartmental collaboration and cooperation, which he had sought to institutionalize on campus. He lauded the general education program, specifically mentioning its ability to get scholars to cooperate across departments and disciplines and also noting its need for evaluation and continuing improvement. The professional schools were praised as largely successful. One notable factor in determining that success was their ability to increase their budgets over the years. Conant could not resist a final shot at the Divinity School, noting that it was the only professional school that during his presidency had been unable to succeed financially. In regard to the School of Education, he added that new funds had been scarce and that this was the reason that "the School of Education, which I have long put first on my list of priorities, is still in a precarious financial position." He concluded his analysis with an endorsement of the universities as exceptionally important in the future of the United States: "As vital centers of sound learning, as strongpoints defending individual liberty, as communities of creative thinkers, no industrialized democracy can do without them; each year will demonstrate their indispensability to this society of free men."[60]

Notes

1 As noted in earlier chapters, Conant's defense work was extensive and important. It has been dealt with at length in Hershberg, *James Bryant Conant*.

2 For the statesman metaphor, see Vannevar Bush, "James Bryant Conant, President of the AAAS (American Association for the Advancement of Science) for 1946," *The Scientific Monthly* 62 (March 1946), 197–200. Bush calls Conant a "statesman of the intellect" on p. 197. For Conant's own version of himself as an analyst, see *My Several Lives*, p. 613.

3 Bush, "James Bryant Conant: President of the AAAS for 1946," p. 197.

4 Virginia Proctor, "Bibliography of James B. Conant," *Journal of General Education* 5 (October, 1950): 48–56.

5 Ibid.

6 Conant's interaction with physicists is described in an oral history interview with noted Harvard physicist and philosopher of science, Gerald Holton. See Katherine Sopka, Interview with Dr. Gerald Holton (January 11, 1977); American Institute of Physics, http://www/aip/org/history/ohilist.31279.html.

7 Conant, "The Role of a Liberal Arts College in a Total War," in *The Inauguration of A Everett Needham Case as the Ninth President of Colgate University*; cited in Proctor, "Bibliography of James B. Conant," p. 52.

8 "Colleges and the Spirit of the Times," *Bulletin of the Association of American Colleges* (December 1948), cited in Proctor, "Bibliography if James B. Conant," p. 55.

9 James B. Conant, "Our College System: A Re-Evaluation," *New York Times* (June 4, 1950).

10 James Bryant Conant, "The Future of Our Higher Education System," *Harper's Magazine* 178 (May 1938): 561–70.

11 James B. Conant, "Wanted: American Radicals," *The Atlantic Monthly* 171 (May 1943): 41–45; quotation p. 45.

12 Conant, "Function of the School and College in Educating for Social and Cultural Leadership," 329–31; quotation, p. 331. Also see *School and Society* 41 (January 5, 1947): 1–7.

13 Conant and Spaulding, *Education for a Classless Society*.

14 See note 12 of this chapter.

15 James B. Conant, "Education for a Classless Society," *The Atlantic Monthly* 146 (May 1940): 593–602.

16 Conant and Spaulding, *Education for a Classless Society*, chapter 3.

17 Nicholas Lemann argues that the consolidation was stopped mainly by Carl Brigham, developer of the SAT. Brigham was in the process of having second thoughts about the restrictive limits that the SAT could place on democratic opportunity if used indiscriminately. See Lemann, *The Big Test: The Secret History of the American Meritocracy* (New York: Farrar Strauss and Giroux, 1999), pp. 40–41.

18 SMS, "Notes on the Origin of ETS," (10/23/58) Carnegie Corporation Papers, Series IIIA, Box 563, Folder 1. For Conant's indication of his unsuccessful interest in the issue in the 1930s, see Office of the President, Record of Interview DCJ (Devereaux C. Josephs) and James B. Conant (January 19, 1946), Carnegie Corporation Papers, Series IIIA, Box 137, Folder 4.

19 "Plan for the Future of the Graduate Record Examination and a proposal to Study the Possibilities of a Central Non-Profit Agency for the Construction of Examinations and for Research in This Field" (January 18, 1946), Carnegie Corporation Papers, Series IIIA, Box 137, Folder 4.

20 "Proposed merger of testing services," O. C. Carmichael and James B. Conant (May 7, 1946), Carnegie Corporation Papers, Series IIIA, Box 137, Folder 4.

21 "Educational Testing and the Non-Profit Agencies" (August 16, 1946), Presidential Papers, Box 297, Folder Carnegie Committee on Testing, 1946, 2 of 2.

22 James B. Conant to Oliver C. Carmichael containing the "Preliminary Report of the Committee on Testing to the President, Carnegie Foundation for the Advancement of Teaching," Presidential Papers (October 4, 1946), Box 247, Folder Carnegie Corporation Committee on Testing 1946–1947 (1 of 2).

23 The ACE, headed by the Midwesterner George Zook, had a very different political agenda from the testing agencies. It involved the extension of more educational opportunity to many more students through testing, an approach pioneered by the Iowan, E. F. Lindquist. For a discussion of the various points of view, see Lemann, *The Big Test*, esp. pp. 17–26.

24 PHB to President Conant (16 October 1946) and Henry S. Dyer to Mr. Buck (October 15, 1946), Presidential Papers, Box 297. Folder Carnegie Corporation Committee on Testing, 1946–1947, 1 of 2.

25 Press Release, "Centralized Agency Formed to Improve Educational Tests and Conduct Research" (December 21, 1947), Carnegie Corporation Papers, Series IIIA, Box 137, Folder 9.

26 Ibid.

27 This activity is well described in Biebel, *Politics, Pedagogues and Statesmanship: James Bryant Conant and the Public Schools, 1933-1948*. See also Biebel, "Styles of Educational Leadership: James Bryant Conant and the Making of an Educational Statesman," Occasional Paper No. 2, University of Virginia Social Foundations of Education Symposium (February, 1971).

28 C. B. Glenn to Dr. James B. Conant (July 27, 1937) and Henry B. Holmes to President Conant (July 28, 1937), both in Presidential Papers, Box 100, folder AASA 1937–1938.

29 Conant, *My Several Lives*, pp. 138–39.

30 On the EPC, see Wayne J. Urban, "The Educational Policies Commission, 1936–1968: Notes for an Autopsy," *The Sophist's Bane* 3 (Fall 2005): 15–30.

Extra-Harvard, 1933–52 161

31 Educational Policies Commission of the National Education Association, *The CCC, the NYA, and the Public Schools* (Washington, DC: National Education Association, 1941).

32 National Education Association, Commission on the Reorganization of Secondary Education, *Cardinal Principles of Secondary Education* (Washington, DC: Government Printing Office, 1918).

33 Educational Policies Commission of the National Education Association, *Education for All American Youth* (Washington, DC: National Education Association, 1944).

34 The proceedings of the EPC were bound and boxed in the National Education Archives, now held by the George Washington University Library in Washington, DC. For Conant's participation, see Proceedings, Educational Policies Commission (January 10, 1942); Proceedings, Educational Policies Commission (February 19–20, 1942); Proceedings, Educational Policies Commission (June 5, 1942); and Proceedings, Educational Policies Commission (March 11, 1944).

35 Educational Policies Commission of the National Education Association, *Education for All American Youth*, p. 21.

36 Conant, *My Several Lives*, p. 614.

37 James B. Conant to William G. Carr (October 11, 1944), Presidential Papers, Box 248, Folder Educational Policies Commission, 1943–1944.

38 Wayne J. Urban, "*Education for All American Youth*: A Failed Attempt to Extend the Comprehensive High School," in B. M. Franklin and G. McCulloch, *The Death of the Comprehensive High School: Historical, Contemporary, Comparative Perspectives* (New York: Palgrave Macmillan, 2007).

39 Conant, "Public Education and the Structure of American Democracy, II General Education for American Democracy," pp. 162–79, esp. pp. 175–79.

40 William G. Carr to James B. Conant (April 29, 1946), Presidential Papers Box 298, Folder Educational Policies Commission, 1945–1946.

41 Conant to William G. Carr (May 2, 1946), Ibid.

42 Carr to Conant (April 22, 1948), Presidential Papers, Box 320, Folder Educational Policies Commission, 1947–1948.

43 We have seen in Chapter 3 how Conant's advocacy of comprehensive high schools put him at odds with the archbishop of Boston.

44 Discussed in Chapter 3.

45 Conant to John K. Norton (January 3, 1949), Presidential Papers, Box 340, Folder Educational Policies Commission, 1948–1949.

46 Conant to William G. Carr (February 27, 1950), Presidential Papers, Box 367, Folder Educational Policies Commission, 1949–1950.

47 Memorandum concerning "Education and National Security" (June 12, 1951), Presidential Papers, Box 3397, Folder Educational Policies Commission, 1950–1951.

48 Conant to William G. Carr (March 11, 1952), Presidential Papers, Box 429, Folder Educational Policies Commission, 1951–1952.

162   *Scholarly Leadership in Higher Education*

49 Willard E. Givens to President James B. Conant (May 5, 1947) and Conant to Givens (May 5, 1947), both in Presidential Papers, Box 305, Folder National Education Association, 1946–1947.

50 "Conant Says Public Schools National Policy Instrument: Strongly Favors Federal Aid," in *United States Municipal News* (February 19, 1948); copy in Presidential Papers, Box 305, Folder National Education Association, 1947–1948.

51 William G. Carr [NEA] to Conant (November 4, 1946), Presidential Papers, Box 298, Folder Commission on the Public Schools; Report on the January 11, 1948, Meeting of the Exploratory Committee for the Commission for the Public Schools and Roy E. Larsen, A Report on the January 31 Meeting of the Exploratory Committee, both in Presidential Papers, Box 326, Folder National Citizens' Commission for the Public Schools, 1947–1948. Larsen to Conant (May 10, 1949), Presidential Papers, Box 338, Folder National Citizens' Commission for the Public Schools, 1947–1948.

52 NEA Seventh National Conference on Citizenship (September 17–19, 1952), Carnegie Corporation Papers, Series IIIA, Box 250, Folder 4.

53 Conant to William G. Carr (March 11, 1952), Presidential Papers, Box 429, Folder Educational Policies Commission, 1951–1952.

54 James Bryant Conant, "Public Education and the Structure of American Society," *Teachers College Record* 47 (December, 1945): 145–92.

55 Hal to Dear Jim [Cowley to Conant] (October 21, 1946), Presidential Papers, Box 298, Folder Cowley, W. H. 1946–1947). This is one of several folders of Cowley-Conant correspondence found in the Conant Presidential Papers throughout the 1940s.

56 Ibid., p. 3.

57 Ibid., p. 7.

58 Conant, *My Several Lives*, pp. 506–17.

59 Ibid., pp. 533–42; Saltonstall, p. 543, Kennedy, p. 544. Also see US Congress: Senate Committee on Foreign Relations, Nomination of James B. Conant. Hearings before the Committee on Foreign Relations, US Senate, Eighty-Third Congress (February 2 and 3, 1953), The Nomination of James B. Conant to be US High Commissioner for Germany. Conant was not overtly partisan politically, but he was identified as a Republican and usually was associated with Republicans and Republicanism.

60 Presidential Report 1951–52; quotations, pp. 35, 39.

6

Educational Statesmanship and
Its Discontents, 1955–71

James Bryant Conant spent nearly four years in West Germany in his diplomatic position. However, it was clear early on in his diplomatic career that his time there would be relatively short and he quickly began making arrangements for his return to the United States and the role he would play after he returned. That role was to be an educational statesman, that is, one who would comment critically, intelligently, and practically on American education and one whose comments would be heeded by the decision makers in this arena. We will see that Conant's comments were many and usually received good public reaction. We will also see, however, that their implementation was far less than their favorable reaction might have predicted. The significance of this situation will be addressed in our final chapter.

As early as April 1954, a bit more than a year from the beginning of his diplomatic career, Conant was discussing a possible return to work on public education with the Carnegie Corporation. The philanthropy reiterated its interest in supporting whatever he chose to do that was "in the public interest."[1] After his return to the United States in 1957, he produced four major works on American education in ten years, works that concentrated, for the most part, on the elementary and secondary sectors. In those works, he built on, or perhaps reechoed, arguments made while he was Harvard president about various aspects of the educational problems in the lower schools. This chapter looks first at his preparations for the educational work he undertook after the end of his diplomatic assignment and then considers the major published works he produced in this period. It ends with a consideration of his autobiography, published in 1970, in which he reprised his entire career.

Conant's own account of his German diplomatic tour mentions that he was called on several times to discuss American education with one or another German group. In fact, he arranged to have his book, *Education and Liberty*,

164   *Scholarly Leadership in Higher Education*

translated by American diplomatic staff members into German for use in these discussions. His major point to his German audiences was that the United States had a unique secondary school, the comprehensive high school, that was quite different from the selective principle that characterized the German academic secondary school, the *gymnasium*. The comprehensive high school addressed vocational, social, and cultural concerns that were unknown in the German academic secondary school. It concentrated on academic studies in preparation for the single examination that qualified a student for university studies. Conant recalled that he was somewhat uncomfortable in these discussions, given that his knowledge of American comprehensive high schools was not first hand. That is, he had seldom if ever visited one of these institutions and considered this a weakness that needed to be repaired if he wanted to continue working in education after he returned to the United States. It was in this context that he began to conceive his project on the comprehensive high school.[2]

In pursuit of this projected effort, Conant contacted William G. Carr, the former administrative officer of the Educational Policies Commission (EPC) of the NEA, with whom Conant had worked closely as a member and then executive officer of that body. By this time, Carr had become the chief staff officer (executive secretary) of the NEA, by far the largest organization of public school educators in the United States. Conant envisioned a loose but real relationship with the NEA, believing that he needed the support from this giant organization to get his ideas and proposals to be seriously considered by the public school people, by school board members who determined policy, and by parents of public school students. Conant had conversations with John Gardner, head of the Carnegie Corporation, who rather quickly agreed to underwrite Conant's effort on the high school, whatever form it took. Conant combined the influence of Carr with the financial backing of Gardner to provide a solid underwriting for his work on the high school. To these two bases, he added the organizational and administrative support of the Educational Testing Service (ETS). ETS would be the facilitator of his efforts and arranged for an office and a residence in New York City, where he would be based for the duration of the project.[3] Conant was taking advantage of his Harvard and his non-Harvard contacts here to help him assemble a powerful and complete platform from which to discourse on the topic of American schooling.

Late in 1956, Conant prepared a memorandum for the Carnegie Corporation outlining his proposed study of the comprehensive high school. He began with some assumptions: (1) that the comprehensive high school provided the

Educational Statesmanship and Its Discontents, 1955–71   165

"proper framework for the education of American youth"; (2) that this form of high school was superior for American society to the separate schools for talented youth that existed in some big cities (and one of which he himself had attended); (3) that the treatment of academically talented youth within the comprehensive high school was exceptionally important; and (4) that the curriculum for those youth should have rigorous requirements in foreign language, mathematics, history, English language and composition, and the sciences. He stated that meeting the curricular stipulations for talented youth was his first criterion for evaluating the worth of a comprehensive high school. He described academically talented youth as students of inherent ability, "perhaps an IQ of 115 and greater." The social function of the comprehensive high school constituted Conant's second major criterion for evaluation. This referred to the nonacademic concerns of the high school and related to both the social interaction and future employment of the various student groups served by a school.[4] It involved issues such as social solidarity, citizenship education, and technical training.

Interaction between the two major criteria was of major importance to Conant. He asked "to what extent it was possible in a comprehensive school which provided orthodox academic opportunities for their talented youth to also provide some intellectual meeting ground for all of the students in the high school." He went on to add that such opportunities, if they existed, would be the "integrating forces" that he wanted to find. Of course, he was just as interested, perhaps even more interested, in seeing the rapid development of the intellectual capacity of talented youth.[5]

The reader of earlier chapters of this book will note that both criteria were important for Conant well before undertaking his study. Academic talent was his top priority for the Harvard student body from the beginning of his presidency and was institutionalized in his National Scholarship Program. Socially integrating factors became important beginning in the late 1930s when he worked with Frank Spaulding and others on the faculty of the Harvard Graduate School of Education. Conant believed that finding high schools that met both of his criteria was exceptionally important in order to quiet public-school critics who were becoming increasingly vocal in the 1950s. Addressing both academic talent and social concerns in comprehensive high schools "would silence the unthinking critic" and would "assist those who are working for the support of American public education."[6] A look at the methodology and findings of the report he undertook is in order before returning to a discussion of how his assumptions and purposes influenced those findings.

166   *Scholarly Leadership in Higher Education*

The American High School Today (1959)

Conant's proposal was commented on by the ETS before its approval for funding. ETS attempted to make Conant's work more sophisticated methodologically and more powerful as a piece of educational research.[7] Conversely, Conant was on record that he wanted his work to be of practical use to citizens' groups, members of school boards, and to school people, rather than beset with academic concerns. He employed a professional staff of four established educators to help him in his work. One could conclude here that Conant was acting in conformity with his own views of the nature and value of scientific knowledge. Recall that he spent much of his general education course in science and his writing on the history of science for that course, and for the general public, on the theme that science needed to be demystified for the nonscientists. He often equated science with a sophisticated common sense.[8]

His methods in the study of high schools for his 1959 book were, thus, less than the quantitative, rigorous analysis that ETS and other working educational researchers sought. Intent on reaching a lay audience, he practiced what we call today a kind of survey research, though the methods Conant used in his study were not sophisticated statistically as was much academic survey work of that time and after. Most importantly for Conant, he and his team visited high schools and undertook analysis of their records and their practice that spoke to his priorities of academic talent and social relevance. On his own, he visited fifty-five high schools in several states, though they were concentrated in the northeast and midwestern sections of the country. His team of four also conducted numerous school visits; in total, they visited over 100 schools in 26 states, with no state getting any more than four schools visited. In all of these activities, the Conant team was on the lookout for comprehensive high schools that worked, that is, that combined his objectives of academic education for the talented and solid ties between the gifted and the other students in the high schools. By the time of the study, Conant's two purposes for a comprehensive high school, however, had evolved into three. The education of the gifted was still the first of his purposes, but the second purpose had become twofold; it still stressed social understandings and contact among all students but also included vocational and vocationally oriented studies that would prepare the bulk of students for "developing a particular skill which may be useful . . . directly upon graduation."[9]

Conant reported the major finding of his study, *The American High School Today*, as follows: "I found eight schools which, in my judgment, were

Educational Statesmanship and Its Discontents, 1955–71   167

satisfactorily fulfilling the three main objectives of a comprehensive high school."[10] This finding could have led to a critical analysis about what he had found, and not found, if Conant had been conducting an evaluative study. That is, he could have considered why only eight of more than 100 schools did what he wanted them to do. But, recall that what he wanted to know is if there were any schools doing what he wanted them to do. And in this case, he found eight to be in conformity. This allowed him, not to conclude that only 8 of over 100 were meeting his 3 objectives but, rather, to note that the 8 were doing so. This in turn allowed him to spend the remaining pages in his book not in analyzing the reasons why the large majority of schools were not performing according to his purposes but in making recommendations for how the rest of the schools could reform themselves to be like the eight satisfactory institutions. Given this orientation, Conant reported the major finding of his study in a way that encouraged the educators in the NEA about their work: "I believe no radical alteration in the basic pattern of American education is necessary in order to improve our public high schools. If all the high schools were functioning as well as some I have visited, the education of American youth would be satisfactory."[11]

The context that made Conant's analysis more than palatable to the nation's school people was the climate of biting criticism of public schools in which it was offered. The 1950s were a decade punctuated by critiques of public schools as anti-intellectual playgrounds made by many conservative authors, most notably Arthur Bestor and Hyman Rickover.[12] These analyses specified progressive education as the chief agent of the intellectual coddling that was going on in the schools. The launch of Sputnik in 1957 intensified critiques of public schools as woefully inadequate particularly in science education.[13] Conant heeded these critiques but only by implication. He acknowledged imperfection in public education but outlined a way out of the situation that could be accomplished without major upheavals, either in education or in the politics and policies related to education. Conant took a middle position here between the critics and defenders of the public schools but took it in a way that allowed the defenders to deal with the criticism by considering and adopting his recommendations.

Conant spent a good deal of time indicating the kind of changes that were needed for improvement of the high schools that he had studied. He made a total of twenty-one recommendations in his report. The first, and because of its place perhaps the most important for Conant, was for a comprehensive counseling system. He advocated starting counseling in the elementary school and a ratio of one counselor to every 250 to 300 pupils in the high school. The counselor's role was multifaceted. Among its most important aspects was guiding the brightest boys and girls toward the maximum use of their academic potential. To achieve this objective, he advocated using aptitude tests to identify those who were underachieving and encouraging these students to take the most challenging courses available. Also, provisions for the other students were to be made by the counselor so that their experience would be conducive to success in the work world after high school. A recommendation for required programs for all students, the talented and the rest of the student body, involved a general education for every student requiring four years of English, three or four years of social studies, mathematics in the ninth grade, and a year of science in the ninth or tenth grade—and seven more elective courses, carefully chosen for each student. Electives were to be advanced academic courses for the talented and occupationally or technically relevant courses for the other students. Conant advocated ability grouping in all required and some elective courses, recommending that students be divided into three groups in each course, the advanced, the middle, and the slow readers. He called for at least half the time spent in English to be devoted to writing; he added that the academically able especially should be given the chance to develop their writing. He proposed a school-wide testing of English composition skills in the eleventh grade and a requirement for more composition for students judged to be able by their aptitude but who had done poorly on the composition test. The longest particular recommendation given by Conant was the one on the academically talented. Here Conant advocated a rigorous curriculum in science, mathematics, social studies, and foreign languages, with a stipulation that homework be carefully assigned, as well as specially designed courses for those who were musically or artistically gifted. In this recommendation, he stated that the academically talented constituted "about 15 per cent of the high school population" and advocated a less rigorous but still academically challenging program for the next 10 to 20 percent of the students. Another recommendation was for the highly gifted, about 3 percent nationally, who should be in separate classes if numbers warranted it or, alternatively, should have their own guidance counselor as a tutor while they were in regular classes. These highly gifted students were to be made aware of, and encouraged to take, advanced placement classes in mathematics, English, or history. The stress on the gifted was clearly obvious in these and other of Conant's recommendations, such as those in the specific subject areas of science and foreign languages. Another way of recognizing the gifted would be to follow his recommendation to publish an academic honors list of those who succeeded in advanced academic courses. Still another way of achieving real recognition was through the deletion of class rankings that did not discriminate

Educational Statesmanship and Its Discontents, 1955–71   169

between those taking basic and advanced courses. College admissions officers were encouraged to look at performance in advanced academic classes rather than at a class ranking, which could be influenced by doing well in less rigorous classes.[14]

From these recommendations, and the ways in which they were given, one could conclude that Conant was committed to the education of the academically gifted as his major priority. There were a few recommendations, however, that met his other purposes. Among these were one that discussed diversified programs for marketable skills. These skills were identified as typing, stenography, other clerically related tasks, as well as home economics instruction for girls. Business, or distributive, education was recommended for those wanting to work in sales, and vocational agricultural education and vocational education in skills related to industry were touted for boys who intended to enter the workforce after graduation. Two other recommendations discussed instruction in reading, one for the very slow reader and a second for developmental reading instruction; this latter recommendation stressed the utility of the course for talented students as well as others. Finally, two recommendations related to the social and citizenship aspects of comprehensive schools. One prescribed a homeroom for all students in which they were mixed in their backgrounds and abilities and in which activities were structured to encourage interaction across the student backgrounds. The second was for a problems of democracy course in the twelfth grade in which students of all abilities were present in each section and which discussed issues and concerns related to democratic citizenship.[15]

Immediately after the listing of his recommendations, Conant began a discussion of small high schools that caused considerable consternation among public school educators. Conant believed that the changes he recommended for existing high schools could not be implemented in schools that were smaller than 100 students per class (400 students in a four-year high school or 300 students in a three-year high school). To implement this priority, he recommended consolidating all high schools that did not meet the minimum size requirement. This put him at odds with school administrators in most of the existing public high schools. An appendix in the *American High School Today* revealed that only the states of California, Connecticut, Massachusetts, New Jersey, Pennsylvania, and Rhode Island had a majority of high schools that met his size criterion. The total number of high schools nationally that did not meet the size criterion was over 14,000, almost three-fourths of the extant high schools in the nation.[16] This recommendation put Conant visibly on one side of an enormous political battle that was going in many states, the battle to consolidate small, and usually rural, schools. That battle was undertaken in many states as Conant was writing and not just in the rural states in the South and the West. The Midwest, in some ways a major setting for the urbanization and industrialization that was taking place nationally, was riven with political turmoil over the issue of school consolidation. Conant himself had discussions with political leaders in Indiana, Illinois, and Minnesota about the need to eliminate the educational inefficiency of the small high school.[17] Conant did not anticipate the controversy that erupted over his small school critique and, other than reiterate his reasons for elimination of small high schools, did little to engage with opponents of consolidation. He was here operating as he often had done in the past. He chose not to respond to negative reactions, preferring to restate his own views rather than answer critics.

In the same section of Conant's book on the high school that discussed the weaknesses of small schools, two other topics were covered. They were called the Large City High School and the Suburban High School. These two types of schools received only six and five pages of discussion, respectively. Within two years, he produced a small volume on these schools, which allowed him to address the problems in each environment more fully.

Urban and Suburban Schools

Conant's book on urban and suburban schools was entitled, catchily but perhaps a bit condescendingly, Slums and Suburbs.[18] He here considered two types of schools that were further from the comprehensive ideal than the mainly small-town schools he studied in his first book on the American high school. Conant's views on inner-city, or what he called "slum" schools, were given more attention, more appreciation, and more criticism than his views on suburban schools. His analysis and recommendations for the latter group can be dealt with rather quickly.

Conant was dealing specifically with the more affluent suburban communities, and their schools, that surrounded the nation's major cities. He found those schools to have an overwhelmingly academic curriculum, though he thought it to be not of the quality that he wanted. He judged about half of the students in these suburban high schools to be academically talented, as defined in his earlier work as in the top 15 percent of their age group. For these students, he recommended a more rigorous academic curriculum than what they were currently receiving. For the rest of suburban high school students, the less than

Educational Statesmanship and Its Discontents, 1955–71   171

academically talented, he recommended more vocationally oriented studies and less emphasis on enrolling in academically elite colleges and universities. He recommended improved guidance services to give students and parents a more realistic idea of student ability and a future based on that reality. This meant more attention to enrollment for the less than talented in two-year colleges or state colleges, rather than in liberal arts colleges or elite universities. Reviewers discussing this part of Conant's analysis commented on how hard it would be to get suburban parents of the less than talented to be realistic about their student's prospects.[19]

Turning to the treatment of urban schools, Conant generated both critical acclaim and vigorous criticism. The acclaim came for Conant's hard-hitting description of the wretched economic conditions in which the schools were located. He noted the dilapidated buildings that urban students often attended, the equally disturbing conditions of many of the neighborhoods in which the schools were located, and the futility of trying to remedy these conditions without genuine economic or political reform for the communities. He frequently noted that the "slum" schools in the inner cities were attended mostly by Negro students, but he also, though less frequently, noted that the urban poor were not all black. He advocated improved guidance services in these schools to identify academic talent, in the student bodies, and to help the many less than talented students prepare for the world of work they would encounter after completion. He suggested meaningful vocational programs other than the traditional wood working and various kinds of shops that often existed. He cautioned educators and citizens that there was "social dynamite" in the student bodies of these institutions, and that the situation was, indeed, potentially explosive.[20]

Conant's most controversial recommendation was allied to his point that the community pathology in which students often lived seriously affected their educational achievement. That recommendation was that there was little to be done effectively to counter the racial segregation, de facto segregation, that afflicted the schools in the inner cities of the Northeast and the Midwest. At a time less than a decade after the ruling in the 1954 *Brown v. Board* decision outlawing de jure segregation in southern and border states, Conant put himself on the opposite side to many if not most advocates of civil rights for African Americans who were pushing to apply *Brown* outside of the South. Conant's position was positive, on the one hand. He believed that black communities were not inherently incapable of providing educational opportunities for their young people, a position that would become more advocated in black circles perhaps a decade or two later than when Conant wrote. But he specifically argued that

172   *Scholarly Leadership in Higher Education*

desegregation in the large cities he studied was impractical. "The answer to improving Negro education in the large Northern cities is to spend more money and to upgrade Negro Schools, many of which are in slums, rather than to effect token integration by transporting pupils across attendance lines"[21] This argument against desegregation policies such as school busing put Conant squarely at odds with civil rights groups such as the National Association for the Advancement of Colored People (NAACP). These groups were interested in voluntary school desegregation plans such as were being implemented in New York City, as well as in strategies such as busing students, redrawing school districts, or providing incentives for black students who wished to attend white schools in other cities.

The civil rights leadership, and many black political leaders, pounced on Conant as a defender, though perhaps not an enthusiastic defender, of segregated schools. Rather than fight segregation, he seemed to advocate accommodation to the situation, at least in the urban North. His accommodation, however, was accompanied by support for needed additional funding in urban communities and in their schools—and, also, by support for the full integration of school faculties in urban schools. Though Conant himself thought in later years that he should have done more to communicate with leaders of the black community and civil rights organizations, he failed to do so.[22] In the face of strident criticism that suggested he was advancing racist opposition of desegregation, he backed off from the controversy over inner-city schools and, instead, turned his educational efforts toward another topic, teacher education.

The Education of American Teachers (1963)

In addition to opposition to his ideas from consolidation opponents and from minority communities seeking meaningful desegregation, Conant was beginning to see himself as increasingly at odds with the professional educators from bodies like the NEA who were vocally supportive of his work. In a confidential note written shortly after publication of his book on the American high school, he recounted the effort he made in the book and, more fully, in talks to various groups, to be positive about the public schools, as positive as he could be. He also noted that the evidence presented in his book could easily have generated a more critical set of conclusions than the ones he offered. He was, in a sense, pulling his punches because of the siege the public schools were under because of Sputnik and the ideas of critics like Bestor and Rickover. He indicated that he was becoming increasingly concerned with the lack of response within the professional education communities to his recommendations: "As of

Educational Statesmanship and Its Discontents, 1955–71   173

today, I feel less sympathetic with my friends in public education than I did a year ago." He went on to note that "there is a great deal of justification for the current talk that the professional educators and administrators, abetted by many professors in schools of education have allowed the high school to become too soft." The softness, for Conant, was most evident in the refusal of the school people to attend to the academically talented, especially in the areas of science, mathematics, and foreign language. He went on to reprise the argument in his report: that a few schools were truly comprehensive, caring for the gifted as well as the rest of the students. But he noted, "I have just barely been able, with a good conscience, to say I have found such schools: but I have found many where the third of these functions [education of the academically talented] has been badly neglected." The neglect was due, he believed, to the hardheadedness of the educational professionals. If the school people did not take steps to improve the comprehensive high school's treatment of the academically talented, "they have more trouble awaiting them from the general public."[23]

Conant took this muffled but real opposition to the school people to the level of public acknowledgment and rather vigorous criticism in his next report, on teacher education. In October of 1961, Conant discussed his possible study of teacher education in a confidential memo to John Gardner. He mentioned support for his study from a small group of deans of high-status schools of education: Teachers College (Columbia), the University of California, Harvard, and the University of Colorado and two high officials of the NEA, its executive secretary, William G. Carr, and the administrative officer of an NEA subgroup devoted to Teacher Education and Professional Standards. The memo indicated that he would spend his own time visiting as many as fifteen institutions that prepared teachers and would hire a small staff to aid him in his work, both echoes of his work on the high school. Carnegie was still a main supporter of his work, both in terms of staff support and of his own remuneration.[24]

A little less than two years later, the book was ready for publication. As in his high school studies, Conant worked with a team that conducted visits to institutions and departments of education, this time in sixteen states (most of the largest states were part of the group). The book that resulted from these visits contained, as in most of his works, a restatement of his earlier views. This analysis, like his mid-1940s statement on education, contained a plea for a truce among educators. It also advocated cooperation among arts and science and education faculties in teacher preparation, like what he advocated then and what he had institutionalized in the Master of Arts in Teaching (MAT) program at Harvard in the 1930s. But the major point of the book was that the existing patterns of certification in the United States were woefully inadequate. A major reason for this was the tendency in many if not most states to prescribe course by course certification programs at the state level with little or no institutional involvement in their development. Conant advocated pulling back from this cumbersome, tedious, and largely wasteful and ineffective set of prescriptions. Instead he advocated that states require only two things to begin teaching: a bachelor's degree from a legitimate college or university and evidence of success in a rigorous student teaching assignment. Each institution should be free to devise its own program for teacher education, carefully conceived by both the education and the subject matter (arts and sciences) faculty. His call for a "truce among educators" meant that each side should take a broad view of the issue and not one devoted to protecting its own interests in the result.[25]

In addressing arts and sciences faculty, he criticized them for their inattention to the general education of teachers and other students, as well as for their slipshod way of providing content courses for prospective teachers. In each case, faculty were guided by their own individual and professional purposes, both based on their own disciplinary needs and desires, rather than by the rigorous and appropriate academic experiences needed for effective teaching. The education faculty came in for similar, but really more scathing, criticism. Education courses were described as "dull, repetitive, badly organized, and in many cases concerned with triviality." Introductory courses were usually "worthless," many educational psychology courses were "superficial and repetitious," history and philosophy of education courses were "irrelevant and misleading," and methods courses were often "taught by people who had never worked in a secondary or elementary school classroom" or whose experience was so old as to have left them "out of touch with the realities there." Conant wanted education faculty divided into two groups: clinical faculty who were experienced elementary and secondary teachers who continued to teach and intermediary faculty thoroughly trained in a basic discipline and able to apply that training to the day-to-day problems of the schools. Conant advocated graduate education for teachers in full-time settings, either taken on leave from teaching or during the summer. Part-time graduate education was to be abolished.[26]

He concluded his analysis with a plea for institutional competition and individual institutional innovation in teacher preparation, stating his belief that the best programs would quickly earn a high reputation for preparing good teachers. He warned that if academics did not cease their quarrels over turf and combine to provide their best effort at training excellent teachers, the lay public

Educational Statesmanship and Its Discontents, 1955–71   175

needed to enter the fray. Once the quarreling educators united to address the issue, the need for lay intervention would recede.[27]

While the number of pages devoted to arts and sciences and to education faculty might have been near equivalent in his book, Conant saved his most damning comments for those on the education side of the academic divide. Arts and sciences faculty were guilty of log-rolling, according to Conant, and education faculty were often poorly prepared and woefully unversed in the work that they were undertaking. The discussion of his report by Fred Hechinger, education editor of the *New York Times,* indicated the incendiary nature of the analysis, at least for those on education faculties. Hechinger described "Dr. Conant's Educational Bombshell" and charted its impact in the fall of 1963.[28]

Conant who earlier had aroused animosity in the ranks of civil rights leaders now was becoming more openly critical of public school people. The latter group was one he himself was becoming increasingly uncomfortable with. He noted this discomfort at the same time that he was still being honored by various school groups. In fact, as he was leaving for Berlin for a few years in 1963, with the *Education of American Teachers* within days of publication, he was the guest of honor at an event of the EPC of the NEA. The top ranks of American education were represented in the EPC, and Conant, as discussed earlier, had spent four terms as a member and one stint as the body's executive officer. After receiving a set of bound volumes of EPC documents produced while he was a member, and a series of encomiums from various members and others in attendance, it was Conant's turn to speak. He thanked the group profusely and stated he was well pleased at the event. He also believed, however, though he did not say, that his pleasure might not be reciprocated by those in attendance when they read his book on teacher education. He chose not to discuss teacher education, for it would inject a "sour note" into the festivities. Instead, he spoke of the still unsolved problems in slum schools that he had written about a few years earlier. He thus avoided having to talk with this group about teacher education, a topic about which he was sure they would not wish to hear what he had to say.[29]

Conant produced much more than the three books discussed herein in the late 1950s and early 1960s. He published a pamphlet on the junior high school, a small essay on universities' obligations in the Cold War political climate, and another small volume on Thomas Jefferson.[30] Most of the books, including *The American High School Today,* were less than 100 pages long. The text in that volume was supplemented by appendices and particular recommendations, bringing the total page count to 140. Some works were based on lectures he had

176   *Scholarly Leadership in Higher Education*

given at institutions such as the University of California and Yale University. The ideas in all of them were consonant with those in the three volumes we have covered here and, just as importantly, quite consistent with his views on education during his Harvard years.

It is hard to gauge the impact of Conant's work in these years. One way could be to look at publication figures. The ETS, one of Conant's official sponsors during this period, produced a document on the circulation of Conant's various books in these years. It listed the total circulation of all volumes as 783,000. Of this number, 472,000 were sold and 311,000 were provided without cost. Given his intent to reach a more general audience with his ideas, these numbers are formidable.[31] Academically, as judged by reviews, the works were less impressive, though Conant would not have argued with that judgment. He was intent on reaching a more than academic audience, one that included public educators, school board members, and parents.

In terms of judging its impact on secondary education, his works produced an avalanche of commentary. One assessment of Conant's work, written in 1977 by a noted professor of education for a national high school principals' group, described him as the champion "of the comprehensive high school as a peculiarly America invention." The commentator added that the comprehensive high school, in conformity with Conant's wishes, was "constantly to be critiqued and improved in order to fulfill better its goal of serving *all* American youth." He suggested that Conant would have been alive to conditions and forces that demanded new approaches and strategies to achieve the goal of comprehensiveness, rather than overly defensive about how his own views had become at least partially outdated.[32]

Yet a doctoral dissertation, one of many produced on Conant and his educational thought, concluded that his specific recommendations went largely unfollowed in American public school systems. This dissertation, in turn, reported on eight dissertation studies of the high school in different states after the publication of Conant's report. It concluded that there was more attention paid to Conant's recommendations for the academically talented than to his other recommendations. It noted that this was a part of the larger discovery of the "gifted" student that was going on within American educational circles. It gave Conant credit for increasing the morale of those who worked in American high schools by publicizing their institution and its importance in the larger society. It also looked at enrollment figures in science, mathematics, and foreign languages in high schools prior to and following Conant's report. It found minimal increases in these fields. The final conclusion of the dissertation was not conducive to a positive assessment of Conant's work: "On the basis of high school enrollment figures in mathematics, science, and foreign languages, and on the basis of the [eight] dissertations studies, it appears that James Conant's *The American High School Today* had no significant impact on the content or structure of American secondary education."[33]

This is a harsh conclusion and, also, one that might be offered about many, if not most, and quite possibly all authors who have attempted to induce tangible changes in American schools. It is not offered here to denigrate Conant and his work but to stress the difficulty of the task he attempted. His work in secondary education was ambitious in its reach but he was not ultimately able to achieve most of the things he wanted. Yet, he surely should be credited for his efforts and the public attention they received, if not for their success. What remains to be covered in this chapter are two of Conant's last publications in the years before his death in 1978, one more in the area of education and a final autobiography.

Education Policy and Autobiography

Conant left for Berlin in mid-1963 to spend two years as an education adviser to the mayor of West Berlin, Willy Brandt. His task was to help in the creation of an education center in the city, which would serve local, national, and international audiences with educational advice. There seemed a nebulousness attached to the post, but provision for living expenses from the Ford Foundation supplemented the municipal funds he received and furthered the sense that the work was meaningful. He discussed the opaque nature of the new body, and his role in it, in a letter to Francis Keppel, the US Commissioner of Education and the former dean of the Harvard Graduate School of Education. He explained that the appointment was fundamentally a political device to boost the morale of educators, and citizens in general, who were living in a West Berlin enclave surrounded by communist East Germany.[34] Conant worked hard to get the center he was visiting permanently funded, and, shortly after achieving that goal, he returned to the United States.

While Conant was in Germany for substantial parts of two years, he made several trips back to the United States and spent a good bit of his time continuing to worry about American schools. In conjunction with these activities, he came up with some new ideas about American educational policies that he thought would help achieve his goals for the public schools. He published these ideas in late 1964, in a book entitled *Shaping Educational Policy*.[35] In that volume,

178   *Scholarly Leadership in Higher Education*

Conant grappled with a problem, the effective control of educational policy, that had to be handled in the United States in a way quite different from how it was handled in most nations. In most European countries, education was managed at the national level, through a ministry of education. The minister was usually also a member of parliament and education was thus addressed through the national legislature as well as through the political administration in place. In the United States, however, education could not be handled as a policy at the federal level, given its absence from the Constitution and the stipulation that things not discussed in the Constitution were the purview of the states. Conant was here dealing with a problem that had long handcuffed the NEA in its search for educational improvement. The NEA, and Conant, had advocated federal aid for states and local public school systems, but general federal aid, that is funds without stipulations about how they were to be spent. This policy, in spite of the fervent advocacy by NEA, seemed to be a nonstarter. Asking the federal government to appropriate funds for public schools without influencing how the funds were to be spent was, at the least, politically impractical.

Conant's solution to the federal education issue was directly related to a problem he had identified in his teacher education study one year earlier. One prominent theme of that study was the weakness of state departments of education. Conant developed that theme in his book on education policy and thought that its resolution lay in invigorating the states as education policy makers. A major reason that this step was necessary was because of the ineffectiveness of a loosely organized coalition of school people, teacher association leaders, school administrators, and professors of education who were often powerfully connected with state legislators and able to frustrate real change. In his teacher education book, and increasingly in his other writing, he referred to this group, not in a flattering tone, as the "educational establishment."[36]

As a way of countering the ability of the educational establishment to successfully oppose needed change, he pointed to one example of a constructive state policy in elementary and secondary education. That example was in the State of New York. In that state, the state department was efficiently organized, well led, and sufficiently staffed to be able to exert significant, constructive influence on policy at the state level and policy and practice at the local level as well. In higher education, Conant pointed approvingly to the state of California and its elaborate higher education system, headed by a powerful state board and having three institutional tiers, with clear mission statements for institutions at each tier to accomplish. The specific issues Conant raised that needed to be solved statewide, in higher education and in elementary and secondary education, were

Educational Statesmanship and Its Discontents, 1955–71   179

familiar to those who had read his other works. Identification and education of the academically talented was important, as was vocational education and the problem of the high dropout rate, especially dropouts by some academically talented students.[37]

Conant's desire to strengthen education policy significantly at the state level was, as mentioned earlier, related to the fact that issues were extremely difficult to address at the national level in a government system with a constitutional mandate that excluded education from federal purview.[38] Conant wanted to weld strong state education policies into what he called a "nationwide," rather than a national, educational policy. To achieve this result, he advocated creation of an interstate educational compact where state educational leaders would meet with each other, discuss and debate solutions to various educational problems and issues, and achieve results through a process that took these discussions and applied them in their own state settings.

Reviewers were generally unkind to Conant's book. They noted that he skated over multiple problems and issues that cast into doubt his desire to invigorate state education policies. One reviewer argued specifically with Conant's praise of New York's state education arrangements. He maintained that Conant's contention that New York was able to control the educational establishment was not true and cited a study by four political scientists that documented the ways that organized school people-influenced policy in the state.[39] The review went on to compare Conant's entire analysis, negatively, to the serious scholarly work of these political scientists and other conscientious scholarly analysts of American education policy. The conclusion reached was that Conant had mistaken the form of educational policy for the substance of the matter itself. Concentrating on a governmental level while ignoring the content of what went on in policy making at any level was a solution that skated only on the surface of the problems. The review ended, like many of Conant's works, with a listing of fifteen propositions about effective education policy making that had been ignored by Conant.[40]

Conant, as he almost always did, chose not to respond to this, or any other review. He was able to report, however, that his idea of a compact was one of his greatest contributions to American education. He noted that the idea would not have received much attention had it not been enthusiastically approved by John Gardner, head of the Carnegie Corporation. Gardner and Carnegie, the major funder of Conant's work in education, were proud of both the work and the individual who had produced it. In a long memorandum devoted to assessing Conant's work, Gardner praised his high school study, his work on slum and suburban schools, and his efforts in teacher education. He discussed evaluation

180   *Scholarly Leadership in Higher Education*

of *Shaping Educational Policy* as a task that was yet to be accomplished. He did say, however, that it "touched on a crucial problem in American education" and identified that problem as "the weakness of state educational machinery."[41]

Conant's proposed interstate compact idea involved approaching state legislators as the avenue of entry for achieving such a compact. Gardner discussed this idea with Terry Sanford, governor of North Carolina who had a significant record of educational improvement in his state. Sanford looked closely at the structure of the compact and discussed it with Conant. Sanford's idea was that the best way to implement successfully the compact was through the executive officers of states, the governors, rather than through the legislatures. Sanford sold his idea to several other governors in the national governors' conference and shepherded it into being as the Education Commission of the States (ECS). That body, still in existence today, is a powerful voice in educational policy at the national level, though only one of many voices.[42] It has annual meetings of state officials and conducts and publishes research in areas such as accountability, assessment, civic education, finance, and governance.[43] It also acknowledged Conant's influence in its creation in a variety of ways, most notably through an annual James B. Conant award for achievement in educational policy. In 2018, the award went to the governor of Tennessee for his leadership in improving educational attainment in his state and for bridging the gap between education and the workforce.[44]

Conant described the creation of the ECS as one of his major social inventions in his autobiography, subtitled "memoirs of a social inventor."[45] In fact, the creation of ECS is described on the last two pages of that volume. It ends abruptly with that discussion, offering nothing in the way of conclusion. That is not the only unusual characteristic of this autobiography. It started almost immediately after the educational policy book was finished. It began as a projected three-volume series on various aspects of his career in education. It underwent a change in venue for Conant's work from one New York City office to another and a change in administrative responsibility for his work from the ETS to Teachers Insurance and Annuity Association (TIAA), a group that had emerged from the early work by the Carnegie philanthropies in establishing pensions for higher education personnel. The constant in these changes was the Carnegie Corporation, which continued to sponsor Conant's work, considering the autobiography the conclusion to his efforts on American education begun in the 1950s.[46]

Conant was never comfortable with one autobiographical volume, but this eventual outcome was the result of a series of exchanges between him and several editors at Harper and Row, with whom he had contracted to publish

Educational Statesmanship and Its Discontents, 1955–71   181

his educational writings in 1966. Conant here, as in earlier works, had a team of three to help him, a professor of education from the University of Wisconsin and two doctoral students from the department of history in Madison. These individuals were supported by Carnegie and the two students divided the work with one deciding to concentrate on the field of education and the other to deal with almost everything else. This latter category encompassed Conant's dealings in war advocacy, issues relating to war, particularly to the Second World War, and his diplomatic efforts in Germany. In mid-1969, as his autobiography was nearing completion after a series of false starts, Conant wrote a small essay on the topic of writing an autobiography. He attributed the idea of an autobiography, as he had attributed much of his earlier work in education, to John Gardner, president on the Carnegie Corporation. Gardner read something Conant had written about his childhood and was excited about the possibility of an autobiography.[47] Conant was not enthusiastic about the autobiography from the beginning and that lack of enthusiasm may have colored the whole project. Harper and Row provided a series of editors, who changed because of personal and professional circumstances. These editors managed to get him to start writing, assuring him that organizational concerns could be handled once the material was in hand. They also encouraged him to be as personal about his life as he could in the autobiography. The final result was a volume of 650 pages of text that, as noted earlier, simply ended abruptly with the creation of the ECS.

Reaction to Conant's autobiography was not positive. Theodore Hesburgh, president of Notre Dame, read the galleys for the publisher. He recounted to a Carnegie Corporation official his largely negative views. He stated that to him the book was "dull" but added that his liking for Conant influenced him to pull his punches in responding to the galleys.[48] The reviews of the published autobiography were largely akin to Hesburgh's analysis. One example, published in a journal of the American Educational Research Association, hit hard at Conant for a lack of intellectual depth in the analysis, for being pragmatic and functional in all of the work, and for ignoring theoretical or, more accurately to the reviewer, ideological concerns that might deepen the issues addressed. For example, the review criticized Conant's view of class as basically hereditary, thereby enhancing the possibility of treating class as an issue of social mobility, as Conant did at Harvard and advocated in his many writings on education. Class as a more than hereditary concept would have involved Conant much more directly in issues such as class maintenance and class conflict, rather than seeing the issue simply as one of increasing individual mobility.[49] The theoretical issues raised in this review were different from, but analogous to, the methodological issues raised in the review noted above of *Shaping Educational Policy*. Conant's work was unsatisfactory to academic critics because it ignored methodological and theoretical concerns at the expense of trying to arouse popular interest and shape policy and practice.

Conant, however, largely failed even to reach a wide audience in his autobiography. The review in the *New York Times* was as negative as that in the scholarly journal. It was entitled "Good Man, Dull Book." The reviewer referred to the volume as a "swamp of an autobiography" and contrasted the liveliness and significance of Conant's life with the tedium of the account of it in the book. The important issues addressed in the life, such as standardized testing, general education, or educational equality, were not addressed in any convincing way in the autobiography. Rather, Conant chose to report his life, like an "obituary writer," in lieu of examining it. The result was dreary and disappointing to the reviewer, something that in no way satisfied the reader. The reviewer ended by noting that he was still fascinated by the life that Conant led, but severely disappointed by the book he wrote about it.[50] Thus, Conant, by failing to overcome his own reticence to let readers inside the reasons for his thoughts and actions, failed on his final effort to reach the popular audience that he had sought in his educational writings since the 1950s.

Conclusion

What may be said in an evaluation of Conant's educational statesmanship from the late 1950s to the end of his published writings in the early 1970s? Two views constitute the ends of a continuum on which to find that evaluation. The first is that of John W. Gardner, president of the Carnegie Corporation during most of the years in which Conant did this work. Gardner, writing early in 1965, was highly complementary of Conant. He began by noting that Conant's book on the high school, published in 1959, had by 1965 seen 450,000 copies produced. Particularly important in that effort, according to Gardner, were the recommendations for ability grouping, programs for the academically talented, programs for slow readers, and standards for school counseling. Gardner also praised Conant's book on urban education, *Slums and Suburbs*, arguing that it was the first book to bring national attention to urban school problems. He then praised Conant's more recent books on teacher education and on educational policy, although noting that their long-term influence had yet to be determined. Gardner commended Conant for, though being a gentle critic

Educational Statesmanship and Its Discontents, 1955–71　　　183

of professional educators, also being one who was able to "shake professional complacency." Similarly, though not as radical in tone as many, if not even most, educational critics, Conant had "stimulated more widespread change than have any of the radicals." Gardner concluded his evaluation by noting the vastness and complexity of the American educational enterprise. Conant's strength as a critic lay in his knowledge of the whole enterprise, allowing him to be more than the fragmentary critic that made a large splash in one or another aspect of education but had little lasting effect. For Gardner, Conant knew both the grass roots of practice and the loftiness of policy, the organizational problems and the intellectual issues, and the comparative international dimensions of all of these facets. For Gardner, Conant was the convincing critic, able to see the whole enterprise and the place of his recommendations in that enterprise. Gardner ended by noting of Conant that his "performance as independent appraiser of American education is a remarkable capstone to a great public career."[51]

A competing view of Conant was not too hard to find. He had many critics, particularly in the world of professional educators. A rather profound criticism, though from within the broad ranks of the professional education community, was not by someone directly in the line of Conant's criticisms. A noted analytic philosopher of education made Conant the lead chapter in his analysis of five leading writers in the field of educational policy in 1968. He was not kind to Conant in his treatment of his works. He claimed that Conant's total work in education and educational policy, since the 1950s, was characterized "by the absence of clear logical argument," lapses and inconsistencies in "the factual information" offered in his analyses, and "contradictions between the high, universal values he espouses and the narrow, parochial values which his policies actually serve." In support of this thesis, the author offered an extremely close reading of Conant's books on educational policy and on teacher education. The analysis is too dense to repeat here, but it did seem to expose Conant as a less than systematic thinker and a casual user of data in support of his various arguments. The author considered how, if Conant's work was so flawed, to explain its considerable influence. That explanation was twofold: First, Conant had been in the national eye since the 1930s when he became the president of Harvard University, and second, Conant's views, though theoretically undernourished and factually not well substantiated, rang true with a kind of conventional wisdom about educational issues and a continuation of an educational status quo with minimal change.[52]

Conant's voice then had a power far beyond any ability to think deeply or look systematically at American education. His power related to his influence on both sides of the disciplinary divide in American education, the subject matter specialists and the professional educational community, and his vision of a democratic society and the schooling it deserved. The vision, however, was so flawed that it allowed a utopian end to cloud the undemocratic means, such as standardized testing and ability grouping, that were seen as a part of its accomplishment. So, though Conant's views often sounded "sane and sensible," they were "unlike anything real or serious."[53]

One is hard-pressed to adjudicate between the lavish praise of John Gardner and the total condemnation of an analytic philosopher. It, of course, is easy to say that they were talking past each other. It was also the case, however, that they were dealing in different conceptual universes. Gardner saw a world of educational institutions in search of better operating policies and practices. The philosopher saw a world of educational analysis and policy prescription that cried out for rigorous solutions appropriate to the circumstances of 1960s America, a world awash in conflict and confusion.

One other point may be offered in critique of Gardner and his praise of Conant. The Carnegie Corporation spent an enormous amount of money in support of the educational writing of James Conant from 1957 until 1968. In that latter year, an internal accounting noted that $1.1 million of Carnegie funds had been expended up to that time. Under consideration was an additional amount of at least $15,000 and potentially more to carry Conant through the completion of what eventually became his autobiography. Difficulties in completing that work were noted, with strategies such as further use of graduate assistants suggested to help it to completion. It was hard for the lead official of a philanthropic organization who had spent an enormous amount of money in support of someone, who had known that someone for thirty years and directed substantial funding to that someone and to his institutions over those years, and who had encouraged that individual at every stage of his work, to be anything but supportive about the work.[54]

The critique of Conant by the philosopher of education can also be itself critiqued. The work in which Conant was studied featured chapters on four other analysts of American education. None of them came out much better evaluated than did Conant. The rigors of analytic philosophy found all subjects, including Conant, to have failed in their analyses, arguments, and prescriptions. One is moved to suggest that analytic philosophy is such a rigorous discipline that it may have found itself unable to really judge anyone other than other analytic philosophers as adequate. The rigors of the field are such that those outside of it can hardly measure up to the criteria of its own practitioners. And

Educational Statesmanship and Its Discontents, 1955–71   185

we have seen a similar disconnect between Conant the educational advocate and the educational researchers who had found his work wanting in social scientific rigor.

The extremes of a uniformly positive and a totally negative evaluation of Conant then, are not especially helpful. We may place his work firmly between these two extremes, in a world of public advocacy rather than one of rigorous scholarship and analysis. But even here, as seen in the dissertations on the Conant report on the high school, he seems not to have accomplished all that much. Yet it must be said that James B. Conant was perhaps the leading analyst of American education in the 1950s and 1960s, as judged by things such as notoriety, acceptance by professional educators and leading lay publications, and publication records. Further, he was responsible to a great extent for the creation of the ECS. And even further, he can be said to be have been largely responsible for the creation of the ETS, another body that continues to exert great influence in American educational circles. Yet ECS and ETS were, and are, both subject to criticism. The former in that it is only one body among several that seeks to bridge the gap between the reality of a locally and state-based educational system and the educational needs of a nation. The latter in that it still seems to want a world in which its standardized tests are dominant in a political climate that sees those tests not as expanding, but as severely limiting, educational opportunity and social mobility.

Conant, then, was a powerful, but flawed, educational statesman in the 1950s and 1960s. By the time of his death in 1978, however, his ideas had become even more contested than they were when they were proffered. Let us return, then, in the last chapter, to a final consideration of his Harvard presidency and its relation to his educational statesmanship after that presidency.

Notes

1 Record of interview James Bryant Conant (April 30, 1954), Carnegie Corporation Papers, Series IIIA, Box 121, Folder 2.

2 Conant, *My Several Lives*, pp. 613–16.

3 Carnegie Corporation, Record of Interview, National Education Association, James B. Conant (10/17/55). Carnegie Corporation Papers, Series IIIA, Box 250, Folder 4. The three-headed support system, while potentially cumbersome, was powerful enough politically and economically to give Conant a secure base from which to do his work. It was certainly a formidable trio and unlike almost anything ever encountered since then in educational research.

4 Confidential Memorandum Prepared by James B. Conant for Mr. John Gardner, President of the Carnegie Corporation, Subject: Proposed Study of Certain Problems Connected with the American Comprehensive High School (December 21, 1956); Carnegie Corporation Papers, Series IIIA, Box 563, Folder 7.

5 Ibid.

6 Ibid.

7 Educational Testing Service, Critique of the Conant Proposal (January 23, 1957), Carnegie Corporation Papers, Series IIIA, Box 563, Folder 7.

8 See the discussion of Conant and history of science in Chapter 4.

9 James B. Conant, *The American High School Today: A Report to Interested Citizens* (New York: McGraw-Hill, 1959), p. 23.

10 Ibid., p. 22.

11 Ibid., p. 40.

12 Arthur Bestor, *Educational Wastelands: The Retreat from Learning in Our Public Schools* (Urbana: University of Illinois Press, 1953); and Hyman G, Rickover, *Education and Freedom* (New York: Dutton, 1959). A few years later, Rickover continued his assault on the public schools in *American Education, A National Failure; The Problem of Our Schools and What We Can Learn from England* (New York: Dutton, 1963).

13 See Wayne J. Urban, *More Than Science and Sputnik: The National Defense Education Act of 1958* (Tuscaloosa, AL: University of Alabama Press, 2011).

14 Conant, *American High School Today*, pp. 41–70; quotation, p. 58. Of the twenty-one recommendations, by far the longest (six out of a total of twenty-nine pages) was devoted to the academically talented, another was devoted to the highly gifted, and the ability grouping and several subject matter recommendations spent considerable time identifying and prescribing for the talented.

15 Conant, *American High School Today*, pp. 52–56, 67–68, 74–76.

16 Ibid., pp. 132–33.

17 Robert Hampel, "The American High School Today: James Bryant Conant's Reservations and Reconsiderations," *Phi Delta Kappan* 64 (May 1983): 607–12; especially p. 610.

18 James B. Conant, *Slums and Suburbs: A Commentary on Schools in Metropolitan Areas* (New York: McGraw-Hill, 1961).

19 For example, see Robert Havighurst, "Conant on Problems of Slums and Suburbs," *Phi Delta Kappan* 43 (January 1962): 173–75.

20 Some thought that the term "social dynamite" was extremely novel and worthy of attention. Readers of this manuscript, however, should recall that he used the term as early as the mid-1940s. See Chapter 3, note 62.

21 As quoted in Conant, *My Several Lives*, p. 622.

22 Ibid., p. 623.

Educational Statesmanship and Its Discontents, 1955–71   187

23 Confidential Supplement to J. B. Conant's The American High School Today: A First Report to Interested Citizens (January 12, 1959), Carnegie Corporation Papers, Series IIIA, Box 563, Folder 8; quotations, pp. 5, 7.

24 James B. Conant to John Gardner, Confidential Memorandum: The Possible Study of Teacher Education (October 26, 1960), Carnegie Corporation Papers, Series IIIA, Box 567, Folder 7.

25 Conant, *The Education of American Teachers*.

26 Teacher Certification (September 18, 1963), Carnegie Corporation Papers, Series IIIA, Box 567, Folder 3.

27 Ibid.

28 Fred M. Hechinger, Dr. Conant's Educational Bombshell, *New York Times* (September 26, 1963).

29 Conant, *My Several Lives*, p. 626.

30 James B. Conant, *The Citadel of Learning* (np: Yale University Press, 1956); Conant, *Recommendations for Education in the Junior High School Years: A Memorandum to School Boards* (Princeton: Educational Testing Service, 1960); and Conant, *Thomas Jefferson and the Development of American Public Education* (Berkeley: University of California Press, 1962).

31 John Holliister to Margaret Mahoney (October 7, 1963), Carnegie Corporation Papers, Series IIIA, Box 564, Folder 2.

32 A. Harry Passow, *American Secondary Education: The Conant Influence* (Reston, VA: National Association of Secondary School Principals, 1977), p. 50.

33 Barry James Teicher, "James Bryant Conant and the *American High School Today*" (PhD Dissertation, University of Wisconsin, Madison, 1977); quotation, p. 276.

34 James B. Conant to Commissioner Francis Keppel (September 21, 1964), Carnegie Corporation Papers, Series IIIA, Box 522, Folder 3.

35 James B. Conant, *Shaping Educational Policy* (New York: McGraw-Hill, 1964).

36 Conant criticizes the educational establishment and makes specific reference to the NEA and its influence in *The Education of American Teachers*, p. 15.

37 Conant summarized his book in an address to state government leaders. See Conant, Shaping Educational Policy: An Address before the Council of State Governments (December 2, 1964), Carnegie Corporation Papers, IIIA, Box 564, Folder 1.

38 Article Ten of the Constitution excluded from the federal government concerns that were not specified in the Constitution. This meant that constitutionally, education was a state, not a federal, government concern.

39 Richard Wynn, "An Inept Lesson in Educational Policy Making," *Phi Delta Kappan* 46 (February, 1965): 251–56.

40 Ibid., p. 255.

41 John W. Gardner, The Conant Studies of American Education (January 5, 1965), Carnegie Corporation Papers, Series IIIA, Box 564, Folder 1.

42 Conant, *My Several Lives,* pp. 648–49.

43 https://www/ecs.org/research-reports/issues.

44 Tennessee Gov. Bill Haslam to Receive the 2018 Education Commission of the States James Bryant Conant Award (May 22, 1918).

45 Conant, *My Several Lives,* p. 649.

46 See Carnegie Corporation Memorandum EAD (E. Alden Dunham) to AP, LM, FA, JWC (April 18, 1967), Carnegie Corporation Papers, Series IIICA, Box 564, Folder 1.

47 James B. Conant, Notes on Writing an Autobiography (May 22, 1969), Carnegie Corporation Papers. S IIIA, Box 405, Folder 7.

48 Ted Hesburgh to Alan Pifer (March 19, 1970), Carnegie Corporation Papers, Series IIIA, Box 405, Folder 7.

49 Paul H. Mattingly, Review of *My Several Lived: Memoirs of a Social Inventor* (New York: Harper & Row, 1970), *American Educational Research Journal* 8 (March, 1971): 396–401.

50 John Leonard, Good Man, Dull Book, *New York Times* (March 4, 1970).

51 John W. Gardner, The Conant Studies of American Education (January 5, 1965), Carnegie Corporation Papers, Series IIIA, Box 564, Folder 1.

52 James E. McClellan, *Toward an Effective Critique of American Education* (Philadelphia: J. B. Lippincott, 1968), pp. 59–127; quotations, p. 59.

53 Ibid., p. 118.

54 EAD to LM, Memorandum, James B. Conant Discretionary Grant—$15,000 (March 22, 1968), Carnegie Corporation Papers, Series IIIA, Box 405, Folder 7.

7

James Bryant Conant and Educational Statesmanship

To this point, I have largely avoided lengthy consideration of James Bryant Conant as a leader. I have spent four chapters on his presidency of Harvard and a fifth on his educational activities in support of public schools in the 1950s and 1960s. In all of these chapters, I have stressed Conant's wide-ranging intellectual interests, in addition to his competence as a chemist and a university president. It is this intellectual breadth, in large part, that helped him to succeed as a university president. In this final chapter, I want first to reprise the major points of Conant's Harvard presidency and come to some, conclusive evaluative position on that presidency. After that, I will look again at Conant's total educational career including his advocacy of the comprehensive high school and discuss its relationship to his reputation as an educational statesman.

I have argued that a major strength of Conant as president of Harvard was that he had a clear sense of what he wanted to accomplish, a respect for the larger university environment in which he operated that came from his several years on the faculty, and a sense of how that environment might limit what he could accomplish. I traced Conant's actions over two decades of his presidency and found a great deal of continuity in them. Excellence in students and faculty was the touchstone of Conant's presidential program for Harvard from the time he took office. He was largely, though not completely, successful in achieving these goals. He understood, more than many university presidents understand, that achieving things was much easier if a president had his faculty with him, rather than against him. And a major learning experience for Conant was the near rebellion of his faculty over faculty personnel policies in the late 1930s. His decision to apologize to faculty for his actions in a very real sense saved his presidency, allowing him to continue in office for another fifteen years.

Almost as important, and in some tension with his respect for faculty, was Conant's profound ambivalence about academic departments. He understood, as

190 *Scholarly Leadership in Higher Education*

a former department head, the allegiance that faculty had to their departments, especially in terms of their own research and the specialized doctoral programs based to a great extent on that research. He also understood, as an advocate of academic excellence not constrained by disciplinary boundaries, that departments could hinder innovation, frustrate interdisciplinary research, and provide substantial obstacles to revisions in curriculum, especially at the undergraduate level. Conant seemed, in most cases, to leave graduate education to the faculty and departments. He saw undergraduate education, however, as a university responsibility that needed to be considered outside of departmental boundaries. Professional schools represented a kind of academic third force for Conant, another place where interdisciplinary values were important to success. His presidency-long interest in the Graduate School of Education yielded a set of interests and a commitment to follow those interests that would carry him through his life after the presidency.

The Second World War had an enormous impact on Conant the man, on his presidency, and on Harvard. His increasing responsibilities in federal science policy and the war effort took him away from campus. His understanding of the potential negative consequences of absence from campus for him as university president influenced him to give more and more responsibility to Paul Buck, who was dean of the Faculty of Arts and Sciences when Conant began to leave Cambridge for long periods and who was made provost late in the war. Conant was, thus, humble and/or savvy enough to recognize that the institution was not dependent on him for its survival, and that the increasing profile of Paul Buck on campus furthered both Conant's presidency and the realization of the temporality of that, or any, presidency. Having been away for a substantial time during the war, Conant never really returned to the kind of full-time, hands-on, micromanagement style that characterizes many contemporary university presidencies, at least the ones that I have been familiar with in my near fifty years in academe.

The major curricular revision undertaken at Harvard during Conant's presidency was the general education reform sparked by the Harvard Committee on General Education. General education became, as shown in several chapters of this book, an increasingly important concern for Conant, both on and off campus. Though he was absent for most of the committee's deliberations, the compatibility of his and their views is striking. Even more striking was Conant's decision to develop and teach a history of science course in the reformed general education curriculum and to publish his syllabus and other syllabuses that ensued from the reform. This effort both put Harvard in the forefront of an

James Bryant Conant and Educational Statesmanship   191

educational discussion going on across the country and allowed others to see directly exactly what was going on in Cambridge in pursuit of general education reform.

Comparative insight into Conant's presidency emerges if he and it are considered in relation to other presidencies. First of all, Conant stood in relation to his predecessors and successors at Harvard. In that context, one name stood out for Conant. A noted educational historian remarked that for Conant, "any other Harvard president is referred to as 'one of my predecessors, or my successor'; only Charles Eliot is always addressed as Mr. Eliot."[1] Eliot's eminence has been noted by numerous scholars of Harvard's history and of larger American history. For Conant, who was an undergraduate when he first encountered Eliot, Eliot's commitments to scholars and scholarship, to student choice, to education in the secondary school, and to the necessary relationship between Harvard and the nation stood out.[2]

Conant's relationship to his immediate predecessor, Abbott Lawrence Lowell, was more complex. Lowell's reforms of Harvard College—the house system, the tutorials, and concentration and distribution requirements—were accepted, for the most part, by Conant.[3] He remarked that his predecessor's refusal to meddle in campus affairs, particularly at the inception of his presidency, and Lowell's fiscal stewardship were important to his own success. While Conant had more regard for graduate study, and for the professional schools, than did Lowell, Conant came increasingly to share his predecessor's interest in the priority of liberal education at Harvard College. Though Conant extended that interest beyond Harvard, something Lowell was unlikely to entertain, and though Conant's general education reforms drastically changed Lowell's distribution requirements, the devotion of the two men to Harvard College was never in question.

As president, my description of Conant as largely, if not completely successful, is a generally held view. My sense of Conant as a man with a constant and consistent support of excellence in students and faculty at Harvard is one that animates the treatment of Conant by Morton and Phyllis Keller, as well as by Richard N. Smith. Both of these works see Conant as one who pursued his "vision" of student and faculty excellence at Harvard throughout his presidency.[4] Perhaps the leading scholar of Harvard University and its history, Samuel Eliot Morison, also pointed to the greatness of Conant and his presidency. He described Conant's accomplishments as a scientist and as president a "humanist," one who cared about undergraduate and graduate students and worked hard to improve their lives on campus. Morison also credits Conant's off-campus eminence and influence as a testament to his, and Harvard's, greatness.[5]

Interestingly, considering Conant's immediate successor leads to some questions about Conant's complete success as a president. On the one hand, Nathan Pusey was a living example of Conant's commitment to the geographical diversification of Harvard. Born in Iowa, Pusey came to Harvard College a few years prior to Conant's accession to the presidency. Pusey was one of the students from the Midwest whom Conant sought to lure to Harvard through his National Scholarship Program. Other attributes of Pusey, however, were less in keeping with Conant's own commitments. Especially interesting, in light of Conant's longtime suspicion of dogmatic religion and the Harvard Divinity School, was Pusey's background. When chosen, Pusey was president of Lawrence College in Appleton, Wisconsin, a solid liberal arts institution, but one not near Harvard in academic accomplishment. He was neither an author of a book nor had he published significant articles, either in number or in content. Some opponents of Pusey wondered about choosing a president who obviously could not have gotten tenure at Harvard. Pusey had a background in the humanities, studying with famous classicist Irving Babbitt and exhibiting many of the conservative ideas and commitments of his mentor. Forays by journalists into Pusey's background discovered "a family man who went to church twice on Sundays [and] didn't own a television." Further, Pusey had left a "trail of controversy at Lawrence, where . . . [his] religious convictions made him alternately steadfast or obstinate." Pusey's election to the presidency was in tandem with a publicized campaign "to restore religion at Harvard." His election encouraged the campaign and, within days of his election, Pusey had launched a major fund drive for the moribund Divinity School.[6]

Several members of the corporation and the Board of Visitors had clashed with Conant over his indifference, if not animosity, to the Divinity School. And they were now intent on reinstalling it, and Harvard College, as the jewels of the university. Pusey promised that the "queen of theology" would again receive her due in Cambridge. Pusey's critics contrasted his "listless presence" and "nominal participation" in faculty meetings with Conant's vigorous involvement. One professor described Pusey as "an academic ball bearing" with little insight or interest in genuine academic concerns.[7] In short, "Pusey wasn't Conant. The most conspicuous dynamic in the Harvard presidential selection process—get someone unlike his predecessor—had once again kicked into gear." A classicist, not a scientist, Pusey was a "devout and active Episcopalian layman."[8] In short, Pusey was, in many ways, the anti-Conant. And the selection of Pusey, if not a repudiation of Conant, was at the least a comment on the constituencies that Conant had neglected.

James Bryant Conant and Educational Statesmanship   193

Still another perspective on Conant's presidency, and his academic leadership, can be gleaned through a comparison with one of the most noted of his contemporaries, Robert Maynard Hutchins. President of the University of Chicago, an institution that became increasingly competitive with Harvard through the twentieth century, Hutchins differed from Conant in numerous respects. Perhaps the basic difference between the two leaders was the contrast between Conant's tendency to consider and consult with faculty, which was reflected in much of what he tried to do at Harvard, and Hutchins's inclination to go with his own prescriptions and work around or override faculty opposition.[9] This likely was due, at least in part, to Conant's PhD and tenured faculty status at Harvard before ascending to the presidency, contrasted with Hutchins lack of a doctoral degree. Hutchins had a legal education and rose meteorically to the deanship of the Yale Law School. Known as the "boy wonder," Hutchins spent little time in the faculty ranks before his administrative career.

There were also several substantive differences between Conant and Hutchins. Conant, as we have seen, was an advocate of American entry into the Second World War several years before Pearl Harbor and campaigned publicly for American intervention in the late 1930s. Hutchins, on the other hand, was a confirmed isolationist who did not want the nation to become entangled in the swamp of disputes between European powers. Once the United States became formally involved in the war, however, Chicago under Hutchins, like Harvard under Conant, participated vigorously in the war effort. In fact, the atomic bomb project that Conant served in Washington in an administrative capacity was facilitated directly by scientists at Chicago who engineered a nuclear chain reaction in an underground facility below the university's football field.[10] Both presidents, as they enthusiastically embraced the war, also worried about the survival and prosperity of academic and intellectual work on their campuses, during and, especially, after the end of hostilities. Each sought to accommodate the military need for training while also maintaining the opportunity for academic studies unrelated to that training.

A relatively unnoticed difference between the two presidents, and one not easily interpreted as favorable to Conant, was that Hutchins's Chicago embraced intellectual exiles from Nazi Germany far more than did Conant's Harvard. We have seen that Harvard, under Conant, hired only a few refugees from Nazi Germany, and the most prominent of the few were not Jewish. Chicago, on the other hand, hired nearly fifty refugee scholars in the late 1930s and early 1940s, and several of these men were Jewish. Hutchins's Chicago, then, which had experienced significant financial support from Jewish department store magnate

194   *Scholarly Leadership in Higher Education*

Julius Rosenwald in its early years, was less riven by anti-Semitism than was Conant's Harvard.[11]

There is no doubt that Hutchins was a strong leader, but there is considerable doubt about the consequences of his leadership. A recent history of the University of Chicago called Hutchins's presidency "revolutionary" but noted that the revolution came in fits and starts. Hutchins's interventions were "stunning" but accompanied by "tensions with the faculty" and other university constituencies. His successful Great Books reform of undergraduate education was paralleled by a markedly unsuccessful attempt to reduce departmental influence in graduate education. The net result of Hutchins's presidency, according to this account, was that "the University of Chicago was left with the contradictory legacy of a powerful vision of intellectualism and a weakened intellectual framework in which students and faculty could live out that vision."[12]

Conant's PhD in a natural science and his academic eminence as a scientist before his presidency and during it in an entirely different realm, perhaps best characterized as educational policy, meant that he was much less likely to antagonize and confront his faculty than Hutchins. Conant was especially attuned to not participating in, and/or backing away from, battles that he likely could not win. Conant was pragmatic at the same time he was visionary and disciplined his vision by what he thought he would be realistically able to accomplish. For example, the Conant-inspired general education reform at Harvard was an alternative to the more radical, Great Books curriculum that Hutchins and Mortimer Adler installed at Chicago. A major difference in the two was that Conant's general education was the product of a faculty committee on the topic, made up largely of senior professors appointed by the president. Hutchins and Adler were much more assertive in the curriculum reform at Chicago. And they all but mocked the Harvard effort as a pale imitation of a "genuine" reform effort like the Great Books curriculum at Chicago.[13] The Chicago reform was imposed through creation of an undergraduate college that divorced itself from the rest of the university. Creating a faculty for the college that also was separate from the academic departments that dominated the rest of the university reinforced the divide between the president and his allies and the rest of the university.

Moving back to Harvard concerns and issues, Conant's works on science and science education in the general education curriculum were part of his own foray into larger educational concerns, begun earlier in his presidency and continuing long after it. They were also a part of a larger intellectual movement at Harvard and elsewhere analyzed in a recent work on the sciences and social sciences at Harvard from the 1920s through the 1960s. In *Working Knowledge*, Joel Isaac

James Bryant Conant and Educational Statesmanship 195

depicted the development of the "human sciences" at Harvard in these years. Isaac showed how the most creative work in the human sciences at Harvard took place in an "intramural gray zone of marginal professional schools, special seminars, interfaculty discussion groups, and non-professionalized societies and teaching programs." He described these places as "interstitial, underutilized academic spaces" and noted that, within them, "scientific philosophy's identification of epistemology with pedagogy and research practices offered a means of defending the human sciences." Isaac elaborated on both of these points when he noted that in "this 'Harvard Complex'—which consisted in a set of irregular institutional arrangements and the attitudes toward science and knowledge that those institutions fostered—epistemology was embodied by and sustained in practices of pedagogy and inquiry."[14]

Isaac's book is part of a wave of recent work in the "human sciences," a larger category than social sciences that allows for transfer of knowledge and understanding between some of the natural sciences and the social sciences. This is not an inappropriate description of much of what Conant attempted in his own work.[15] Further, as Conant argued in his discussions of history of science, it was in the research activities and pedagogical experiences of Harvard faculty and graduate students that progress was facilitated, rather than in theoretical studies. Conant's affinity for science pedagogy, as exhibited in his cases in the history of science in the general education program, was an exemplar of what Isaac found most stimulating in the Harvard "complex" for philosophy of science. That stimulation came through research and teaching discussions and practices like those discussed in Conant's books on science in the late 1940s and early 1950s. Conant's suspicions of departments and traditional disciplines certainly aided the development of various interdisciplinary and extradisciplinary institutions at Harvard. And his efforts in helping to create the general education program, and his teaching actively and enthusiastically in that program, were particular examples of the larger phenomenon charted by Isaac.

Still, it is the case that some specific parts of Conant's legacy at Harvard did not survive his presidency. For example, his cherished general education courses in science and other studies diminished in significance as the program itself fell under the sway of administrators with commitments far distant from Conant's. In spite of substantial, though not universal, support from faculty, the program atrophied under an unsympathetic administration. The nadir was reached in the 1960s when a physicist who was vice chairman of the general education program resigned his position. He cited as his reason for resigning, a dean, an economist who "had no interest in General Education at all" and who "allowed

196   *Scholarly Leadership in Higher Education*

[it] essentially to go to hell." Faculty supporters managed to save the program but not to prevent it from being largely taken out of the spotlight that it had enjoyed under Conant's administration.[16]

Discussion of general education also turns our attention to Conant as a teacher. He excelled as a teacher with graduate students in chemistry as well as in the general education program. His excellence as a chemist and teacher of chemistry graduate students was readily acknowledged by many of his colleagues. He supervised sixty graduate students in his field while in the chemistry department and most went on to successful careers in academe or industry.[17] One account described Conant as a task master but anything but the "slave driver" that Conant himself claimed to be. He treated students, according to this doctoral student, as coworkers in the scientific enterprise and exhibited an attitude of open-mindedness toward work that might not be in conformity with his own findings. He would ask a student whose work resulted in questions of his own findings, "What are you going to do next?" The attitude and phrase illustrated Conant's expectation "that the student would have good ideas of his own," thereby providing "a constant stimulus" toward "student fulfillment."[18] Another graduate student described Conant as a teacher in most attractive terms: for this young researcher, Conant was "a stimulating teacher of graduate students, having a magnetic attraction for budding chemists." And Conant's treatment of junior colleagues in his field was as respectful as his treatment of graduate students. One young scientist testified to Conant's "extraordinary quality of being able to treat very junior colleagues as equals." He summarized the situation as follows: "It was a stimulating experience for any young scholar to be able to work with or for him: and his genuine kindness and sincere interest in the ideas, research, and career of the young scholars who were associated with him can only be describe as memorable."[19]

Conant was equally, if not more, impressive as a teacher of the history of science, the general education course that he developed and taught for three years during his presidency. His enthusiasm for the subject rubbed off in expected, and unexpected, ways on the graduate students who worked with him in developing and teaching the course. One, a young physicist, noted the opportunity provided by Conant's "shop club" of the post–Second World War years, the meetings of which were devoted mainly to the problems of teaching in general education. This group allowed young teachers of general education to interact with the impressive array of scientists, social scientists, and humanists who participated in general education at Harvard.[20]

James Bryant Conant and Educational Statesmanship 197

Conant had a profound impact on the work of Thomas Kuhn, his first teaching assistant in the general education course in science at Harvard. Kuhn dedicated his landmark volume, *The Structure of Scientific Revolutions*, "To James B. Conant, Who Started It." Kuhn expanded on his relationship with Conant when he noted in the first of three paragraphs of acknowledgments in his preface, "It was James B. Conant, the president of Harvard University, who first introduced me to the history of science and thus initiated the transformation in my conception of the nature of scientific advance." Kuhn added, "Ever since that process began, he has been generous of his ideas, criticisms, and time—including the time required to read and suggest important changes in the draft of my manuscript." The bulk of the preface was given over to discussing particular experiences that fueled Kuhn's ideas, and the first experience he mentioned was a "fortunate involvement with an experimental college course treating physical science for the non-scientist," which "provided my first experience in the history of science."[21]

Kuhn took over Conant's general education history of science course when the president stepped down from teaching it after three years. Kuhn, who was working on his dissertation in theoretical physics at the time he began teaching with Conant, switched his interest from scientific theory to the history of science and to teaching that history of science. It would take fifteen years for that interest to culminate in publication of *The Structure of Scientific Revolutions*, arguably the greatest volume in the history and philosophy of science in the twentieth century. While one should not overemphasize Conant's influence on Kuhn, it is significant enough that Kuhn started his history of science studies working with Conant and continued to work in the history of science, and to think about that work, before publishing his seminal volume on scientific revolutions. Conant's influence here was intellectual and not in any way related to his presidency. Rather, his approach to the history of science helped to yield one of the classic works in the history and philosophy of science in the twentieth century.

All of this is to say that Conant's eminence as a leader in higher education was due, as much, or more, to his intellectual work as to any specific approach he took to the presidency or characteristics he exhibited as president. It is difficult to divorce the president from the intellectual in Conant's Harvard years. And the same difficulty comes in describing Conant's presidency in terms of specific qualities of leadership. For my own analysis, two things are enough to distinguish Conant as an academic leader. The first is just what has been discussed here, his intellectual interests and his ability to act on those interests as a teacher, and write about them as an analyst and commentator.

The second has been alluded to periodically throughout this work. It is Conant's regard for, respect for, and identification with faculty and faculty work. Two examples are offered here to illustrate the affinity of faculty for Conant, one from the sciences and one from the humanities. Conant as president developed a special relationship with the Physics Department. This began with a joint research project he conducted with Percy Bridgman long before becoming president that, according to one department member, resulted in a president who had "a feeling for the work that was being done by at least part of the department." The affinity was reinforced by Conant's participation in faculty recruitment, a process that yielded several excellent appointments in the department. And finally, the president and the physicists cooperated in developing the general education courses in the sciences. In accounting for the reasons for this empathic relationship, one historian of physics and physicists saw the most important factor as the intellectual makeup of the president. To illustrate the primacy of the intellectual commitment of President Conant, the historian discussed the well-known situation on campus that the president was unavailable for any appointments on one day of the week. On that day, according to this source, Conant stayed at home the entire day, not bothering to dress up but choosing to spend the day "on his books and papers and background reading." This account, taken from an interview in the Harvard Physics Department in 1977, argued that the issue was that "the presidents in those days were different."[22] The source of the difference was intellectual interest and intellectual curiosity about the world on the part of a university president who was interested in those facets of academic life and made them a part of his own life.

Another noted Harvard faculty member, Arthur Schlesinger of the History Department, also highlighted Conant's abilities to relate to faculty. Schlesinger was a member of the committee appointed by the faculty to consider the personnel claims of the two teacher unionists with radical political views who were slated for nonrenewal by Conant in the late 1930s. As discussed in Chapter 2, Conant made that faculty committee his own committee to address issues of appointment and renewal at Harvard. Schlesinger, in discussing Conant's actions here, noted, "This evidenced that absence of self-pride—that willingness always to reconsider a decision—which characterized his make-up." He added that this was a rare quality in a university president, claiming specifically that President Lowell was unlikely to have acted in such manner. Schlesinger also recounted an instance of Conant arranging a time to visit with Harvard historians as a part of Winston Churchill's visit to Harvard in the midst of the Second World War.[23]

James Bryant Conant and Educational Statesmanship   199

The point in both cases was Conant's regard for faculty, and particularly, for history faculty, as important members of the university community.

And Schlesinger, a member of the Harvard Committee on General Education, pointed to Conant's leadership in establishing another innovative program, not previously discussed herein, the Nieman Fellowship Program for working journalists. The Nieman program, established under Conant through a gift from the Nieman Foundation, provided support for working journalists to come to Harvard for a year, study what they wanted to study, work with any faculty with whom they shared an interest, and take advantage of whatever university resources they thought would be helpful. This program resembled, in large part, the desire of the president to link practitioners to academics embodied in the early years of the Littauer School and in the move in the Graduate School of Education to work with practicing school administrators, both discussed in Chapter 2. The Nieman program was enormously successful in luring top-flight journalists to come to Harvard for a period of study and reflection. It still is able to do that. Schlesinger credited Conant with the creation of the program, and the historian was one of several faculty who committed themselves to work with the Nieman fellows in whatever ways seemed to serve their interests.[24]

The point of these two reports, one from physicists and one from a noted member of the history faculty, was, and is, that President Conant was an academic leader who made it his business to establish, and to cultivate, productive relations with his faculty. Perhaps contemporary university presidents, burdened with all sorts of heightened responsibilities in all aspects of university life, have little time for such activities. They ignore them, however, at their peril. The importance of respect for the faculty was also noted by two of the speakers at Conant's memorial service, held at Harvard in April of 1978. The classicist John H. Finley and the then president of Harvard, Derek Bok, both alluded to Conant's respect for the faculty as a critical, no the critical, factor in his successful presidency.[25] Finley mentioned the successful resolution of the dispute over the faculty personnel policies achieved through the presidential apology in the late 1930s, while Bok mentioned the promotion and tenure policies eventually approved in the aftermath of the dispute as the ultimate guarantor of the excellence of Harvard University.[26]

Many of the things offered herein to illustrate Conant's success as president were alluded to at that memorial. The National Scholarship Program, the General Education Program, the decisive step taken toward coeducation during the Second World War, and the devotion to the Graduate School of Education and the ensuing embrace of public education were all referred to at the memorial.

The notion of Conant's vision for Harvard as an institution providing service to the nation was also a strong theme in this volume. President Bok alluded to the National Scholarship Program as a particularly strong indication of this commitment. And he added that the innovation in this program was in getting a private institution to recognize and act on a commitment to national service through the selection of its students. This commitment quickly gravitated to most of the other prestigious private college and universities.[27]

In discussing general education, Bok also referred to Conant's fundamental respect for students at Harvard. Bok mentioned that Conant's initial idea of general education was based on a commitment to American history as the fundamental thread. Harvard students, however, wanted required courses in the humanities, sciences, and social science as the core of a new program. Conant was insightful enough to see that his own preference was not likely to be enacted and became a strong enthusiast of the program that emerged from his committee, one that resembled the plan of the students much more than his own initial desires. Bok described this as an example of "just how flexible Mr. Conant could be—and how open to good ideas from any quarter."[28]

The success of President Conant, then, was noted and applauded at the memorial session shortly after his demise. Memorial sessions are not usually a good time for qualifying one's judgment of success. But monographs on a presidency in a series in leadership in higher education have no such restriction. Let me state again the reservations that have accompanied this analysis throughout its production. I have voiced my questions as to Conant's unbridled devotion to standardized tests, his too easy connections with the Carnegie Corporation, his unabashed support of wars, hot and cold, and his tendency to ignore critical reviews of his work as, arguably, chinks in his reputation.

Conant's devotion to meritocracy, particularly as embodied with his continued support of standardized testing, overriding opposition wherever he could and simply ignoring it on most occasions, ignored how individual merit falls victim to the many ways that social and economic privilege can "improve" one's merit. The expensive "tutorial" programs for tests like the Scholastic Aptitude Test (SAT), the Graduate Record Examination (GRE), the Law School Admissions Test, and other standardized measures of academic aptitude and achievement are but one way that the wealthy and privileged seek to maintain their advantages in their children. In April and May of 2019, when this manuscript was being completed, a number of criminal indictments of various prominent individuals, including two noted actresses, occurred for illicit actions taken in support of gaining admission for their offspring to various private universities. The particulars have ranged from outright bribes of university admissions officers to payment to alter actual test scores to bogus athletic qualifications. The ingenuity of the American middle and upper middle classes seems unbounded. One wonders how Conant would have reacted to this situation.

Another place where merit might have had its limits in Conant's world was in his cozy, I don't know of a better descriptive word, relationship with the Carnegie Corporation. From his early cultivation of Frederick Keppel, corporation president, through his nomination of Keppel's son to the deanship of the Harvard Graduate School of Education, through the *carte blanch* that Conant was given to underwrite his studies of American education, one is hard pressed to see the relationship between the amount of the support given and the objective accomplishment of the individual who was supported. Conant's service to his nation was also a bit of a two-edged sword. There is no doubt of his commitments to democracy in the United States as well as his pursuit of what he saw as the best ways to advance that value. Yet he seemed dismissive of the ways that his commitments might be seen as politically partisan, especially by those who opposed what he advocated, groups such as those on the political left or the members of the Roman Catholic Church. And this mention of political opponents leads to my final reservation about Conant, his tendency to simply ignore critics, rather than respond to them. It seems to me that this indicates a sort of arrogance in Conant the scholar or intellectual, very much in tension with, if not in opposition to, his respect for intellectual excellence as well as for faculty opinions.

This last point brings us back to a consideration of Conant's writings in relation to public education at the end of his career. It was in this arena that his failure to respond to criticism was most frequent and also a factor in accounting for his failure to see many of his priorities put into practice. Still, as noted in Chapter 6, he was in large part responsible for the creation of the Education Commission of the States (ECS), an organization that remains powerful today in devising and implementing educational policy and practice. And an additional way to interpret Conant's educational advocacy at the end of his career is to note what the *New York Times* pointed out at the time of his death: "There is not now at any major university a leader concerned with the whole of American education."[29] That statement seems as true in 2019 as it was when it was written in 1978. And its truth stands as an indictment of leadership in American higher education in this age and, at the least, an encouragement to leaders to take up the cause of American democratic education, if not necessarily in the particular ways that cause was advocated by James Bryant Conant.

Notes

1 Merle Borrowman, "Conant the Man," *Saturday Review* (September 21, 1963): 58–60, quotation, p. 58.

2 On Eliot, see, among many others, Hugh Hawkins, *Between Harvard and America: The Educational Leadership of Charles W. Eliot* (New York: Oxford University Press, 1972).

3 Chapter 2 showed how the Chemistry Department, with Conant as chair, refused to hire tutors for Harvard College students.

4 Keller and Keller, *Making Harvard Modern*; and Smith, *The Harvard Century*.

5 Samuel Eliot Morison, "The Harvard Presidency," *New England Quarterly* 31 (December, 1958): 435–46.

6 Smith, *The Harvard Century*, pp. 200, 202.

7 Ibid., pp. 188, 202.

8 Keller and Keller, *Making Harvard Modern*, p. 175.

9 On Hutchins, I rely on Mary Ann Dzuback, *Robert M. Hutchins: Portrait of an Educator* (Chicago: University of Chicago Press, 1991), and more recently, John W. Boyer, *The University of Chicago: A History* (Chicago: University of Chicago Press, 2015), pp. 215–320.

10 Boyer, *The University of Chicago*, p. 301.

11 This is not to say that there was no anti-Semitism at Chicago, however. For trustee opposition to the hiring of Edward Levi as the university's first provost in 1950 because of his Jewish background, see Boyer, *The University of Chicago*, p. 359.

12 Ibid., p. 320.

13 Kridel, "Student Participation in General Education Reform," pp. 154–64.

14 Joel Isaac, *Working Knowledge: Making the Human Sciences from Parsons to Kuhn* (Cambridge, MA: Harvard University Press, 2014), p. 6.

15 Dorothy Ross, "Getting over It: From the Social Sciences to the Human Sciences," *Modern Intellectual History* 11 (April, 2014): 191–209.

16 Oral History Transcript, Dr. Gerald Holton (January 11, 1977), Center for the History of Physics at the American Institute of Physics: http://www.aip.org/history/ohilist/31279.html.

17 *James Bryant Conant: A Remembrance* (Cambridge: Harvard University, 1978).

18 Paul D. Bartlett, *James Bryant Conant, 1893-1978: A Biographical Memoir* (Washington, DC: National Academy of Sciences, 1983), pp. 91–124; quotation p. 106. For other evidence of Conant's academic achievement as a chemical researcher and teacher, see G. B. Kistiakowsky and B. F. Westheimer, James Bryant Conant, 26 March 1893–11 February, 1978, *Biographical Memoirs of Fellows of the Royal Society* 25 (November, 1979): 208–32.

19 I. B. Cohen, "James Bryant Conant," *Proceedings of the Massachusetts Historical Society* 90 (1978): 122–30; quotation pp. 123, 130.

20 Holton, *Thematic Origins of Scientific Thought*, p. 42.

21 Thomas Kuhn, *The Structure of Scientific Revolutions* (Chicago: University of Chicago Press, 1970), pp. v, xiii, vii.

22 Oral History Transcript, Dr. Gerald Holton (January 11, 1977), p. 7.

23 Arthur M. Schlesinger, *In Retrospect: The History of a Historian* (New York: Harcourt, Brace & World, Inc. 1983), pp. 95, 143.

24 Ibid., p. 98.

25 *James Bryant Conant: A Remembrance.*

26 Ibid., pp. 6, 29.

27 Ibid., p. 25.

28 Ibid., p. 26.

29 As quoted in Smith, *The Harvard Century*, p. 192.

Bibliography

Primary Sources

There are two major primary source collections relevant to this work. The first is the James Bryant Conant Presidential Papers, housed in the Archives in Widener Library at Harvard University. The second collection is the Carnegie Corporation Papers, housed in the Buller Library on the campus of Columbia University. Additionally, Conant produced an autobiography that stands as a source for much of this work. See Janes B. Conant, *My Several Lives: Memoirs of a Social Inventor* (New York: Harper and Row, 1970). Finally, Conant produced an annual report for each year of his presidency. These reports, full of presidential opinions as well as institutional information, were published and are available electronically or through the Archives at the Harvard University Library. The ones I used in this manuscript are cited immediately below.

Conant, James Bryant. "President's Report for 1932-33," *Official Register of Harvard University* 31 (February 5, 1934): 5–20.

Conant, James Bryant. "President's Report for 1934-35," *Official Register of Harvard University* 33 (February 29, 1936): 5–32.

Conant, James Bryant. "President's Report for 1935-36," *Official Register of Harvard University* 34 (March 22, 1937): 5–28.

Conant, James Bryant. "President's Report for 1936-37," *Official Register of Harvard University* 35 (February 28, 1938): 5–36.

Conant, James Bryant. "President's Report for 1937-38," *Official Register of Harvard University* 36 (February 28, 1939): 5–33.

Conant, James Bryant. "President's Report for 1938-39," *Official Register of Harvard University* 37 (March 30, 1940): 5–39.

Conant, James Bryant. "President's Report for 1939-40," *Official Register of Harvard University* 38 (April 10, 1941): 5–38.

Conant, James Bryant. "President's Report for 1940-41," *Official Register of Harvard University* 39 (February 25, 1942): 5–36.

Conant, James Bryant. "President's Report for 1941-42," *Official Register of Harvard University* 41 (September 26, 1944): 5–34.

Conant, James Bryant. "President's Report for 1942-43," *Official Register of Harvard University* 41 (September 28, 1944): 5–26.

Conant, James Bryant, "President's Report for 1943-44," *Official Register of Harvard University* 44 (July 7, 1947): 5–23.

Conant, James Bryant, "President's Report for 1944-45," *Official Register of Harvard University* 45 (December 1, 1948): 5–26.

206   *Bibliography*

Conant, James Bryant. "President's Report for 1945-46," *Official Register of Harvard University* 45 (May 20, 1948): 5–31.

Conant, James Bryant. "President's Report for 1946-47," *Official Register of Harvard University* 46 (December 1, 1949): 5–30.

Conant, James Bryant. "President's Report for 1947-48," *Official Register of Harvard University* 47 (May 16, 1950): 5–32.

Conant, James Bryant, "President's Report for 1948-49," *Official Register of Harvard University* 49 (April 30, 1952): 5–33.

Conant, James Bryant. "President's Report for 1949-50," *Official Register of Harvard University* 51 (April 2, 1954): 5–30.

Conant, James Bryant. "President's Report for 1950-51," *Official Register of Harvard University* 51 (April 20, 1954): 5–37.

Conant, James Bryant. "President's Report for 1951-52," *Official Register of Harvard University* 51 (August 27, 1954): 5–58.

Books, Dissertations, and Reports

Bestor, Arthur. *Educational Wastelands: The Retreat from Learning in Our Public Schools* (Urbana, IL: University of Illinois Press, 1953).

Biebel, Charles D. Politics, Pedagogues, and the Public Schools (Ph. D. Dissertation, University of Wisconsin, 1971).

Boyer, John. *The University of Chicago: A History* (Chicago: University of Chicago Press, 2015).

Buck, Paul H. *The Road to Reunion: 1865-1900* (Boston: Little Brown and Company, 1937).

Committee on the Objectives of General Education in a Free Society, *General Education in a Free Society* (Cambridge: Harvard University Press, 1945).

Conant, James B. *On Understanding Science* (New Haven: Yale University Press, 1947).

Conant, James Bryant. *Education in a Divided World* (Cambridge: Harvard University Press, 1948).

Conant, James Bryant. *The Growth of the Experimental Sciences: An Experiment in General Education: Progress Report on the Use of the Case Method in the Teaching of the Principles of the Tactics and Strategy of Science* (Cambridge: Harvard University Press, 1949).

Conant, James Bryant. *Harvard Case Histories in Experimental Science* (Cambridge: Harvard University Press, 1950).

Conant, James B. *Science and Common Sense* (New Haven: Yale University Press, 1951).

Conant, James B. *Modern Science and Modern Man* (New York: Columbia University Press, 1952).

Conant, James B. *The Citadel of Learning* (np: Yale University Press, 1956).

Bibliography 207

Conant, James Bryant., general ed., and others, *Harvard Case Histories in Experimental Science* (Cambridge: Harvard University Press, 1957).

Conant, James B. *The American High School Today* (New York: McGraw-Hill, 1959).

Conant, James B. *Recommendations for Education in the Junior High School Years: A Memorandum to School Boards* (Princeton: Educational Testing Service, 1960).

Conant, James B. *Thomas Jefferson and the Development of American Public Education* (Berkeley: University of California Press, 1962).

Conant, James B. *Shaping Educational Policy* (New York: McGraw-Hill, 1964).

Conant, James Bryant. *The Education of American Teachers* (New York: McGraw-Hill, 1963).

Conant, James B. and Francis Spaulding, eds., *Education for a Classless Society* (Cambridge: Harvard University Graduate School of Education, 1940).

Conant, Jennett. *Tuxedo Park: A Wall Street Tycoon and the Secret Palace of Science That Changed the Course of World War II* (New York: Simon and Schuster, 2002).

Conant, Jennett. *109 East Palace: Robert Oppenheimer and the Secret City of Los Alamos* (New York: Simon and Schuster, 2005).

Conant, Jennett. *Man of the Hour: James B. Conant: Warrior Scientist* (New York: Simon and Schuster, 2017).

Diamond, Sigmund. *Compromised Campus: The Collaboration of the Universities with the Intelligence Community* (New York: Oxford University Press, 1992).

Dzuback, Mary Ann. *Robert M. Hutchins: Portrait of an Educator* (Chicago: University of Chicago Press, 1991).

Educational Policies Commission [of the National Education Association]. *The CCC the NYA and the Public Schools* (Washington, DC: National Education Association, 1941).

Educational Policies Commission [of the National Education Association]. *Education for All American Youth* (Washington, DC: National Education Association, 1944).

Gruber, Carol S. *Mars and Minerva: World War I and the Uses of the Higher Learning in America* (Baton Rouge, LA: Louisiana State University Press, 1976).

Hawkins, Hugh. *Between Harvard and America: The Educational Leadership of Charles W. Eliot* (New York: Oxford University Press, 1972).

Holton, Gerald. *Thematic Origins of Scientific Thought* (Cambridge: Harvard University Press, 1973).

Isaac, Joel. *Working Knowledge: Making the Human Sciences from Parsons to Kuhn* (Cambridge: Harvard University Press, 2014).

Karabel, Jerome. *The Chosen: The Hidden History of Discrimination and Admissions at Harvard, Yale, and Princeton* (New York: Houghton Mifflin, 2005).

Keller, Morton and Phyllis Keller. *Making Harvard Modern: The Rise of America's University* (New York: Oxford University Press, 2007).

Krug, Edward A. *The Shaping of the American High School, 1890-1920* (New York: Harper & Row, 1961).

Kuhn, Thomas. *The Structure of Scientific Revolutions* (Chicago: University of Chicago Press, 1970).

208   *Bibliography*

Lemann, Nicholas. *The Big Test: The Secret History of the American Meritocracy* (New York: Farrar Strauss, and Giroux, 1999).

Lipset, Seymour Martin and David Riesman. *Education and Politics at Harvard: Two Essays Prepared for the Carnegie Commission on Higher Education* (New York: McGraw-Hill, 1975).

McClellan, James E. *Toward an Effective Critique of American Education* (Philadelphia: J. B. Lippincott, 1968).

National Education Association, Committee on the Reorganization of Secondary Education. *The Cardinal Principles of Secondary Education* (Washington, DC: Government Printing Office, 1918).

Passow, A. Harry. *American Secondary Education: The Conant Influence* (Reston, VA: National Association of Secondary School Principals, 1977).

Powell, Arthur G. *The Uncertain Profession: Harvard and the Search for Educational Authority* (Cambridge: Harvard University Press, 1980).

Rickover, Hyman G. *Education and Freedom* (New York: Dutton, 1959).

Rickover, Hyman G. *American Education, A National Failure: The Problem of Our Schools and What We Can Learn from England* (New York: Dutton, 1963).

Schlesinger, Arthur M. *In Retrospect: The History of a Historian* (New York: Harcourt, Brace & World, Inc., 1983).

Schrecker, Ellen. *No Ivory Tower: McCarthyism and the Universities* (New York: Oxford University Press, 1986).

Smith, Richard Norton. *The Harvard Century: The Making of a University to a Nation* (New York: Simon and Schuster, 1986).

Synnott, Marcia Graham. *The Half-Opened Door: Discrimination and Admissions at Harvard, Yale, and Princeton, 1900-1930* (Westport, CT: Greenwood Press, 1974).

Teicher, Barry James. James Bryant Conant and The American High School Today (Ph. D. Dissertation, University of Wisconsin, 1977).

Urban Wayne and Jennings Wagoner, Jr. *American Education: A History* (New York: Routledge, 2014).

Warner, W. Lloyd, Robert Havighurst, and Martin B. Loeb, *Who Shall be Educated: The Challenge of Unequal Opportunity* (New York: Harper and Brothers, 1944).

Wechsler, Harold. *The Qualified Student: A History of Selective College Admissions in America* (New York: John Wiley, 1977).

White, Theodore H. *In Search of History: A Personal Adventure* (New York: Harper & Row, 1978).

Articles, Chapters, and Reviews

Barber, Bernard. Review of *Science and Common Sense, American Sociological Review* 16 (October, 1951): 735–36.

Bibliography 209

Boring, Edwin G. Review of *Modern Science and Modern Man, American Journal of Psychology* 67 (March 1954): 192–94.

Borrowman, Merle. "Conant the Man," *Saturday Review* 46 (September 21, 1963): 58–60.

Bush, Vannevar. "James Bryant Conant: President of the AAAS for 1946," *Scientific Monthly* 67. (March 1946): 197–200.

Cohen, I. B. "James Bryant Conant," *Proceedings of the Massachusetts Historical Society* 90 (1978): 122–30.

Cohen, I. Bernard. "George Sarton," *Isis* 48 (September 1957): 286–300.

Conant, James B. "Function of the School and College in Educating for Social and Cultural Leadership," *Bulletin of the American Association of University Professors* 21 (April 1935): 329–31.

Conant, James B. The Future of Our Higher Education System," *Harper's Magazine* 178 (May 1938): 561–70.

Conant, James B. "Education for a Classless Society," *Atlantic Monthly* 146 (May 1940): 593–602.

Conant, James B. "How Can a Democratic Nation Fight a War and Still Stay Free," *School and Society* 54 (October 18, 1941): 313–15.

Conant, James B. "A Truce among Educators," *NASSP Bulletin* [National Association of Secondary School Principals] (January 1945): 1–8.

Conant, James Bryant. "Public Education and the Structure of American Society," *Teachers College Record* 47 (December 1947): 145–92.

Conant, James B. "Our College System: A Re-evaluation," *New York Times* (June 4, 1950).

Conant, James B. "Academic independence," *Bulletin of the American Association of University Professors* (Winter 1952–53): 517–19.

Conant, James B. "George Sarton and Harvard University," *Isis* 48 (September 1957): 301–305.

Conant, James B. "Unity and Diversity in American Secondary Education," in *My Several Lives: Memoirs of a Social Inventor* (New York: Harper and Row, 1970): 665–70.

Conant, James Bryant. "An Autobiographical Fragment," in Robert J. Havighurst ed., *Leaders in Education*, The Seventieth Yearbook of the National Society for Studies in Education, Part II (Chicago: University of Chicago Press, 1971).

Cutter, George B. "A Book to Be Studied," *Journal of Higher Education* 17 (February 1946): 109–10.

Hampel, Robert. "The American High School Today: James Bryant Conant's Reservations and Recommendations," *Phi Delta Kappan* 64 (May 1983): 607–12.

Havighurst, Robert. "Conant on Problems of Slums and Suburbs," *Phi Delta Kappan* 43 (January 1962): 173–75.

Hechingher, Fred M. "Dr. Conant's Educational Bombshell," *New York Times* (September 26, 1963).

Kistiakowsky, G. B. and B. F. Westheimer. "James Bryant Conant, 26 March 1893 – 11 February 1978," *Biographical Memoirs of Fellows of the Royal Society* 25 (November 1979): 208–32.

Kridel, Craig. "Student Participation in General Education Reform," *Journal of General Education* 35 (1983): 154–64.

Leonard, John. "Good Man, Dull Book," *New York Times* (March 4, 1970).

Mattingly, Paul H. Review of *My Several Lives: Memoirs of a Social Inventor*, *American Educational Research Journal* 8 (March 1971): 396–401.

Mones, Leon. "Harvard Report: A Socially Important Education?" *The Clearing House* 20 (January 1946): 262–66.0; 364–66.

Morison, Samuel Eliot. "The Harvard Presidency," *New England Quarterly* 31 (December 1958).

Oppenheimer, Jane. Review of *Science and Common Sense*, *Quarterly Review of Biology* 26 (December 1951).

Pei, Mario A. "Some Reflections on the Harvard Report," *The French Review* 19 (January 1946): 168–73.

Proctor, Virginia. "Bibliography of James B. Conant," *Journal of General Education* (October 1950): 48–56.

R.L.A. Review of *Harvard Case Histories in Experimental Science*, *Philosophy of Science* 20 (October 1953).

Ross, Dorothy. "Getting over It: From the Social Sciences to the Human Sciences," *Modern intellectual History* 11 (April 2014): 191–209.

Tead, Ordway. Review of *Science and Common Sense*, *Journal of Higher Education* 22 (November 1951): 453–54.

Urban, Wayne J. "The Educational Policies Commission, 1936-1968: Notes Toward an Autopsy," *The Sophist's Bane* 3 (Fall 2005): 15–30.

Urban, Wayne J. "Social Reconstructionism and Educational Policy: The Educational Policies Commission, 1936-1941," in Karen Riley ed., *Social Reconstructionism: People, Politics, Perspectives* (Charlotte, NC: Information Age Publishing, 2006).

Urban, W. J. "Education for all American Youth: A Failed Attempt to Extend the Comprehensive High School," in B. M. Franklin and G. McCulloch eds., *The Death of the Comprehensive High School: Historical, Contemporary, Comparative Perspectives* (New York: Palgrave Macmillan, 2007).

Urban, Wayne J. "James Bryant Conant and Equality of Opportunity," *Paedagogica Historica* 46 (February–April 2010): 193–205.

Urban, Wayne J. and Marybeth Smith. "Much Ado about Something: James Bryant Conant, Harvard University, and Nazi Germany in the 1930s," *Paedagogica Historica* 51 (February–April 2015): 152–65.

Wynn, Richard, "An Inept Lesson in Educational Policy Making," *Pi Delta Kappan* 46 (February 1965): 251–56.

Zirkle, Conway. Review of *Science and Common Sense*, *Isis* 42 (October 1951): 268–71.

Index

AASA. *See* American Association of
    School Administrators
academic departments 37–8
academic freedom 80–3
academic nationalism 59, 105
ACE. *See* American Council on Education
ad hoc committee 41, 42
Adler, Mortimer 194
adult education 58, 107, 114
African Americans 46
allied organizations, National Education
    Association and 145–53
American Association of School
    Administrators (AASA) 97,
    144, 146
American Association of University
    Professors 41
The American Commonwealth (Bryce)
    116
American Council on Education
    (ACE) 143
American cultural history 4, 57, 58
American Defense-Harvard Group 70–1
The American Dilemma (Myrdal) 116
American educational policies 177
American Educational Research
    Association 181
The American High School Today (1959)
    166–70, 175
American public education 9, 146, 150,
    165
American public schools 54, 95, 150
American radicalism 139
"The Anglo-Saxon Tradition"
    (Conant) 94
anti-Catholicism 97
anti-communism 68, 83
anti-intellectualism 49
anti-Semitism 61
   Nazi regime 45
"an up or out" policy 40
Atlantic Monthly 137, 139

atomic bomb project 193
Atomic Energy Commission 145
atomic policy 145
autobiography, Conant, James Bryant
    177–82

Babbitt, Irving 192
Bestor, Arthur 167, 172
biological sciences 116
Black, Henry 14, 15, 34
black political leaders 172
Board of Overseers 26, 38, 40–2
Bok, Derek 199, 200
books on education, Conant, James Bryant
    92–7
Boring, Edwin G. 129, 130
Boston Brahmins 10, 27, 33
Boyle, Robert 123
Brandt, Willy 177
Bridgman, Percy 18, 198
Brown v. Board decision (1954) 171
Bruner, Jerome 120
Bryan, Williams Jennings 11
Buck, Paul 72–3, 80, 106, 107, 143,
    190
*Bulletin of the American Association of
    University Professors* 87, 140
Bundy, McGeorge 82
Bush, Vannevar 137

California Institute of Technology 75
*Cardinal Principles of Secondary
    Education* 147
Carmichael, Oliver C. 142, 144
Carnegie, Andrew 56, 179, 181
Carnegie Corporation 80, 142, 153, 181,
    184, 201
   funding 78–9, 85–6
   memorandum for 164–5
   philanthropies 136, 180
   public education 163
   standardized aptitude tests 31

Carnegie Foundation for the Advancement
of Teaching 142
Carr, William G. 150, 164, 173
Catholic enrollment 46
CCC. *See* Civilian Conservation Corps
CEEB. *See* College Entrance Examination
Board
Chauncey, Henry 31
citizenship education 118
Civilian Conservation Corps (CCC)
114, 147
civil rights leadership 172
Claflin, William 73
classless society 140–1
The Clearing House 117–18
Coeducation 5, 78, 199
Cold War 28, 42, 61, 79, 80–3, 97, 175
and Korean conflict 76, 95, 127
political systems 119
Soviet Union 68, 92
United States 92, 151
college admissions officers 169
College Entrance Examination Board
(CEEB) 30, 141
communism, and democracy 127
community education 114
community pathology 171
The Compromised Campus
(Diamond) 82
Compton, Arthur Holly 48
Conant, James Bryant 1, 6, 7, 25
academic freedom 80–3
advocacy of public schools 136
advocate of academic excellence 190
"The Anglo-Saxon Tradition" 94
autobiography 177–82
bibliography 137
birth 9
books on education 92–7
Chandler Medal 19
chemistry faculty 3
classless society 140–1
Cold War 80–3
criticisms on 183
diplomatic career 163–4
doctoral programs 105
educational activities 156
educational career 9, 189
educational statesmanship 182

Education and Liberty 94–7, 163–4
Education in a Divided World 92–4,
151, 156
education policy 177–83
education, public administration,
history 50–60
enrollment in Harvard College 14–22
Extra-Harvard, 1933–52 135–58
faculty excellence 35–43
faculty promotion and tenure policies
77
family 10–12
full professorship 18–19
general education 103, 106, 108, 119,
194, 197
in sciences 121–30
General Education in a Free Society 4,
120, 149
Harvard Committee Report 107
history of science 4
internationalization 80–3
leadership role 120
leaving Harvard 156–8
Letter of Transmittal 108
liberal education 103, 104, 106, 108,
109
Manhattan Project 2, 67
meritocracy 43, 61, 62 n.10, 74, 95,
200
National Education Association
153–6
National Scholarship plan 114
national scholarships and standardized
tests 29–34
non-priorities of 43–8
participation in faculty recruitment
198
philosopher of education 184
and Physics Department 198
policy decisions 126
presidential program for Harvard
189–91
program in history of science (1930)
104
publication record 135, 137
publications 137–41
public education 86–92, 136, 201
retirement system reform 26
as scholar 2–3, 5

school education   12–14
and Second World War   69–75
Teachers College lectures   91–3, 154
tercentenary celebration   48–50
undergraduate education   105
university professorships   104
urban education   182
Conference on the Arts and Sciences   48
Coolidge, Charles   73
Cooperative Test Service   141
Cowley, W. H.   106, 154–5
Crimson   14–15
cultural anthropology   79
cultural history   58–9
curriculum reform, at Chicago   194
Cushing, Richard   97

Davis, Allison   151
democracy, communism and   127
Democracy in America (De Tocqueville)   116
democratization of Harvard   9–10
Department of Social Relations   78–80, 84
Department of Sociology   78
Diamond, Sigmund   82–3
Divinity School   1, 27, 50, 60, 120, 158, 192
funds for   47–8
Dollard, Charles   86
Dyer, Henry S.   143

ECS. *See* Education Commission of the States
Eddington, Arthur   48
educational establishment   178, 179
Educational Policies Commission (EPC)   146, 147, 155, 175
of National Education Association   164, 175
Educational Records Bureau   142
Educational Testing Service (ETS)   7, 135, 164, 166, 180
creation   141–5
initial capital assets of   145
Education and International Tensions   151
Education and Liberty (Conant)   94–7, 163–4

Education Commission of the States (ECS)   7, 180, 181, 185, 201
Education for All American Youth   147–9, 154, 155
Education in a Divided World (Conant)   92–4, 151, 156
The Education of American Teachers (1963)   172–7
Education of the Gifted (1951)   151
education policy, Conant, James Bryant   177–82
Eisenhower, Dwight D.   157
Eliot, Charles W.   4, 14, 21, 25–7, 191
elitism   xii–xiii
Emerson, Ralph Waldo   139
employment procedure   38–9
EPC. *See* Educational Policies Commission
ETS. *See* Educational Testing Service

Faculty of Arts and Sciences   35–6, 39–41, 57, 72, 73, 78
FBI. *See* Federal Bureau of Investigation
Federal Bureau of Investigation (FBI)   82, 83
federal funds   68, 75, 76
Finley, John   27, 199
First World War   16, 18, 69
Ford Foundation   177
Freedom of Information Act   83
Friedrich, Carl   51
Frost, Robert   21
Fulbright, J. W.   144
funds
Carnegie Corporation   78, 79, 85–6
for Divinity School   47–8
for Harvard University   43–5

Galbraith, John Kenneth   81
Gardner, John W.   164, 173, 179, 182–4
general education   6, 15, 22, 49, 58, 93–5, 194, 196, 197
committee   110–11
courses   118–19
in humanities   116
in natural science   121
faculty   117
fundamental issue   117
in Harvard College   103, 114–21
objectives of   117

political relevance of   119
program   118, 119
reforms   124, 191
renaissance of   120
science instruction   113
in sciences   121–30
and special education   113
of teachers and students   174
General Education in a Free Society
(Conant)   4, 120, 149
General Education Program   199
General Education report, Harvard
Committee on   106, 107,
109–14, 117
German secondary schools   94, 164
German universities   45
GI Bill   67–8, 73–5
Gifted (students)   xiii, 13, 93–6, 148,
151–55, 166, 173
Gilson, Etienne   48
Givens, Willard   152
Graduate Record Examination
(GRE)   31–2, 200
Graduate School of Arts and
Sciences   60, 76
Graduate School of Education   1, 52,
53–5, 61, 83–6, 190, 199
Graduate School of Public
Administration   51
GRE. *See* Graduate Record Examination
Great Depression   22, 28, 44, 46, 146
"Great Texts of Literature"   115
Greek classics   116
Gropius, Walter   45, 75
Gunmere, Richard   143
gymnasium   164

Harper and Row   180, 181
Harper's Magazine   137, 139, 140
Harvard Business School for the Defense
Department   76–7
Harvard College
committee's recommendations for
121
faculty   118
general education   103, 114–21
liberal arts colleges   118
liberal education   103, 104, 191
social science faculty members   116
Harvard Committee   106, 110, 111

on General Education report   106,
107, 109–14, 117
Harvard Committee on General
Education   190
Harvard community   30, 39, 158
Harvard Corporation   72, 73
Harvard Graduate School of Education
136, 140, 201
Harvard Law School   123
Harvard Physics Department   198
Harvard Reading List in American
History   58
Harvard Redbook   49
Harvard Society of Fellows   35–6
Harvard University   1
administrative issues and academic
concerns   75–80
Catholic enrollment   46
Conant, James Bryant (*see* Conant,
James Bryant)
development of   67
enrollment   71
funds for   43–5
nationalization of   68
national scholarships and standardized
tests in   29–34
Harvard University Press   121
Hechinger, Fred   175
Henderson, Lawrence   17–18
Hesburgh, Theodore   181
Hicks, Granville   81
higher education opportunity   139
high school curriculum   111, 113
Hiss, Alger   81
history of science   56–60
"History of Science and Learning"   56
Holmes, Dean   54–5
Homans, Robert   20
House Plan of President Lowell   104
house system   19, 20, 25, 35
Hughes, H. Stuart   80
humanities   111–12, 115, 116
Hutchins, Robert Maynard   193, 194

The Idea of the University (Newman)   49
inherent ability   165
interdisciplinary discussion group   120
internationalization   80–3
Isaac, Joel   194–5
Isis   56

Jackson, Andrew   109, 139
Jefferson, Thomas   109, 139, 146, 175
Jim, Greasy   27
Journal of Higher Education   118, 127
Jung, Carl   48

Keller, Morton and Phyllis   191
Kennedy, John F.   158
Keppel, Francis   85, 86, 177
Keppel, Frederick   201
Kittredge, George   26
Kohler, Elmer   16
Korean War/conflict   76, 77, 81, 95, 156–7
    American involvement in   151
K-12 school   144
Kuhn, Thomas   197

Laboratory of Social Relations   78
language studies   112
Large City High School   170
Larsen, Roy E.   152
Law School Admissions Test   200
lectures and discussion sessions   116
Levin, Harry   120
liberal education   49, 58–9, 104, 106, 109
    Harvard College   103, 104, 191
    problem for   103
Life magazine   149–50
Lippmann, Walter   28
Littauer School   45, 51, 55, 61, 84, 199
Locke, Alain   46
Lowell, Abbott Lawrence   17, 19–21, 25–7, 39, 48, 198
    administration   44
    Catholic enrollment   46
    curricular solution   105
    free electives for students   60
    Harvard College reform   14, 191
    Harvard Society of Fellows   35–6
    House Plan of   104
    Jewish admission   33
    Jewish refugee employment   45

McCarthy, Joseph   6, 81, 82, 158
McKinley, William   11
Malinowski, Bronislaw   48
Manhattan Project   67, 72
Manpower Commission Policy   71

Massachusetts Institute of Technology   75
Master of Arts in Teaching (MAT)
    program   52, 53, 88, 158, 173
May, Ernst   120
meatballs (non-status Harvard students)   22. 34
Meinecke, Frederick   48
memorial sessions   200
meritocracy   28, 33, 43, 61, 62 n.10, 74, 95, 200
Modern Science and Modern Man   128
Moral and Spiritual Ideals in Education (1950)   150
Morison, Samuel Eliot   191
Murdock, Kenneth   19–21
Murray, Henry   120

National Association for the Advancement of Colored People (NAACP)   172
National Citizens Commission   153
National Defense Research Council (NDRC)   72, 75
National Education Association (NEA)   7, 97, 136, 167, 172, 178
    and allied organizations   145–53
    Educational Policies Commission of   175
    evaluation   153–6
nationalism   105
National Scholarship plan   77, 114
National Scholarship Program   13, 77, 141, 165, 192, 199, 200
national scholarships   29–34, 74, 77
National Science Foundation (NSF)   76, 128, 145
National Youth Administration (NYA)   114, 147
natural science   121, 124–7, 149
Natural Science 4 course   121
natural sciences   56, 111, 124–6
Nazi Germany   45, 49
NDRC. *See* National Defense Research Council
NEA. *See* National Education Association
needs-based approach   30
Newman, John Henry   49
New York Times   139, 182
Niebuhr, Reinhold   47

Nieman Fellowship Program   199
Nieman Foundation   199
Noyes, Edward   144
NSF. *See* National Science Foundation
NYA. *See* National Youth Administration

Oxford-Cambridge tradition   39

Palmer, George Herbert   14
parochialism   26
Parsons, Talcott   120
part-time graduate education   174
Pearl Harbor   73, 193
philanthropic organization   184
physical science   124, 125
Piaget, Jean   48
pneumatics, Robert Boyle's
        experiments   123
politics in Harvard campus   143
Popular Science Monthly   138
private secondary education   96
professional education
        communities   172–3
professionalization of science   122
professional schools   51–2, 74, 76
    student enrollment in   70
professorships program   36–7
psychoanalytic psychology   79
publications, Conant, James Bryant
        137–41
public education   86–92, 136, 141, 163,
        167, 201
public schools
    Conant's advocacy of   136
    criticism of   167
Pusey, Nathan   192

Radcliffe College   78
radicalism   139
Reserve Officers Training Corps
        (ROTC)   70
retention procedure   38–9
retirement system reform   26
Richards, Grace Thayer   17
Richards, Theodore   4, 15–17, 36
Rickover, Hyman G.   167, 172
Riesman, David   79, 120
Roman Catholic Church   6, 97
Roman classics   116

Roosevelt, Franklin Delano   48
Roosevelt, Theodore   11
Rosenberg, Ethel   81
Rosenberg, Julius   81
Rosenwald, Julius   194
ROTC. *See* Reserve Officers Training
        Corps
roving professors   3
Roxbury Latin School   12–14
Russian Research Center   79–80

Salem City Guide   10
Sanford, Terry   180
Sarton, George   4, 56, 57
SAT. *See* Scholastic Aptitude Test
SATC. *See* Student Army Training Corps
Schlesinger, Arthur   198, 199
scholastic aptitude   89
Scholastic Aptitude Test (SAT)   30, 31,
        141
School and Society   137, 140
School of Education   52–4, 60
School of Medicine, enrollment in   70
School of Public Health   70
Schrecker, Ellen   81–2
Science and Common Sense (1951)   124,
        127, 129
Science journal   138
sciences, general education in   121–30
secondary schools
    Harvard Committee report on   111
    humanities instruction in   111–12
Second World War   67–8, 81, 181, 193,
        198, 199. *See also* Cold War
    American participation in   138
    and Conant presidency   28, 190
    end of   76–7
    Harvard University and   61, 69–75,
        84
    mistreatment of African Americans
        46
Servicemen's Readjustment Act of   1944
        73
Shaping Educational Policy   177, 180,
        182
"Shop Club"   3, 17, 196
Skinner, B. F.   130
Slums and Suburbs   170, 182
Smith, Marybeth   63 n.63

Smith, Richard N.   191
social dynamite   90, 171
social efficiency progressivism   88
social science approach   55–6
social sciences   78, 116, 122, 124, 126–30,
        195
Soviet Union   67, 81, 92
    Cold War conflict   68
Spaulding, Francis T.   55, 83–4, 88,
        141–2, 144, 165
    secondary school   87
specialized education   106, 107, 110, 111,
        119
standardized aptitude tests   29–34
standardized testing   xiii, 89, 92, 110,
        135, 142–3, 151, 182, 200
Standing Committee on General
        Education   117
Structure of Scientific Revolutions, The
        (Kuhn)   197
Student Army Training Corps (SATC)
        69
Student Council Committee (1939)
        105
suburban school   170–7
Swedenborgianism   27
Sweezey, Alan R.   39, 40

Taussig, Frank   14, 26
Teachers College lectures   91–3, 154
Teachers Insurance and Annuity
        Association (TIAA)   180
tercentenary celebration   48–50
TIAA. *See* Teachers Insurance and
        Annuity Association

Tillich, Paul   120
"A Truce Among Educators"   88
Turner, Frederick Jackson   14, 36
tutorial method   35

Ulich, Robert   45
undergraduate education   190
On Understanding Science, On
        (1947)   124
"uniform coverage" method   112
United States
    citizenship   107
    Cold War with Soviet Union   92
    private secondary education   96
    radicalism   139
    secondary and higher education   94
    Second World War   69
    universal education   108
University Professorships program   36–8
urban schools   170–7. *See also* suburban
        school

vocational agricultural education   169

Wald, George   120
Wallace, Henry   80
Walsh, Raymond   39, 40
Whitehead, Alfred North   21, 36
White, Morton   120
Wood, Ben D.   32
Working Knowledge   194–5

Yale University Press   121, 124

Zook, George F.   144